THE MINISTRY OF THE CELEBRATION OF THE SACRAMENTS

VOL. I
SACRAMENTS OF INITIATION AND UNION

CELEBRATION OF BAPTISM
CELEBRATION OF CONFIRMATION
CELEBRATION OF THE EUCHARIST

VOL. II
SACRAMENTS OF RECONCILIATION

CELEBRATION OF PENANCE
CELEBRATION OF ANOINTING OF THE SICK

VOL. III
SACRAMENTS OF COMMUNITY RENEWAL

CELEBRATION OF HOLY ORDERS
CELEBRATION OF MATRIMONY

THE MINISTRY OF
THE CELEBRATION OF THE SACRAMENTS

Sacraments of Reconciliation

Nicholas Halligan, O.P.

Volume II
Penance, Anointing of the Sick

ALBA · HOUSE   NEW · YORK

SOCIETY OF ST. PAUL, 2187 VICTORY BLVD., STATEN ISLAND, NEW YORK 10314

NIHIL OBSTAT:
Very Rev. Joseph C. Taylor, O.P., S.T.M., Ph.D.
Very Rev. William B. Ryan, O.P., S.T.M., J.C.D.

IMPRIMI POTEST:
Very Rev. Charles T. Quinn, O.P., S.T.L.
Provincial

NIHIL OBSTAT:
Very Rev. Joseph C. Taylor, O.P.
Censor Deputatus

IMPRIMATUR:
Patrick Cardinal O'Boyle
Archbishop of Washington
August 28, 1972

The Nihil Obstat and Imprimatur are a declaration that a book or pamphlet is considered to be free from doctrinal or moral error. It is not implied that those who have granted the Nihil Obstat and Imprimatur agree with the contents, opinions or statements expressed.

LIBRARY OF CONGRESS
CATALOGING IN PUBLICATION DATA

Halligan, Francis Nicholas, 1917-
The sacraments of reconciliation.

(His The ministry of the celebration of the sacraments, v. 2)
Includes bibliographical references.
1. Penance. 2. Unction. I. Title.
II. Series.
BX2200.H25 vol. 2 [BX2260] 264'.02'008s [265'.6]
ISBN 0-8189-0279-5 (v. 2)   73-9604
ISBN 0-8189-0271-X (set)

Current Printing (last digit):

9   8   7   6   5   4   3   2

Copyright 1973 by the Society of St. Paul.

Designed, printed and bound in the United States of America by the Fathers and Brothers of the Society of St. Paul, 2187 Victory Boulevard, Staten Island, N. Y. 10314 as part of their communications apostolate.

Foreword

The sacraments of initiation and unity, received in faith, inaugurate the life of Christ in the soul of the faithful, strengthen it, and establish in full stature the unity of the Mystical Body of Christ among men. They identify the disciple of Christ. In a threefold manner they bring the presence of Christ into intimate union with each individual Christian and provide him with the capacity to realize the meaning of his discipleship and of achieving its eternal fulfilment.

Man, however, is a free and responsible agent. Even the grace of Christ does not compel him against his will. He may respond to the invitation of Christ in faith and sacrament; he is also capable of refusing, of failing to respond. Similarly, having received any one or all of the sacraments of initiation and unity, he is still a responsible disciple who continues his free acceptance of Christ and deepens this union; yet he is capable withal of neglecting, weakening, and even totally severing this union in love won at so great a price by the crucified and risen Savior. The mystery of personal sin in man is also the mystery of man redeemed by Christ.

Once the bond with Christ is severed by the conscious effort of the Christian, the hope of reconciliation and at the same time of restoration of former status in the Mystical Body is possible only through the gratuitously offered saving grace of the Redeemer, which is embodied in the Sacrament of Penance.

On the other hand, where the union of charity has been impaired by personal sins, even though subsequently forgiven by sacramental absolution, in some way these sins (over and above the abiding presence of fallen nature as it exists in this pilgrim life) more or less leave their consequences upon the individual. When he comes to be in a condition of dangerous debility of health, he is less able to cope with and to control the inner forces to which this condition is susceptible. In this event, through the Sacrament of the Anointing of the Sick he is strengthened, comforted, and enabled to overcome the residue or remnants of former sins, at times even reconciled to Christ in charity through the remission of sins not previously forgiven.

The sacraments of reconciliation—Penance and the Anointing of the Sick—principally regard the sins and the sinfulness of the pilgrim disciple reconciling him in different ways to Christ and to the Church. They purify and prepare the soul for a wholehearted witness of discipleship; they dispose to a more fruitful reception of the graces of the other sacraments.

TABLE OF CONTENTS

Foreword v

THE CELEBRATION OF PENANCE

I. Penance, the Abiding Vehicle of Reconciliation
   with Divine Goodness 3
   A. Necessity of Acts of Penance 3
   B. Role of the Sacrament 6
II. Requirements for the Celebration of Penance 8
   A. Requisite Material 8
   B. Prescribed Words or Formula 8
      1. Individual Absolution 8
      2. Common or General Absolution 11
      3. Oral Recitation of the Formula 16
      4. In the Presence of the Penitent 17
         a. Outside of necessity 17
         b. In a case of necessity 18
      5. Unconditioned Formula 19
      6. Repeatable Formula 20
   C. Time and Place of the Celebration of Penance . . 20
III. Minister of the Celebration of Penance 21
   A. Requisite Sacerdotal Power 21
   B. Penitential Jurisdiction 22
      1. Necessity of Jurisdiction 22
      2. General Types of Jurisdiction 23
      3. Ordinary Jurisdiction 24
      4. Delegated Jurisdiction 26
         a. Function 26
         b. Use 27
         c. Concession 29
         d. Cessation 29
      5. Special Delegated Jurisdiction 30
         a. Danger of death 30
         b. Maritime and air faculties 33
         c. Paschal precept 34
         d. Irregularities 34
         e. Vindictive penalties 34

f. Vows and oaths	35
g. Fast and abstinence	35
h. Reserved cases	35
i. Indulgences	36
6. Expired Delegated Jurisdiction	36
7. Common Error and Doubtful Jurisdiction	36
a. Common error	36
b. Positive and probable doubt	38
8. Confessors of Religious	39
9. Confessors in Seminaries	41
10. Confessors who are Regulars	41
C. Manifestation of Conscience	44
D. Qualities of a Confessor	45
1. Goodness	47
2. Knowledge	48
3. Prudence	50
E. Duties in the Celebration of Penance	52
1. Hearing of Confessions	52
a. With the care of souls	52
b. Without the care of souls	53
2. Attitude of the Confessor	54
3. Correction of Defects and Errors	59
4. Preservation of the Sacramental Seal	61
a. Obligation of the seal	61
b. Material under the seal	64
c. Violation of the seal	66
d. Penalties	68
5. Proper Respect for Confessional Knowledge	68
a. Unlawful use	69
b. Lawful use	69
6. Assistance to Penitents	71
a. The dying	71
b. Occasionists	73
c. Habitual sinners	76
d. Recidivists	78
e. Scrupulous	80
f. Children	82

g. Religious and clerics	83
F. Abuses	86
1. Solicitation	86
2. Absolution of an Accomplice in Sin	93
IV. Candidates for the Sacrament of Penance	97
A. Frequency of Sacramental Confession	97
B. Devout and Frequent Confession	99
C. First Confession	99
D. Material for Sacramental Confession	100
1. Necessary Material	100
2. Sufficient Material	101
3. Free Material	102
4. Certain Material	103
5. Doubtful Material	103
E. General Accusation of Sins	104
1. In Case of Necessity	104
2. Outside of Necessity	104
F. Acts of the Penitent	105
1. Contrition	106
2. Confession	109
a. Characteristics of sacramental confession	109
b. Integrity or completeness of confession	111
c. Excusing causes	115
General norms	115
Physical inability	116
Moral inability	117
d. Examination of conscience	120
e. General confession	121
3. Satisfaction or Penance to be Fulfilled	121
a. Commutation	125

RESERVED CASES

I. Ecclesiastical Censures	127
A. Notion of Censure	127
B. Manner of Establishment	128

SACRAMENTS OF RECONCILIATION

  C. Manner of Incurrence 128
  D. Manner of Reservation 129
  E. Subject of Censures 130
  F. Material for Censures 132
  G. Binding Force and Multiplication 133
  H. Causes Excusing from Incurrence 134
   1. Fear 134
   2. Ignorance 134
  I. Manner of Absolving Censures 136
  J. Jurisdiction to Absolve 138
   1. In Danger of Death 138
   2. Outside the Danger of Death 138
  K. Excommunication 143
   1. Notion 143
   2. Effects 143
   3. *Specialissimo Modo* 144
   4. *Speciali Modo* 145
   5. *Simpliciter* 147
   6. Reserved to the Local Ordinary 148
   7. Reserved to No One 150
  L. Suspension 150
   1. Notion 150
   2. Division 151
   3. Effects of Particular Suspensions 151
   4. Reserved to the Apostolic See 152
   5. Reserved to the Ordinary 153
   6. Reserved to No One 153
  M. Interdict 154
II. Reserved Sins 154
  A. Notion of Reserved Sin 154
  B. Manner of Establishment 154
  C. Excusing Cause 155
  D. Jurisdiction to Absolve 155
  E. Cessation of Reservation 156

CHASTITY AND ITS VIOLATIONS

Chastity

I. Role of Chastity 159
II. Kinds of Pleasures 161

Violations of Chastity

I. Inordinate Character of the Violation of Chastity . . . 163
II. Objective Moral Norms 165
III. Sins Against Chastity Complete in a Manner Apt to Achieve Natural Generation 169
    A. Fornication 169
    B. Adultery 171
    C. Rape 171
    D. Abduction 172
    E. Incest 173
    F. Carnal Sacrilege 173
    G. Obligations in Justice 174
IV. Sins Against Chastity Completed in a Manner Precluding the Achievement of Nature's Purpose 176
    A. Pollution or Masturbation 176
    B. Sodomy and Homosexuality 182
    C. Bestiality 184
    D. Some Sexual Conditions and Perversions . . . 185
V. Internal Sins Against Chastity 188
    A. Morose Delectation 188
    B. Sinful Desire 188
    C. Sinful Joy 189
VI. External Uncompleted Sins Against Chastity . . . 190
    A. Carnal Disturbance 190
    B. Impure Actions 190

THE CELEBRATION OF THE ANOINTING OF THE SICK

I. Role of the Sacrament of the Anointing of the Sick . . 195

II. Requisite Material 197
III. Prescribed Words or Formula 199
IV. Minister of the Celebration of the Unction of the Sick . 199
V. Candidates for the Sacrament of the Anointing of the Sick . 201
VI. Repeated and Conditional Celebrations 203
VII. Visitation and Communion of the Sick 205
VIII. Rite of the Anointing of the Sick 206
IX. Viaticum 207
X. Continuous Rite of Sacramental Celebration
in Danger of Death 208

THE MINISTRY OF THE CELEBRATION OF THE SACRAMENTS

THE CELEBRATION OF PENANCE

I *Penance, the abiding vehicle of reconciliation with divine goodness*

If all those who had been regenerated in Baptism had enough gratitude to God to keep forever the justice received in Baptism by his grace and bounty, there would have been no need to institute any other sacrament than Baptism for the remission of sins. But since God is rich in mercy and knows our frail structure, he has also prepared a remedy of life for those who, after Baptism, have given themselves over to the slavery of sin and to the power of the devil. This remedy is the sacrament of Penance, and through it the benefit of Christ's death is applied to those who have fallen after Baptism.[1] However, Penance was not a sacrament before the coming of Christ, and even after his coming it is not a sacrament for anyone who has not been baptized.[2]

A. *Necessity of Acts of Penance*

At all times all men who were stained by serious sin have needed penance to obtain grace and justice.[3] Properly speaking, penance is a moderated grief for past sins inasmuch as they have offended God, with the intention of removing them.[4] Although a natural virtue of penance is possible, it is of itself of no avail for salvation.[5] Thus a true penitent is one moved by divine grace or a supernatural virtue to detest and to grieve over his sin, inasmuch as it is an injury and an offense to God, and firmly to resolve correction and satisfaction.[6] The benefit or value, as viewed in faith, which is the reparation due to God, is the formal

1. Trent, Denz.-Schön. 1668. **Ordo Paenitentiae**, 1, 3-5 (S.C.C.D. 2 dec. 1973).
2. **Ibid.**, 1670.
3. **Ibid.**, 1669; cf. Ezech. 18:30; Luke 13:3; Acts 2:38.
4. Cf. **Summa Theol.**, III, q. 85, aa. 1, 3.
5. Trent, Denz.-Schön. 1525, 1553. Penance is derived from expressions indicating a condition of pain or penalty: **poenitentia, poenam tenere, poenire, poenae tenentia**, etc.; it may also be called repentance or penitence.
6. Cf. **Summa Theol.**, loc. cit.; Suppl., q. 16, aa. 1, 3.

motivation of the penitent. Any person guilty of or even capable of sin is an apt subject of the virtue of penance. Detestation and sorrow are principal in penance; presupposed is the operation of faith, hope, fear, and initial love.[7]

Christian faith teaches that true penance can take away all sins.[8] This means perfect penance or contrition made perfect through charity.[9] For one in a state of serious sin it is necessary for salvation by a necessity both of means and of precept.[10] The virtue of penance operates to justify the sinner solely through the personal penitential act.

The precept of penance does not oblige immediately after the commission of serious sin, although a sinner is obliged to desist immediately from sin and actual affection for it. Being an affirmative precept, it does not always and at every moment oblige but only when a special reason urges. Otherwise one would sin every time he averted to the obligation of penance; an ill person is not taking medicine every time he thinks of it, but only when necessary.

However, precisely when the precept of penance obliges is not so clear. Of itself it certainly urges at the moment of death and in probable danger of death (in warfare, a dangerous journey, difficult childbirth, etc.) or of perpetual loss of reason. Outside of such danger, how often in life this obligation of itself binds, or how long one can refrain from eliciting an act of penance before incurring another sin by delaying this act, is not certain. However, a notable delay in repenting is reprobated in Scripture,[11] as it

---

7. Cf. Trent, Denz.-Schön. 1526.
8. Ibid., Denz.-Schön. 1669.
9. Ibid., 1677-1678: Imperfect contrition or attrition springs from a consideration of the malice of sin or from the fear of hell and its punishments. It excludes the will to sin and hopes for pardon; thus it does not make a man a hypocrite or a greater sinner but is a gift of God and an inspiration of the Holy Spirit, not as already dwelling in the soul but as merely giving an impulse that helps the penitent make his way toward justice.
10. Cf. Eccles. 2:22; Matt. 4:17; Lk. 13:3; Denz.-Schön. 1526-1527. Necessary as **means** for salvation signifies that without it salvation cannot be obtained; necessary by **precept** means required inasmuch as it is prescribed.
11. Eccles. 5:8-9; Rom. 2:4-5. Cf. **Summa Theol.**, II-II, 1. 14, a. 2; **Suppl.**, q. 6, a. 5; **IV. Sent.**, d. 17, q. 3, a. 1, qcla. 4.

indicates a neglect and contempt of God and a failure in the grave obligation to tend to one's ultimate end.

The precept of penance obliges accidentally or because of the fulfilment of some other duty or obligation: a) when a sacrament is celebrated or received; b) when another precept or virtue, e.g., charity, requires a previous act of penance; c) when an act of penance is necessary to overcome a serious temptation inasmuch as it restores friendship with God; d) when one wishes to evidence penance externally, which otherwise would be simulation. The violation of the precept of penance obliging only accidentally is not a special sin. Of itself there is no special precept of penance for slight sins, as they may even be left for expiation in the next life; an obligation may arise accidentally, e.g., when they are the only matter in the reception of the sacrament of Penance.

A deliberate will not to do penance or not to repent is a special sin of impenitence; the simple omission of penance is not a special sin unless the obligation binds of itself. Failure in the obligation that binds only accidentally would not be a special sin of impenitence but a transgression of the precept or virtue against which one offends by sinning. Nevertheless, at all times sinners must be warned to sorrow for their sins as soon as they are aware of them, since a protracted enmity with God is an injury to his majesty and most dangerous and destructive for the penitent who must rely on the mercy of God. Confessors inquire about such repentance for the purpose of ascertaining the fulfilment of the positive precept of annual confession and of judging the penitent's state of conscience in order that it might be formed rightly.

Penance or repentance embraces all personal sins. All actual serious sins fully offend God and render the sinner perfectly turned away from God, and thus they are the proper and principal material of penance. Proper but secondary material is all slight sins, since as sins they also in some way offend God. Sins already forgiven are also matter for repentance, since their remission is not infallibly certain to us, their retraction not always perfect, their satisfaction not always full. Mere imperfections are generally not material for penance but rather for the zeal of charity and the motivation of perfection.

B. *Role of the Sacrament*

The exteriorly manifested acts of the virtue of penance have been raised by Christ to the sacramental level; they have become the material of an effective sign of grace. Faith teaches[12] that, given its institution by Christ, the sacrament of Penance must by a necessity of means be received actually (*in re*) or, when that cannot be done, at least in desire (*in voto*), in order to remove serious sins committed after Baptism. It is certain[13] that after the institution of the sacrament perfect contrition alone is no longer able to destroy sin except through an order or relationship to the sacrament itself which, if not always received actually, is received at least in desire with perfect contrition. An explicit desire is not required, an implicit desire suffices. This is necessarily included in perfect contrition itself, inasmuch as the perfectly contrite will also be prepared to fulfill everything necessary for salvation, even if here and now through inadvertence, forgetfulness, or invincible ignorance the penitent does not think of what these necessary things are. (However sin is remitted, the obligation of receiving absolution remains). The sacrament obliges also by a necessity of precept,[14] operating by the very fact of its celebration with at least imperfect contrition or attrition.

The sacrament of Penance is repeatable.[15] The divine precept of itself obliges seriously at the moment of death and in very probable danger of death or of permanent loss of reason. It cannot be determined with certainty if and when the obligation binds of itself also sometimes in life, or even after every lapse into mortal sin. The sacrament of Penance obliges accidentally, by reason of a natural or positive precept: a) when the Eucharist is to be received and serious sins have not been confessed or indirectly

12. Trent. Denz.-Schön. 1670, 1672, 1674.
13. Ibid., 1677-1678.
14. Ibid., 1706. Interior penance or sorrow for sin committed must last a lifetime, as sin must always be displeasing. The external signs of this sorrow will last for a determined time in proportion to the sin. Penance must be habitually continual (the act itself must necessarily be interrupted) by doing nothing contrary to penance and resolving to maintain displeasure of past sins.
15. Trent, Denz.-Schön. 1701.

remitted;[16] b) when a sacrament must be received or *ex officio* celebrated or administered and an act of perfect contrition cannot be elicited; c) when a grave temptation or evil habit cannot be overcome without confession. The omission of the sacrament in these cases is not a sin against the divine precept of confessing but a violation of the other obligation which requires confession. The precept does not require immediate confession of sins, lest they be forgotten, but only a confession of those sins of which the penitent is conscious after a diligent examination of conscience. The positive precept of ecclesiastical law (since the IV Lateran Council in 1215) obliges those conscious of mortal sin to an annual confession.[17]

The sacrament of Penance has the power to remit through the infusion of sanctifying grace all sins however grievous and however often repeated, and to restore the state of divine friendship.[18] It brings to the well disposed peace and serenity of conscience joined to great consolation of soul.[19] As with the virtue, it takes away the eternal debt or punishment,[20] diminishes the temporal punishment and sometimes (but not always) takes it away fully,[21] revives previous meritorious works,[22] and lessens evil dispositions. It confers a sacramental grace or special supernatural help moving the penitent to an ever-growing hatred of sin and more surely preserving him from sin in the future. Many other benefits are gained from this sacrament by well-disposed penitents.

The sacrament of Penance is distinctive especially in the fact that it is administered in the manner of a judgment[23] or by a judicial act, whereas the other sacraments consist in a certain consecration: the sinner is the culprit, witness, and accuser; the priest is the judge rendering sentence. Unlike other judgments which tend toward the punishment of the guilty, sacramental judgment is directed to

16. c. 856.
17. c. 906. Cf. **Ordo Paenitentiae**, 7.
18. Trent, Denz.-Schön. 1712; cf. c. 870.
19. Trent, Denz.-Schön. 1674-1675.
20. **Ibid.**, 1542-1543.
21. **Ibid.**, 922, 1672, 1580, 1542-1543, 1712.
22. Pius XI, Denz.-Schön. 3670.
23. Trent, Denz.-Schön. 1671-1672, 1709.

the absolution of the sinner and his reconciliation with God. In this sacrament instituted by Christ all sins committed after Baptism are remitted by the conjunction of the absolution of the priest and the precise placing of certain acts by the penitent.

II *Requirements for the Celebration of Penance*

A. *Requisite Material*

Faith teaches that the remote and necessary material of the sacrament of Penance is all serious sin committed after Baptism and not yet duly submitted to the power of the keys of the Church.[24] It is certain also that slight sins not yet confessed and all actual sins already confessed and remitted are the remote, free, and sufficient material of the sacrament.[25]

The proximate material of the sacrament is the three acts of the penitent: contrition, confession, and satisfaction.[26] Because they are the free acts of the penitent in this sacrament, although judgment on them in view of absolution is the competency of the confessor, they will be examined at length below.[27]

B. *Prescribed Words or Formula*

1. *Individual Absolution*

The formula of this sacrament is the words by which the priest as judge passes sentence or absolution on sins; it signifies the use and effect of the power of the keys in the remission of sins. The formula should express the exercise of the judicial power given to the ministers of the Church, to be exercised in the name of God, and the actual effect.[28]

It is certain that the words "I absolve you" are required for

24. **Ibid.**, 1679, 1707.
25. **Ibid.**
26. Florence, Denz.-Schön. 1323; Trent, 1671, 1673. **Ordo Paenitentiae**, 6, 11.
27. Cf. III **Candidates for the Reception of Penance.**
28. Cf. Florence, Denz.-Schön. 1323; Trent, 1673; **Summa Theol.**, III, q. 84, a. 3.

The Celebration of Penance

a *valid* formula.[29] It is probable that the words "from your sins" also pertain to validity, since the previous words are not sufficiently determined and may be as readily applied to absolution from censures as from sins. In practice, therefore, these words must be included, lest the sacrament be exposed to nullity; where they are omitted the formula is to be repeated conditionally. The words "in the name of the Father, and of the Son, and of the Holy Spirit" are not required for validity, but their omission is a slight sin. The voluntary omission of an essential word of the formula or of one probably required for validity is a serious sin. However, whether voluntary or not, the omission invalidates the sacrament or at least exposes it to the danger of nullity and thus deprives the penitent of sacramental grace. Absolution imparted in an equivalent form would be gravely unlawful but valid.

The *lawful* formula is the integral rubrical formula which the Church prescribes to be employed in absolution. Although the prayers added to the formula by the Church are not necessary for the absolution itself, in the absence of a justifying cause (number of penitents, frequency and brevity of a confession, etc.) they are not to be omitted.[30] The minister ought carefully to observe the prescribed formula with the accompanying prayers and ceremonies, such as are found in the *Roman Ritual* or in approved vernacular rendition. The prescribed[31] formulas are:

Common Formula of Absolution:

When the priest wishes to absolve a penitent, he imposes a salutary penance and, after the penance has been accepted, with his hands (or at least his right hand) extended over the head of the penitent, says:

> *May God, the Father of mercies, who through the death and resurrection of his Son reconciled the world to himself and poured forth the Holy Spirit for the remission of sins, grant you through the ministry of the Church pardon and peace. And*

---

29. Ibid., Cf. **Ordo Paenitentiae**, 19.
30. c. 885. This canon does not seem to express a strict precept.
31. **Ordo Paenitentiae**, 21, 46, 62.

I absolve you from your sins in the name of the Father, and of the Son, ✠ and of the Holy Spirit.

The penitent responds: *Amen.*

When grave necessity urges in danger of death, the priest may say briefly:

I absolve you from your sins, in the name of the Father, and of the Son, ✠ and of the Holy Spirit.

The penitent responds: *Amen.*[32]

It is not obligatory to give the introductory blessing before the penitent begins his confession, but this custom should be preserved. The penitent opens his confession by blessing himself in the usual manner. The priest may also give his blessing at the same time. The confessor imparts his absolution while sitting, after the manner of a judge pronouncing sentence; any just cause will excuse from this. The raising of the hand in absolution and the making of the sign of the cross are not required under pain of sin, but the custom and the rubrics are to be observed in this matter.

If sins are confessed which are of themselves (*ratione sui*) reserved or to which a censure is attached (*ratione censurae*) it suffices for the confessor, observing the norms of law in reserved cases, to intend to absolve a properly disposed penitent also from them when pronouncing the formula of sacramental absolution. He may, however, before absolving sins, absolve from a censure with the formula which is to be used when a censure is absolved outside the sacrament of Penance:

---

32. **Ordo Paenitentiae,** 62, 65. It is not more than a slight sin to use the short formula without necessity.

The Celebration of Penance

By the power granted me, I absolve you from the bond of excommunication (or suspension or interdict). In the name of the Father, and of the Son, ✠ *and of the Holy Spirit.*[33]

If a penitent has incurred an irregularity the priest, according to the norm of law, may dispense from the same, either in confession and after absolution, or outside the sacrament, and with the formula:

By the power granted me, I dispense you from the irregularity you have incurred. In the name of the Father, and of the Son, ✠ *and of the Holy Spirit.*[34]

2. Common or General Absolution

In time of war soldiers may be absolved in groups as soon as it is judged necessary to absolve them by a general formula or common absolution; likewise groups of citizens may be so absolved in danger of death, when this is necessary. In all cases penitents should, if possible, be warned to confess their serious sins when they next go to confession, to be presently contrite and resolved not to sin in the future, and to manifest this in some way, at least by striking their breast.[35] When there is time, this absolution is to be given with the usual and complete formula; otherwise the short formula may be used.

---

33. **Ordo Paenitentiae, Appendix I.**
34. **Ibid.**
35. S. Poen. 10 dec. 1940; 25 mart. 1944. **Ordo Paenitentiae, 35.**

Concern for the welfare of souls as well as for the right understanding of and the proper ministry and use of the sacrament of Penance prompts the Church to lay down the following pastoral norms:[36]

I The teaching of the Council of Trent must be firmly held and faithfully put into practice. This implies a reprobation of the recent custom which has sprung up in places by which there is a presumption to satisfy the precept of sacramentally confessing serious sins for the purpose of obtaining absolution by confession made only generally or through what is called a community celebration of penance. This reprobation is demanded not only by divine precept as declared by the Council of Trent but also by the very great good of souls deriving, according to centuries-long experience, from individual confession rightly administered. Individual and integral confession and absolution remain the only ordinary way for the faithful to be reconciled to God and the Church unless physical or moral impossibility excuses from such confession.

II It can indeed happen because of particular circumstances occasionally occurring that general absolution may or even should be given to a number of penitents without previous individual confession.

This can happen first of all when there is imminent danger of death and, even though a priest or priests are present, they have no time to hear the confession of each penitent. In this case any priest has the faculty to give general absolution to a number

---

36. Sacramentum Poenitentiae (Normae Pastorales circa Absolutionem Sacramentalem Generali Modo Impertiendam), S.C.D.F. 16 iunii 1972. **Ordo Paenitentiae**, 31-35, 60-63.

of people after first, if there is time, exhorting them briefly to make an act of contrition.

III Apart from the cases of danger of death, it is lawful to give sacramental absolution collectively to a number of faithful who have confessed only generically but have been suitably exhorted to repent, provided that there is serious necessity: namely, when in view of the number of penitents there are not enough confessors at hand to hear properly the confessions of each within an appropriate time, with the result that the penitents through no fault of their own would be forced to do without sacramental grace or Holy Communion for a long time. This can happen especially in mission lands but in places also and within groups where it is clear that this need exists.

This is not lawful, however, when confessors are able to be at hand, merely because of a great concourse of penitents such as can for example occur on a great feast or pilgrimage (cf. Denz.-Schön. 2159).

IV Local Ordinaries and, to the extent that they are concerned, priests are bound in conscience to see that the number of confessors should not become reduced because some priests neglect this noble ministry, while involving themselves in secular affairs or devoting themselves to less necessary ministries, especially if those ministries can be performed by deacons or suitable lay people.

V The judgment as to whether the conditions already mentioned (III) are present and, consequently, the decision as to when it is lawful to grant general sacramental absolution are reserved to the local Ordinary after he has conferred with other members of the episcopal conference.

If a serious need arises of giving general sacramental absolution apart from the cases laid down by the local Ordinary, the priest is obliged, whenever it is possible, to have previous recourse to the local Ordinary in order to grant the absolution lawfully; if this is not possible, he is to inform the Ordinary as soon as possible of the need of the granting of the absolution.

VI In order that the faithful may take advantage of general sacramental absolution it is absolutely required that they be suitably disposed: each should repent of the sins he has committed, have the purpose of keeping from sin, intend to repair any scandal or loss caused, and also have the purpose of confessing in due time each serious sin that he is at present unable to confess. Priests should carefully remind the faithful of these dispositions and conditions, which are required for the validity of the sacrament.

VII Those who have serious sins forgiven by general absolution should make an auricular confession before receiving absolution in this collective form another time, unless a just cause prevents them. They are strictly obliged, unless prevented by moral impossibility, to go to confession within a year. They too are affected by the precept that obliges every Christian to confess privately to a priest once a year at least all his serious sins that he has not yet specifically confessed (cf. Denz-Schön. 1683, 1707-1708, 2031).

VIII Priests are to teach the faithful that those who are aware of being in serious sin are forbidden to refuse deliberately or by neglect to satisfy the obligation of individual confession, when it is possible to have a confessor, while they wait for an occasion for collective absolution.

IX In order that the faithful may easily be able to satisfy the obligation of making an individual confession, let care be taken that confessors are available in the churches on days and at hours that are convenient for the faithful.

In places that are remote or difficult to reach, where the priest can come only at rare intervals during the year, let it be arranged that, as far as possible, the priest shall on each occasion hear the sacramental confessions of a group of penitents and give collective absolution to the other penitents provided that the conditions already mentioned (III) are present, so that in this way all the faithful, if possible, shall be able to make an individual confession at least once a year.

X The faithful are carefully to be taught that liturgical celebrations and community rites of penance are of great usefulness for the preparation of a more fruitful confession of sins and amendment of life. Care must however be taken that such celebrations or rites are not confused with sacramental confession and absolution.

If in the course of such celebrations the penitents make an individual confession, each is to receive absolution singly from the confessor to whom he goes. In the case of general sacramental absolution, it is always to be given in accordance with the special rite laid down. The celebration of this rite is to be kept quite distinct from the celebration of Mass.

XI If one who is in a situation causing actual scandal to the faithful is sincerely penitent and seriously proposes to remove the scandal, he can indeed receive general sacramental absolution along with others, but he is not to go to Holy Communion until, in the judgment of a confessor whom he is first to approach personally, he has removed the scandal.

XII Priests should be careful not to discourage the faithful from frequent or devotional confession. On the contrary, let them draw attention to its fruitfulness for Christian living and always display readiness to hear such a confession whenever a reasonable request is made by the faithful. It must be absolutely prevented that individual confession should be reserved for serious sins only, for this would deprive the faithful of the great benefit of confession and would injure the good name of those who approach the sacrament singly.

XIII The granting of general sacramental absolution without observing the norms given above is to be considered a serious abuse. Let all pastors carefully prevent such abuses out of awareness of the moral duty enjoined upon them for the welfare of souls and for the protection of the dignity of the Sacrament of Penance.

3. *Oral Recitation of the Formula*

By the will and institution of Christ absolution to be *valid* must be oral, even in the greatest necessity.[37] Although not of faith, it is theologically certain and the perpetual practice. Thus, concretely, all expressions of absolution other than in words must be considered invalid.[38] The words need not be heard by the penitent

---

37. Cf. Florence, Denz.-Schön. 1323; Trent, 1673.
38. Clement VIII, S. Off. 20 iun. 1602; 7 iun. 1603; Denz.-Schön. 1994-1995; Paul V, S. Off. 14 iul. 1605. Cf. St. Thomas, **Opusc.** 22, c. 2.

(or even by the minister), but they must be of themselves audible. Absolution cannot be given in writing or by a sign or a nod; in this it differs from the form of matrimony.

4. *In the Presence of the Penitent*

Outside of necessity

Sacramental absolution must be imparted to a penitent who is personally present, and his accusation of sins must be made to a confessor who is present. The absolution cannot be given vocally nor the sense of the words preserved unless the penitent is present, i.e., one who according to the common and ordinary manner of speaking and acting can hear the words or to whom the confessor can speak. To hold that confession can be made to one who is absent or that absolution can be imparted by letter or messenger to one who is absent has been condemned.[39] A serious cause will permit a penitent to write out his sins and even to send them to the confessor, but he must be present to accuse himself of the sins so written and to receive absolution validly. Absolution can be given to the unconscious whose desire for it can be presumed.

The penitent must be physically or at least morally present. Since physical presence cannot be always had in human affairs, by divine institution that presence is required and suffices by which a penitent, according to the common manner of judging of men, is considered to be truly present. Moral presence is that within which men still can and are accustomed to speak among themselves, even though in a loud voice. There is no need for the penitent actually to hear or to understand the words, since it is not the penitent whose action the words must indicate but God. Often the words must be said in a low voice lest bystanders hear. The penitent's presence is required so that the words may have a reasonable meaning. It is not necessary that there be no barrier at all between confessor and penitent, e.g., a grille. However, if a confessor and penitent are in different non-communicating rooms, the absolution is ren-

---

39. Clement VIII; Paul V, **loc. cit.**

dered at least doubtful; it may be imparted only in a case of necessity and conditionally.

It is generally held that within about twenty paces distance sufficient presence is had for the words of absolution to fall upon the penitent. Greater distance, e.g., fifty to one hundred paces may be admitted, if there is a moral union of the persons, e.g., in a street, military field, stadium, courtyard, etc. The opinion that absolution can be given in any case at any distance as long as the penitent is seen or sensibly perceived is untenable, since it does not seem to fulfill the nature of a judgment. An absolution beyond about twenty paces or in some dubious presence is doubtful.

In case of necessity

The penitent can and must be absolved as often as he can be perceived by some sense, at least confusedly, even if due to some accidental hindrance he is not perceived. If he is more than twenty to thirty paces away the absolution is to be conditional. Thus a priest must absolve a person who is seen to fall from a roof, into a river, to drown; also the dying who cannot be approached for some reason, e.g., fire, wreckage, locked door, contagion, time to cover the distance, etc.

A common absolution may be imparted, under the conditions already noted, to many persons in a group, even though the members in the rear are more than twenty to thirty paces distant. When because of the great distance these latter cannot be considered to be morally present, they cannot be validly absolved. The group should then be divided and the single parts absolved to insure validity.

If the penitent, thinking he has been absolved, should leave before receiving absolution, then:

> if he is near the confessional, he can be absolved without recalling him, even though he may have mingled with others, as long as it is prudently judged he is still morally present;
>
> if not, he must be recalled for absolution if this can be conveniently done and he can conveniently return;
>
> if this cannot be done and he is certainly morally present, although not perceived, he must be absolved;

The Celebration of Penance

if he is neither present nor will return later, nothing can be done but recommend him to God;

if he later returns to the same confessor for confession, he should be warned to be sorry for all his sins and absolved;

if the approach is not for confession but for some other reason, he must be warned of the defect of absolution. However, in practice the admonition usually may be omitted, since this is generally a source of uneasiness to penitents and very difficult for the confessor due to the danger of scandal or of infamy to him. The penitent does not suffer spiritual damage, since these sins are also indirectly remitted in the following confession.

Absolution given over the telephone is certainly unlawful and probably invalid. It is not the human voice but an artificially produced sound, and the persons are commonly considered to be absent from each other. This manner of absolving may be used conditionally in extreme necessity. Absolution through a speaking tube is certainly unlawful but probably valid. Although the human voice is heard, the moral presence is doubtful. Absolution by telegraph, radio, or television is certainly unlawful and invalid.

5. *Unconditioned Formula*

All the sacraments are to be conferred absolutely and only conditionally when a peculiar reason or cause demands or permits. A condition does not affect the sense of the form but the will of the minister. The sacraments work their effect when they can; it is not in the power of the minister to suspend it for a future time. Tradition and the practice of the Church has always held that absolution under a future condition is invalid. Absolution under a condition of the present or past is certainly valid and for a just and sufficient grave cause lawful. Absolution may not be given conditionally unless the reason is well founded and grave necessity urges; thus, it must be imparted as often as, if not given, a notable spiritual damage would threaten the penitent, and if given absolutely, nullity or irreverence of the sacrament is risked. This is exemplified in the following cases of doubt: a) of the confessor that he absolved the penitent who is in mortal sin; b) of the dispositions of or the matter submitted by a penitent in danger of death, or whether the penitent is alive or has understood the confessor; c) of the return of the penitent if absolution is not given; d) of the attainment of the use of reason; e) of the sufficiency of the matter confessed by a devout person from whom certain matter cannot be prudently obtained.

It is not necessary but rather generally inadvisable for the confessor to inform the penitent that he has been absolved conditionally. When the penitent is considered in good faith, his later Communion will not be sacrilegious. When conditional absolution is given in the case of serious sins, especially in view of the doubtful dispositions of the penitent, the latter must not receive Communion, as this risks the danger of sacrilege. The confessor, at least, cannot recommend Communion but rather, when asked, leave it to the conscience of the penitent.

An oral or vocal expression of the condition is not necessary; it may be merely mentally expressed. In order to assure the placing of the condition, it is advisable to express it orally in words.

6. *Repeatable Formula*

When a penitent has already received absolution but then remembers a forgotten sin or a gravely changing circumstance or a notably diverse number of sins already confessed, the confessor must repeat the absolution. Otherwise, the penitent must confess this as necessary material in the next confession. The penitent must have contrition for this new material, unless his previously elicited contrition virtually perseveres. In practice, the confessor will ask the penitent if he is sorry for these sins also and confirm the penance given or add to it, as he prudently judges. When a slight sin is confessed after absolution, a new absolution may be imparted, but it is not required.

C. *Time and Place of the Celebration of Penance*

The sacrament of Penance may be celebrated on any day and at any hour. Prudence will direct the confessor in employing the more appropriate hours, especially regarding women penitents.

The proper place for the celebration of Penance is in a church, public oratory, or semipublic oratory,[40] unless there is a justifying cause for the confession to be heard elsewhere. This should take place in the confessional, if possible, even in the latter situation.[41]

For the confessions of women the confessional (always with a fixed and narrowly perforated grating between confessor and penitent) must always be located in an open and conspicuous place, and generally in a church, public or semipublic oratory.[42] For a just cause the local Ordinary may permit the hearing of women's confessions elsewhere, even habitually, but with the use of a confessional set up in an open and conspicuous place. A confessor or religious superioress may make a similar designation, but only for a single occasion, e.g., during a special religious event when many confessions are to be heard, during a retreat, etc.

The confessions of women are not to be heard outside the confessional unless an exception is required by reason of illness or some other true necessity, and in these cases the safeguards which the local Ordinary has judged opportune are to be observed.[43] True necessity or real need would seem to be present when the hearing of the confession in the normal place would cause the penitent serious embarrassment or difficulty. The confessor must make the decision in the particular case, judging the peculiar circumstances and legitimately designating a place for the confession.

III *Minister of the Celebration of Penance*

A. *Requisite Sacerdotal Power*

The ministry of the sacrament of penance requires both the

40. c. 908. Cf. **Ordo Paenitentiae,** 12-14, 38, and 40a for other confessional situation accomodations.
41. The ordinary place for the hearing of the confessions of men is the confessional in the church or public or semipublic oratory (PCI 24 nov. 1920). Men may be heard even in a private house (c. 910, 2). The hard of hearing are customarily heard in the sacristy or some other appropriate place but with a confessional, if possible.
42. c. 909.
43. c. 910, 1.

power of the priesthood and the power of jurisdiction or governance. Catholic faith teaches that Christ gave to the priest alone the power of binding and loosing, of forgiving and retaining sins.[44] The power of Orders is the efficacious instrument of the conferral of grace. It is a power equally received by all in priestly ordination rendering the recipient capable of sanctifying the people. It bestows the proximate aptitude and disposition to receive jurisdiction over subjects for the purpose of sanctifying them and, in the sacrament of Penance, of absolving their sins. The sacrament of Orders thus causes the penitential judgment to be efficacious.

B. *Penitential Jurisdiction*

Jurisdiction is the public power to rule subjects. Ecclesiastical jurisdiction is the public power to rule, to judge, to coerce the baptized with a view to their sanctification and supernatural happiness, which is the end purpose of the Church. This jurisdiction is exercised over all the baptized, as they alone are the subjects of the Church.[45] This includes penitential jurisdiction which is the judicial power to remit or to retain sins in the sacred tribunal of Penance, the faculty of exercising the power of Orders on certain definite persons as legitimately designated subjects, thus making the penitential judgment of the priest to be valid.

1. *Necessity of Jurisdiction*

It is certain that by divine institution, besides Orders, the priest must possess jurisdiction.[46] A judgment can be made only on one who is subject to the authority of the judge; absolution is a judiciary sentence, and thus the subjects or penitents must be assigned to the priest, even for the valid remission of venial sins.[47] Jurisdiction is received by the commission (*missio*) of a competent superior, which commission to certain subjects may be increased

---

44. Trent, Denz.-Schön. 1684, 1710; c. 871; cf. **Summa Theol., Suppl.** q. 8, a. 1; q. 19, a. 4. **Ordo Paenitentiae,** 9.
45. c.87.
46. Cf. c. 872; Trent, Denz.-Schön. 1686; **Summa Theol., Suppl.** q. 8, a. 4. **Ordo Paenitentiae,** 9.
47. Cf. c. 872; S.C.C. 12 feb. 1679.

or lessened, suspended or limited as to persons, places, times, cases, sins.[48] Since the other sacraments are not conferred in the manner of a judgment and do not have judicial acts, jurisdiction of itself is not required for them, except for their lawful administration (*licentia*). Thus *a priest may never validly impart absolution unless he possesses penitential jurisdiction in the Church from some valid title.*

2. General Types of Jurisdiction[49]

Jurisdiction in the external forum primarily and directly guides the external social relations of the faithful toward the society of the Church with the accompanying juridical and social effects. It thus determines whether the faithful in view of their conduct are worthy of praise or of blame *before the visible Church*. It is often exercised publicly by the passing of laws, inflicting of penalties, etc.

Jurisdiction in the internal forum here guides and directs the internal moral relations of the faithful with God, providing for the private welfare of the faithful in their moral conduct with God. It thus determines whether the faithful in view of their conduct are worthy of praise or blame *before God*. Exercised secretly in this forum of conscience the jurisdiction is private with effects before God alone and carries no juridical effects in the Church unless specially provided for. When this jurisdiction must be exercised in the confessional, i.e., in the sacrament of Penance or in connection with it, it is called *sacramental forum* and is bound by the sacramental seal. When it is not subject to this limitation, it is called *extra-sacramental forum*. Some dispensations may be given in this latter manner. The jurisdiction may be exercised over one who is absent and by letter or messenger (with the exception of sacramental absolution).

Jurisdiction may be *universal* or *particular* depending on whether or not it embraces all persons, places, matters, etc., or is limited in any of these. Exercised with a formal judicial process it is called judicial; when exercised without the process it is called *voluntary*,

---

48. c. 878.
49. Cf. c. 196; cc. 1044, 2250; 2254; 2290.

as in the case of dispensations or favors.

A most important distinction in jurisdiction is *ordinary* or *delegated.*

3. *Ordinary Jurisdiction*

Ordinary jurisdiction is that which in virtue of law or of custom the incumbent of an ecclesiastical office[50] automatically acquires from the office, not by privilege or any other act of his superior subsequent to and separated from the acquisition of the office itself, no matter whether his tenure is permanent or temporary. It is *proper* when the office is principal and the jurisdiction is exercised in one's own name, e.g., a residential bishop; it is *vicarious* when the office is accessory and the jurisdiction, although proper in a sense, is exercised in the name of another, e.g., a vicar general.[51]

The ordinary power of hearing confessions is obtained as soon as the office to which the power is attached is lawfully secured. It is personal over the possessor's own subjects and territorial over those not his subjects. Thus, one having ordinary jurisdiction can absolve his own subjects everywhere, but he can absolve those who belong to another diocese or parish or rite only within the limits of his own territory.[52] Ordinary power can be delegated entirely or in part to another, unless the law expressly rules otherwise.[53]

Ordinary jurisdiction comes to an end with the loss of office, with the passing of a condemnatory or declaratory sentence, and by excommunication, suspension from office and interdict.[54]

The following possess ordinary penitential jurisdiction:

Holy Father. The Roman Pontiff enjoys ordinary jurisdiction over all the faithful throughout the world.[55]

50. c. 145, 2.
51. c. 197.
52. c. 881.
53. c. 199, 1.
54. cc. 183; 873, 3; cf. cc. 208; 2261; 2275; 2279, 1; 2284. Some hold that for the sacrament of Penance suspension from divine functions (**a divinis**) or from jurisdiction (**a jurisdictione**) has the effect of suspension from office (**ab officio**).
55. c. 873, 1.

Cardinals. By privilege Cardinals enjoy ordinary jurisdiction everywhere over all the faithful, including religious of both sexes, regarding the sacrament of Penance. They cannot absolve from censures reserved *specialissimo modo* to the Holy See nor from those arising from a violation of the secrecy of the Holy Office.[56] They may not delegate this jurisdiction, except for their own or their household's confessions.[57]

Local ordinaries. Residential bishops, abbots and prelates *nullius*, etc., and their vicars general and episcopal vicars, administrators of an ordinariate, enjoy ordinary jurisdiction within their own territory.[58]

Religious ordinaries. Major superiors of exempt clerical religious institutes enjoy ordinary jurisdiction over their subjects; other superiors in such institutes enjoy ordinary penitential jurisdiction over their own subjects in accordance with the norms of their constitutions.[59] These subjects are postulants, novices, professed, and the laity who live on the premises. They can delegate this jurisdiction to other priests of the secular and regular clergy,[60] in accordance with their constitutions, and no jurisdiction delegated by the local Ordinary is needed.

Pastors. Pastors and those who have the status equivalent to pastors enjoy ordinary penitential jurisdiction. The care of souls entrusted to the pastor implies jurisdiction in the internal forum only,[62] with the ordinary jurisdiction to hear confessions within

---

56. Ibid.; c. 239, 1. 1º.
57. c. 239, 1. 2º. The same power of delegation is also enjoyed by residential and titular bishops. (c. 349, 1. 1º)
58. cc. 873, 1; 198; Vatican II, Decree **Christus Dominus**, 27. Cf. also Paul VI, motu proprio **Pastorale Munus** (30 nov. 1963), I, n. 29: "To use the faculties and privileges, with due observance of their scope and tenor, which religious resident in the diocese enjoy for the welfare of the people."
59. c. 873, 2.
60. c. 875, 1.
61. Cf. **The Celebration of Baptism,** footnote 74. The jurisdiction of military chaplains depends upon the faculties provided by the Military Ordinariate; they may also be delegated by the local Ordinary.
62. The pastor enjoys only limited jurisdiction in the external forum. (cf. cc. 1044; 1045; 1094; 1245, 1)

his own parish of his own subjects and of visitors (*peregrini*) and wanderers (*vagi*) of any rite,[63] and outside his own parish of his own subjects everywhere.[64] During paschal time he may absolve from all cases which the local Ordinary has reserved to himself.[65] By almost universal practice, the pastor is given delegated jurisdiction for the whole diocese. Pastors by office do not have the right to choose their own confessors, i.e., to delegate another priest to hear their own confession.[66] Likewise, a pastor is unable by office to delegate another priest jurisdiction to hear the confessions of his subjects.[67]

4. Delegated Jurisdiction

a. *Function*

Jurisdiction is delegated when it is not attached to an office but is committed to a person.[68] This delegation may be *by law* inasmuch as the law itself grants jurisdiction in certain circumstances, e.g., in danger of death,[69] or *from a competent superior* inasmuch as the special act of the superior expressly grants the jurisdiction whether the person be chosen for his personal qualifications or by reason of the office he holds, e.g., in the case of faculties granted by the Holy See to local Ordinaries.

In the matter of penitential jurisdiction delegated jurisdiction is of itself personal, so that the faculty of *subdelegating* is excluded unless expressly granted. Nor can there be further subdelegation unless this also was expressly granted.[70]

Only those who are capable of ecclesiastical jurisdiction for the sacrament of Penance may be delegated, and it may be exercised only over those who are subjects of the one delegating.[71] The Ordinary of the place where the confessions are to be heard is the authority competent to grant delegated jurisdictions for the con-

63. cc. 873, 1; 881, 1.
64. c. 881, 2.
65. c. 899, 3.
66. Alexander VII, 24 sept. 1665, Denz.-Schön. 2036.
67. PCI 16 oct. 1919.
68. c. 197, 1.
69. c. 882.
70. c. 199, 4-5.
71. c. 201, 1.

fessions of all persons, both lay and religious, to all priests secular and religious, even exempt religious.[72] This power to delegate belongs exclusively to the local Ordinary, if there is question of absolving the laity or clergy, non-exempt religious, or the members of another institute. It is enjoyed cumulatively with the superior of an exempt clerical religious institute, if there is question of absolving the subjects of that superior. Thus a confessor who is a Regular can absolve all penitents in virtue of the jurisdiction received from the local Ordinary, but in virtue of the jurisdiction received from his own superior he can absolve only the subjects of that superior.

Those who are delegated and all who hear confessions should possess the knowledge, prudence, and holiness required for this sacred function. The presence of these qualifications ought to be judged by their own proper superiors. Local Ordinaries may not grant jurisdiction nor religious superiors delegate jurisdiction or grant permission to hear confessions except to those priests who have been qualified by an examination or whose theological doctrine is otherwise known to be satisfactory. If prudent doubt later arises, a confessor may be required to submit to a further examination, even though he is a pastor.[73] The examination is not necessary for the validity of the grant of jurisdiction, unless particular law so determines.[74] A local Ordinary in delegating a religious and a religious superior in delegating an outsider can accept as indicative of worthiness the successfully passed examination given by the respective Ordinaries of those delegated. In the case of their own subjects it seems that the local Ordinary and the religious superior should examine.

b. *Use*

Priests who are religious should not use the delegation received from the local Ordinary without the at least presumed permission of their superior.[75] In practice this permission usually exists, unless

72. cc. 874, 1.
73. c. 877.
74. E.g., religious constitutions may further determine the qualifications and the examinations for hearing confessions.
75. c. 874, 1.

it is clear that the superior has positively forbidden the use of the delegation. Local Ordinaries are not habitually to grant confessional jurisdiction to religious not presented by their own superior, nor without serious reason should they refuse it to qualified religious who are so presented.[76] The validity of the grant or of the use of delegation is not affected in these cases. The local Ordinary may lawfully grant on one or another occasion the delegation and the recipient lawfully exercise it, as presentation is of itself a light obligation from which a just cause excuses, as long as there is no presence of scandal or, on the part of the religious, a serious precept. Revocation or suspension of permission given by the religious superior does not by that fact remove or suspend the jurisdiction granted by the local Ordinary.

Delegated jurisdiction and the permission to hear confessions can be granted with certain limitations; but in the absence of a justifying reason local Ordinaries and religious superiors should guard against too extensive a limitation.[77] The delegating authority cannot limit the faculties conferred by the common law, as such a limitation would be invalid and unlawful. However, should a permissible limitation be invoked without reasonable cause, the restriction would be valid though unlawful, and the delegated priest could not validly absolve. A priest with confessional jurisdiction from the local Ordinary is lightly obligated to have the pastor's permission to exercise lawfully his faculty when hearing confessions in a church subject to the pastor and to have the superior's permission in chapels of regulars or of nuns. The prescribed profession of faith and the oath against Modernism must be taken by a priest before entering upon the office of confessor.[78]

A priest who presumes to hear confessions without jurisdiction is *ipso facto* suspended *a divinis*; if he presumes to absolve from reserved sins without jurisdiction he is automatically suspended *a confessionibus*.[79]

---

76. cc. 874, 2; 880.
77. c. 878. Religious constitutions may place further limitations.
78. c. 1406, 7°; S.C.C. 25 oct. 1910; 20 iun. 1913. For new formula cf. **AAS**, S. Off. 20 dec. 1967 (p. 1058).
79. c. 2366.

c. *Concession*

To hear confessions validly jurisdiction must be granted *expressly*, either orally or in writing.[80] Thus a tacit or presumptive concession is excluded but not one that is implicit; a bishop sending a priest to give a mission or to help out a pastor implicitly delegates jurisdiction. In an urgent case intimation or notice of the grant of jurisdiction is not needed, if the priest is morally certain (e.g., by telephone or telegraph) that it has been granted; he may validly absolve because the rescript or faculty is valid before its acceptance and effective from the moment of its concession.[81] In every instance the concession must be made and a presumption of the future is inadmissible, i.e., that the faculty would be given if requested. No charge can be made for the grant of jurisdiction, which would be simony.[82]

d. *Cessation*

The power of delegated jurisdiction itself ceases when the mandate for which it was given is carried out or completed, or when the purpose of the delegation has been realized, e.g., to hear confessions until the chaplain recovers from his illness, or when the specified period of time has expired or the determined number of cases has been reached.[83] An act placed through inadvertence would not invalidate the absolution.[84]

The one delegating or his successor may directly notify the one delegated that the jurisdiction has been revoked,[85] and thus subsequent absolutions would be invalid; if it were suspended, the absolutions would be only unlawful, unless it were a suspension from office or a sentence.[86] Jurisdiction would not be lost with the demise of the one delegating, unless it were conferred *ad beneplacitum*, etc.[87]

80. c. 879, 1.
81. Cf. cc. 37, 38.
82. c. 879, 2.
83. c. 207, 1.
84. **Ibid.**, 2.
85. **Ibid.**, 1; cf. c. 880.
86. cc. 2264; 2275, 2º; 2284.
87. cc. 183, 2; 61.

Jurisdiction ceases if the one delegated informs the one delegating of his renunciation of the faculty and it is accepted.[88] Suspension and censure with sentence effect cessation. Change of domicile of itself does not affect the existence of delegation, since it is made to the person. The condition of domicile, however, may be expressly stated in the concession or implicitly understood. In the U.S.A. it is generally understood that penitential jurisdiction is revoked when the priest no longer retains domicile in the diocese.

5. *Special Delegated Jurisdiction*

In some instances the common law gives to *all priests* powers to absolve and to dispense; it is not necessary that the priest enjoy habitual ordinary or delegated jurisdiction, i.e., normal powers. In other circumstances special powers are given to *all confessors*, but normal jurisdiction is presupposed. These powers are granted by the common law of the Church to be used in the internal forum and thus the right to use them cannot be denied validly and lawfully. Not every use of these powers, however, will be lawful,[89] even though valid because of the supreme interest of the Church in the good of souls.

a. *Danger of death*

When there is danger of death, all priests, even though they are not approved for confessions, can validly and lawfully absolve any penitent whatsoever from any sin or censure, no matter in what manner it is reserved or how notorious it may be, even in the presence of a duly authorized priest, without prejudice, however, to the regulation of cc. 884, 2252.[90]

A reasonably prudent judgment is to be made from signs and conjectures that the danger of death is present and that it is morally certain that death can follow in a short time. It is not necessary that the final moment (*articulus mortis*) has arrived or that death is imminent or physically certain. In doubt of the existence of the danger or when an erroneous judgment (which is not deliberately

---

88. c. 207, 1.
89. Cf. c. 884 on the absolution of an accomplice.
90. c. 882.

false) has been made, the absolution is certainly valid, since the Church supplies jurisdiction for such contingencies.[91]

Danger of death may threaten from an intrinsic cause, such as a dangerous illness, very difficult childbirth, extreme old age, wound, etc., or from an extrinsic source, such as a sentence of execution, imminent battle, air raid alarm, difficult surgery, a truly perilous trip, etc. Mobilized soldiers may be considered in danger of death for the purposes of this faculty.[92] A person in probable danger of falling into insanity, or who has been captured by pagans with slight hope of release and of ever contacting a priest, or who is suffering under certain forms of religious persecution, may be considered in danger of death.

It suffices that the priest be validly ordained, even though he may be irregular, suspended, excommunicated, or a schismatic, heretic or apostate, and even though a priest with normal jurisdiction is present. It is commonly taught that a *penitent* cannot lawfully seek absolution from an heretical or schismatical priest, if it is possible to summon another priest to whom the penitent can confess without serious difficulty or embarrassment; and even when lawful, precautions must be taken to avoid scandal and to remove the danger of perversion to the penitent.

Absolution in the circumstance of danger of death is valid and lawful in the internal forum only, having no effect in the external forum.[93] An excommunication or personal interdict should be removed before the sins are absolved, as they prevent the lawful reception of the sacraments.[94] A deliberate inversion of the proper order by the confessor would be gravely unlawful but valid. A suspension may be absolved either before or after the sins, since it does not prevent the lawful reception of the sacraments.[95] When absolution is given from censures reserved *ab homine* or *specialissimo modo*, there must be recourse within a month of convalescence, under pain of reincurrence of the censure, to the Sacred Penitentiary

---

91. c. 209.
92. S. Poen. 18 mart. 1912; 29 maii 1915.
93. PCI 28 dec. 1927.
94. cc. 2246, 3; 2250, 2; 2260, 1; 2275, 2º.
95. cc. 2250, 1; 2278, 1.

in the latter case, or in the former case to the competent superior who invoked the penalty or to his successor or his delegate.

Civil marriage is a special case concerning the absolution of (1) priests in danger of death, who, (2) having attempted civil marriage, (3) are prevented by very grave reasons from ceasing to dwell in the same house with their accomplice but promise to observe absolute chastity in the future and wish to be absolved and to receive the sacraments as laymen. The excommunication attached to this crime is simply reserved to the Holy See,[96] but in this special combination of circumstances there is an obligation to have recourse to the Holy See as with a most specially reserved censure.[97]

When the local Ordinary cannot be reached, a confessor in the course of a sacramental confession in danger of death, and for the internal forum only, enjoys the power of dispensing, for the purpose of quieting a conscience and in a proper case of effecting the legitimation of offspring, and provided that scandal is avoided, from the formality required in the celebration of marriage and from ecclesiastical impediments, excepting the priesthood and affinity in the direct line arising from a consummated marriage, provided that the usual promises are given in a disparity of worship or mixed religion dispensation.[98] Being restricted to the internal forum, the confessor cannot dispense from public impediments. Dispensation of impediments public by nature but factually occult is doubtful.[99]

When a dying penitent has been the accomplice *in peccato turpi* of the absolving priest, it is unlawful (but valid) for the priest to absolve, unless there is absolute necessity.[100] By the commission of this sin he would incur an excommunication most specially reserved to the Holy See.[101] If a priest other than the sacerdotal accomplice can hear the confession of the dying penitent without danger of grave infamy to the accomplices or of scandal to others,

96. c. 2388, 1.
97. S. Poen. 18 apr. 1936.
98. c. 1044.
99. Cf. PCI 28 dec. 1927.
100. c. 884.
101. c. 2367, 1.

and the penitent does not refuse to confess to this other priest, the case of necessity is not present.

b. *Maritime and Air Faculties*

All priests who are on a *sea voyage,* provided they have duly obtained the faculty of hearing confessions from their own Ordinary or from the Ordinary of the port where they embark or from the Ordinary of any intervening port at which they stop in the course of the voyage, can throughout the entire voyage hear aboard ship the confessions of all the faithful who are making the voyage with them, even though the ship should in the course of the voyage pass through or even stop awhile at various places subject to the jurisdiction of several Ordinaries. Moreover, as often as the ship in the course of the voyage puts in at a port, they can hear the confessions both of the faithful who for any reason board the ship and also of those who seek to confess to them when they incidentally go ashore, validly and lawfully absolving them even in cases reserved to the local Ordinary.[102] Under identical terms the same faculty is enjoyed by all priests making an *air* journey.[103]

The faculty applies only to an ocean journey as distinguished from river travel[104] and must be a true and proper journey. For the purposes of this faculty the Ordinary designated as "own" may be the Ordinary of the place where jurisdiction to hear confessions is enjoyed and not necessarily where the priest has domicile or quasi-domicile. A religious Ordinary is positively excluded.[105] The priest enjoys this special faculty as soon as he boards the ship (or aircraft); it terminates when he definitely leaves the ship (or aircraft) in the terminal port. He may exercise this faculty for as long as three days, if the ship remains in a port for that length of time, or even if the priest should leave one ship and remain in the place for three days while awaiting another ship. He may not use this faculty for a longer period, if the local Ordinary can be

---

102. c. 883.
103. Pius XII, **motu proprio,** 16 dec. 1947.
104. A voyage on a great river, such as the Mississippi, or an immense lake, such as the Great Lakes, seems to be included.
105. PCI 30 iul. 1934.

easily reached,[106] nor in any other city or place morally distinct from the port city or territory. When at sea and outside of their territory the faithful are not bound by the reservation of a sin or censure by their local Ordinary.[107]

c. *Paschal Precept*

For a reasonable cause the faithful of both sexes may *postpone* for a time the fulfillment of their obligation of annual Communion during the Paschal season, provided they have received this *advice* from a priest who has penitential jurisdiction over them. Such a counsel may be given, e.g., to a person ill at home where it is not convenient to receive Communion, or to one not yet sufficiently instructed to make First Communion.

d. *Irregularities*

Every confessor[109] may dispense from all irregularities arising from an *occult* delict, excepting the case of voluntary homicide or abortion and all cases up for formal trial, but only in the circumstances of a *more urgent occult case* in which it is impossible for the delinquent in person, by letter or by agent to reach the Ordinary and imminent danger exists of serious harm or infamy; but the confessor can thus permit the penitent only the lawful exercise of orders already received and not the reception of further orders. There is no special formula required but a statement of what is being dispensed suffices. A confessor may exercise this faculty extrasacramentally regarding those over whom he has penitential jurisdiction. Recourse is not necessary after the dispensation has been granted.

e. *Vindictive Penalties*

In *occult* cases that are *very urgent,* if the observance of the vindictive penalty imposed by anticipatory sentence (*latae sententiae*) would result in the loss of reputation or scandal, every confessor

---

106. PCI 20 maii 1923. The estimation regarding the approach is to be made by the priest himself.
107. Cf. cc. 900, 3°; 2247, 2.
108. c. 859, 1.
109. c. 990, 2.

is authorized, in the sacramental forum, to suspend the obligation of observing it, with the imposed burden of having recourse at least within a month by letter and through the confessor, if this is possible without serious inconvenience, without the use of names, to the Sacred Penitentiary or to a bishop endowed with the requisite faculty, and of abiding by the mandate then imposed. If recourse is impossible in some unusual case, the confessor himself can then dispense in accordance with c. 2254, 2.[110]

f. *Vows and Oaths*

The common law does not empower a confessor to dispense from vows and oaths. However, confessors may be delegated this faculty over non-reserved vows and oaths by the local Ordinary or by a superior of an exempt clerical institute to be exercised in the sacramental forum only on their respective subjects. Commutation is included.[111]

g. *Fast and Abstinence*

The confessor as such has no faculty to dispense from these obligations but can be delegated by the local Ordinary for the sacramental forum (sometimes contained in diocesan faculties). However, a confessor can always declare, in the case of doubt, whether the penitent has an excusing cause, i.e., a physical or moral inability to observe the law.

h. *Reserved cases*

Missionaries having diocesan faculties in the place, during the time they are giving a mission to the people, enjoy the same powers as pastors to absolve from cases which Ordinaries have reserved to themselves in any way. Some extend this faculty to include those who give novenas or who give retreats to clerics, religious or laypeople whether publicly or privately or individually, and even to those confessors who are delegated to help in the

---

110. c. 2290.
111. cc. 1313; 1314; 1320.

hearing of confessions during such times. Moreover, the local Ordinary may grant to confessors of outstanding knowledge and prudence the faculty to absolve in the act of sacramental confession anyone whomsoever of the faithful from all censures, even though reserved, with the exception of: a) censures *ab homine;* b) censures most specially reserved to the Holy See; c) censures for the violation of the secret of the Holy Office; d) the excommunication for priests and all others who presume to contract marriage, even civilly, with them and are actually living together.[112]

i. *Indulgences*

Confessors can permit the substitution of other designated works for those prescribed for the gaining of indulgences in the case of those who cannot perform the latter because of some impediment justifying the substitution.[113] Confessors can exercise this faculty over those whose confession they can hear, even though such is not made.

6. *Expired Delegated Jurisdiction*

In the case of power granted for the internal forum, an act performed through *inadvertence* after the time limit has elapsed or the number of cases has been exhausted is valid.[114] It is here required that the jurisdiction over the cases has been previously possessed. The enumeration of the situations covered by the principle is taxative.

7. *Common Error and Doubtful Jurisdiction*

In common error *or* in positive and probable doubt of law or of fact, the Church supplies jurisdiction for both the internal and the external forum.[115]

a. *Common Error*

Error is a false judgment about an objective reality. Respecting

---

112. c. 899, 3; Paul VI, motu proprio **Pastorale Munus**, I, 14.
113. c. 935; Paul VI, Apost. Const. **Indulgentiarum Doctrina**, 1 ian. 1967, norms n. 11.
114. c. 207, 2.
115. c. 209.

the sacrament of Penance, it is a false judgment by which a priest is believed to be in possession of the jurisdiction necessary here and now to hear a confession and to grant absolution, although in reality he does not actually so possess it. If the error is commonly held, the Church supplies absolutely the jurisdiction thought to be possessed. In order to safeguard the pastoral and juridical welfare of the faithful, the needed jurisdiction is momentarily or transiently conferred upon the priest who actually exercises it in order to do *validly* what otherwise would be done invalidly.

Error in regard to jurisdiction is common when it is *de facto common*, i.e., when the false judgment has been made by the generality of the people of the place and the cause which would naturally lend them to make this error has been publicly placed and brought to their general notice. For example, a public announcement is made at the opening of a mission that confessions will be heard by the visiting priests. The error of one or even of a few, such as three or four in a town or more in a city, is considered to be private and particular, even though the circumstances founding the error will necessarily lead others to the same judgment. Thus it must be certain, or investigated to become sure, that the majority of the faithful are in error; until that fact is realized, any absolutions of penitents will be invalid due to lack of jurisdiction.

However, beyond this obvious situation of common error, it is safe in practice (and the absolution would be valid) to consider that error is sufficiently common to supply jurisdiction when it is *de iure common*, i.e., when a cause is publicly placed which, if they were aware of it, would lead the generality of the people into error, even if it has not generally been actually brought to their attention. In fact the error is not common, yet it is construed in law to be common because the cause and circumstances are such as are adequate to induce error in the minds of almost all prudent persons in a given place. The error is virtually common. For example, if an unannounced priest entered the confessional as though to hear confessions, as sometimes happens with a weekend supply.

The *use* of supplied jurisdiction is *lawful* only when there is present a reason sufficient to counterbalance the disturbance of right order, since it is normally unlawful to deviate from the established rules of the jurisdictional system laid down by the Church. Thus, without cause one would force the Church to supply jurisdiction. Prescinding from a case of contempt of authority or of scandal to the faithful, it is of itself gravely unlawful to use common error outside of proportionate necessity. A serious cause must be present to deliberately provoke common error or to use it when it arises unintentionally.[116] However, since the jurisdiction is actually supplied, the absolution is valid and the penalty of suspension for presuming to hear confessions without necessary jurisdiction[117] is not incurred. The privilege of supplied jurisdiction is for the benefit of the faithful, and so it is operative, even if the confessor knows he lacks jurisdiction. Necessity may be present if infamy of the priest or scandal must be avoided or the faithful must be turned away from confession with notable inconvenience because of the lack of an approved priest, especially on days of precept or some special ecclesiastical event.

b. *Positive and Probable Doubt*

As long as a doubt of law or of fact is positive and probable, jurisdiction is certainly supplied for the valid conferral of absolution. *Doubt* is a state of mind regarding a proposition in which certain judgment is suspended through fear of error. It is *positive* when there are more or less probable reasons commanding the assent of the mind, though with some fear of error; *negative* when there is no reason or solid reason either to affirm or to deny the possession of requisite jurisdiction in a given case. A positive doubt becomes *probable* when at least some reason in favor of possession of jurisdiction is truly solid or truly probable. The doubt is on the part of the priest. *Doubt of law* refers to the existence, extent, or the meaning of a law respecting jurisdiction in a given case, e.g., the notion of common error. *Doubt of fact* refers to the existence of the conditions required by a law for its

---

116. Some theologians hold that it would be only an abuse of something lawful rather than doing something unlawful, and therefore not more than a slight sin; others hold that a just cause excuses from this fault.
117. c. 2366.

application, e.g., whether a superior has granted jurisdiction, or whether the jurisdiction covers reserved cases, or whether his jurisdiction has lapsed.

The use of supplied jurisdiction here is not a usurpation of power against the mind of the Church, which is supplying only what is necessary, i.e., conditionally, if not already possessed by the priest. Thus, neither a serious reason nor any reason is required for the *lawful* use, even outside of necessity. There will always be a light reason in that the penitent wishes to confess.[118]

8. *Confessors of Religious*

The penitential jurisdiction required for the hearing of the confession of any penitent is valid and lawful also with regard to hearing the confessions of all religious, men and women.[119] Religious, in their desire to strengthen in themselves union with God, should try to go to the sacrament of Penance frequently, that is, twice a month. Superiors should promote this practice and provide this opportunity for the members to go to confession at least every two weeks and even oftener, if they wish to do so.[120]

---

118. Some theologians allow conditional absolution in a case of merely negative doubt but only when grave necessity demands, e.g., the fulfilment of the urgent obligation of annual confession, or the obligation to celebrate Mass or to receive Communion. Unless common error will supply jurisdiction, the priest is bound, all things being equal, to warn the penitent to confess as soon as possible to a certainly approved confessor or at least to elicit an act of perfect contrition.
119. S.C. Rel., 8 dec. 1970. **Normae circa usum et administrationem sacramenti Poenitentiae, praesertim apud Religiosas.** Canons which are contrary to or incompatible with these norms, or which because of them no longer apply, are suspended.
120. Ibid.: "Religious, because of their special union with the Church which 'incessantly pursues the path of penance and renewal' should value highly the sacrament of Penance by which the fundamental gift of 'metanoia,' that is, of conversion to the kingdom of Christ, first received in Baptism, is restored and strengthened in members of the Church who have sinned. Through this sacrament pardon is obtained from the mercy of God for the offenses committed against him, and we are reconciled with the Church which we wound by our sins. Religious should likewise hold in high regard the frequent use of this sacrament by which due knowledge of self is deepened,

All women religious and novices may, for the sake of their freedom in this regard, henceforth validly and lawfully confess to any priest approved for confessions in the place, without need for special jurisdiction or designation.[121] For the good of the community, however, an ordinary confessor should be provided in contemplative monasteries, houses of formation, and larger communities, as well as (at least in such monasteries and houses of formation) an extraordinary confessor, without any obligation of approaching him. In other communities an ordinary confessor may be named, if particular circumstances suggest this, according to the Ordinary's judgment and after request or consultation with the community. As far as possible, lay communities of men fall under these norms.

The local Ordinary should choose confessors carefully, with sufficient maturity and the needed qualities; he should judge their number, age, term of office, and should consult beforehand with the community. The ordinary confessor is considered as the priest habitually available for the confessions of the religious. He should arrange that he is available to hear at least twice a month the confessions of those religious who wish to approach him. The extraordinary confessor should go to the religious community at least four times a year.[122]

In an exempt clerical institute the designation and, if the priest does not otherwise enjoy penitential jurisdiction in that place, even the conferral of jurisdiction belongs to the superior of the religious subjects.[123]

> Christian humility is strengthened, spiritual direction is provided, and grace is increased. These and other wonderful effects not only contribute greatly to daily growth in virtue, but they are highly beneficial also to the common good of the whole community." The superior must make a special point of leaving the religious appropriately free with respect to the sacrament of Penance and the direction of conscience (cf. Vatican II, Decree **Perfectae Caritas,** n. 14).

121. **Ibid.** c. 876 is thus abrogated.
122. c. 521, 1.
123. c. 875, 1.

9. Confessors in Seminaries

A seminary is a college in which young men are trained for the clerical state.[124] As long as the young men dwell there for formation looking toward the clerical state, it is juridically a seminary.[125] There should be in every seminary a rector for government, at least two ordinary confessors, and a spiritual director (who also may hear the confessions).[126] Additional confessors should be provided whom the seminarians will be free to approach. The vote of these confessors is not to be sought when a seminarian's promotion to orders or dismissal is under consideration.[127] The rector enjoys the ordinary jurisdiction of a pastor[128] and can validly hear the confessions of his subjects but not lawfully, unless spontaneously requested and for a grave and urgent cause.[129]

10. Confessors Who Are Regulars

The Apostolic privileges noted here, bestowed by direct grant to a particular religious institute or by a communication of privileges, may be safely used in practice and with prudence by priests who are Regulars or Mendicants whenever they hear confessions, until the Apostolic See determines otherwise.

Regular confessors, when they hear confessions within the diocese for which they have been approved by the local Ordinary may absolve from those automatically incurred (*latae sententiae*) censures which are reserved by the common law to the local Ordinary. This faculty is restricted to the internal forum.

A confessor enjoying jurisdiction solely from a regular superior can absolve the latter's subject from a diocesan reservation but not from cases reserved in the religious institute without special faculty to do so from the competent superior.[130] If the local Ordinary

---

124. Cf. c. 1354, 1.
125. Even though designated a **collegium, academia, convictus,** etc., and regardless of the rank of the seminary.
126. c. 1358.
127. c. 1361. Seminarians also enjoy the usual freedom to approach any approved confessor.
128. c. 1368.
129. cc. 881; 891.
130. Cf. also c. 518, 1, together with S.C. Rel., 8 dec. 1970 (note 119 above).

reserves to himself *ratione censurae* or even *ratione peccati* sins which are already reserved to him *ratione censurae* in the common law, the regular confessor may safely employ in practice his privilege and absolve the penitent. In an individual case prudence may counsel the confessor not to use his faculty.

To use this or other privileges pertaining to absolution in confession it suffices that the Regular be a member of the institute enjoying the privilege and not necessarily that he possess confessional jurisdiction in his own institute. However, he must have the jurisdiction delegated by the local Ordinary for hearing the confessions of the faithful, and at least the presumed permission of his own superior to use the jurisdiction.

Regulars, approved by their superiors when they absolve the faithful who are subjects of the superior,[131] may absolve from sins in any way reserved by the local Ordinary, even though these faithful incurred the reservation before assuming the status of being presently a subject of the superior.

Since the privilege of Regulars to absolve pertains only to the reservations of the common law, sins and censures reserved by particular law to local Ordinaries are beyond this faculty. Thus a Regular confessor may not absolve from automatically incurred censure Catholics who have dared to attempt marriage after obtaining a civil divorce.[132]

Regulars including novices do not incur reservations imposed by the local Ordinary. Members of Mendicant Orders are immune from episcopal reservations, except if they presume 1) to preach in churches without previous permission of the local Ordinary, 2) to hear confessions of the laity without his approbation, 3) to expose scandalous images for public veneration.[133]

The confessional privileges of Regulars have been granted, not for their benefit, but for the good of the penitents who come to them. Thus these privileges should be used, unless a greater good

---

131. c. 514, 1.
132. III Plenary Council of Baltimore, n. 124.
133. When a Regular penitent has not incurred an episcopal reservation, a diocesan confessor may absolve his sin, and probably also in the case of the faithful of 514, 1, when the sin was committed within the religious house.

of the penitent is to be served by not employing them. In certain individual cases the requirements of the external forum may counsel a delay in absolution, e.g., until reparation has been made for the scandal caused by a crime, or in a public case where reconciliation is needed in the external forum and the mandate of the bishop is awaited and when such a delay would serve the good of the penitent, e.g., a repeated abortionist who is led to consider the crime of minor moment because of the ease of approach to a Regular confessor.

Regular confessors with jurisdiction from the local Ordinary can dispense and commute all private non-reserved vows of the faithful (even if confirmed by oath), both within and outside the confessional, provided that the rights of interested parties are not injured thereby. Generally a commutation is more salutary and meritorious for the penitent than a dispensation.

Regular confessors having jurisdiction from the local Ordinary can dispense their penitents from irregularities *ex delicto occulto,* except in a case of voluntary homicide or effectively procured abortion, or in a case which is before a juridical court. Restricted to the sacramental forum but not to more urgent cases, this faculty may be used both to permit the penitent to receive Orders and to exercise lawfully Orders already received. When engaged in missions, retreats or some such public exercises, Regulars[134] can dispense penitents in the internal forum and in confession only from all occult irregularities, even those otherwise requiring express and individual mention.

Members of religious institutes who are Regulars, when on a journey with permission of their superior, may confess to a priest of their own Order suited for hearing confessions, even though not approved by the superior, or in defect of such, to any other priest suited for hearing confessions, even though not approved by the local Ordinary, if the constitutions of the Order do not expressly forbid it. It is sufficiently probable that in granting the legitimate permission to leave the religious house, the superior implicitly grants jurisdiction to delegate.

134. Those communicating with the Passionists. Pius VI, 27 maii 1789.

It is sufficiently probable that a Regular confessor who has obtained and still retains jurisdiction from some local Ordinary may while on a journey validly hear the confessions of the faithful, if he is unable to approach the local Ordinary conveniently for faculties and if the pastor is not opposed to his hearing the confessions.

C. *Manifestation of Conscience*

All religious superiors are strictly forbidden to induce their subjects by any means whatever to manifest their conscience to them. Subjects, however, are not forbidden to open their hearts freely and spontaneously to their superiors; indeed, it is expedient that they should approach their superiors with filial confidence and, if the superiors are priests, they should reveal to them the doubts and anxieties of their conscience.[135]

All categories of superiors in the strict sense are included in this prohibition, prelates and non-prelates, major and local superiors both clerical and lay, in institutes of both men and women religious. Masters and mistresses of novices or of the professed, prefects of clerics, etc., since they are not strictly superiors, are not directly covered by the restriction of the law but rather by reason of the spirit and end of the law, i.e., indirectly they are bound. Spiritual direction is not ruled out by this law but only the necessity of spiritual direction by superiors, because of the danger of abuses; their right to induce it is entirely removed. They may induce their subjects to manifest their conscience to others, such as their confessors or spiritual directors, but never to the superiors themselves. Thus, all means of influencing the subject in this matter with respect to the superior are forbidden superiors. They may, however, counsel their subjects, instruct them in the law and their rights, and explain the advantages of manifestation of conscience. The superiors, moreover, have the care of the community which comprises the preservation of the order, discipline, and regular observance of all members, and the fostering of their religious and spiritual life.

---

135. c. 530.

Thus they may inquire about things which some external manifestation make the natural object of exterior government, such as negligences, infidelities, passions, aversions, etc. Charity and a discreet reserve and delicacy will direct their inquiry in these matters as they are closely connected with the domain of conscience itself. They will be careful not to press insistently a reluctant subject for motives and causes.

Superiors are forbidden to induce only what is in the strict sense a manifestation of conscience, i.e., the secret dispositions, passions, temptations, motives, trials, dislikes, the degree of culpability of hidden faults, hidden acts of virtue or graces received. Spiritual direction by superiors when spontaneously and freely sought by their subjects (novices and professed) is not affected by the restriction of the law, but encouraged. The manifestation of doubts and anxieties to superiors who are priests is positively recommended by the law; the manifestation to lay superiors is not forbidden but neither is it called expedient. Thus this manifestation of conscience to superiors is entirely the concern of the subjects, who in no way are to be induced or constrained. Masters and mistresses of novices (and others mentioned previously, who are strictly superiors) likewise may not induce or constrain their subjects. However, their special function is the spiritual formation and instruction of the novices. For this to be properly and successfully accomplished, some manifestation of conscience from the novices is to be expected and required. Avoiding all inducement and constraint, the master may paternally and discreetly suggest such manifestation. Superiors and novice masters who by their observance, evident virtues, zeal, prudence, sympathy and availableness inspire respect and reverence, filial trust and love, often receive the spontaneous and free confidences of their subjects.

D. *Qualities of a Confessor*

"There is nothing more excellent, or more useful for the Church of God and the welfare of souls, than the office of confessor."[136] "Next to the Holy Sacrifice, the most important and serious act

---

136. II Plenary Council of Baltimore, n. 278.

of the priest is the administration of the sacrament of Penance";[137] "if any power be exalted and venerable, it is surely the power of the priest to whom it is granted, as the instrument and minister of God, to make just men of sinners and to open for them the gates of heaven."[138] It is also one of the gravest responsibilities of a priest. In order to promote the divine honor and the salvation of souls, the priest must remember that in hearing confessions he enjoys not only the function of a *judge* but also the role of a *physician,* and that he has been appointed by God as a minister both of divine *justice* and also of divine *mercy*.[139] The penitential judgment of the confessor, then, is not condemnatory and vindictive but liberative and curative. It belongs to the nature of this sacrament to pass judicial sentence, but its end or purpose is to heal the wounds of sin. As a minister the priest is obliged by religion to procure most carefully the honor of God and the good of the sacrament through its valid and lawful administration. He is bound in justice and charity to secure the good of the penitent by fostering dispositions for a most fruitful reception of the sacrament now and as a safeguard for the future. He is similarly bound to provide for the common good in the exercise of his office by avoiding whatever is injurious to the public good or to individuals through scandal or other evil. Thus, beside sacred orders and the jurisdiction necessary for the sacrament of Penance, the integrity of the con-

137. Pius XII, **Discourse to the Parish Priests and Lenten Preachers of Rome,** 6 feb. 1940: ". . . Take your place in that divine tribunal of self-accusation, sorrow, and forgiveness, as judges in whose breasts beat the hearts of fathers and friends, of physicians and teachers. And while the primary purpose of this sacrament is to reconcile men to God, do not lose sight of the fact that this exalted purpose is splendidly served by spiritual direction. For souls are here brought nearer to the paternal voice of the priest than ever; they bring their pains and troubles and doubts to him, and accept with confidence his advice and his warnings. The people feel keenly the need of confessors who are men of virtue and are skilled in theology and ascetics; men, who, because of their experience and knowledge, will be able to interpret tactfully and kindly for them, and in a clear and dependable manner, the rules which will enable them to travel safely on the road to a good life."
138. **Ibid.,** 17 feb. 1942.
139. c. 888, 1.

fessor's office demands for the spiritual welfare of the souls committed to him certain qualities or characteristics, which can be described as *"goodness, knowledge* and *prudence."*[140] These qualities are only described here; further implications and applications are treated later when the various duties of the confessor toward the penitent are considered.

1. *Goodness*

The probity of life expected of the minister of Christ in the confessional is more than the mere state of grace or freedom from serious sin so that a sacrilegious administration might be avoided. In the celebration of Penance he should be free from all unchristian harshness and severity, impatience and hastiness, human respect and sentimental familiarity, vanity and self-adulation. The virtues directive of his office are several and interrelated, but a supernatural zeal and love for souls, sinners especially, must be his most obvious and principal imitation of the Master. The confessor's apostolate of souls is to all sinners without distinction or favoritism, and without reluctance to accept the burdens of the ministry, uniting kindness and gentlemanliness with necessary firmness.

Patience is a virtue which is never out of demand in the life of a confessor,—patience with all types of sinners, and constancy and long-suffering when the hearing of confessions becomes monotonous, protracted, or a trial.[141] Humility gives the confessor a practical sympathy with penitents, because he is aware of his

140. **Rit. Rom.**, Tit. III, c. 1, c. 1. "The faithful want good confessors, who have a sound and mature grasp of doctrine, who will show to them clearly and accurately what is lawful and unlawful, who will impose no unnecessary burdens or obligations and who will come to their aid when justice or charity require it; they want prudent confessors in whom, as penitents, they can fully confide, without the risk of spiritual harm; confessors full of the spirit of God, who know how to lead them to the perfection which corresponds with their state. Show yourselves, beloved sons, worthy of such a noble ministry" (Pius XII, **loc. cit.**, 17 feb. 1942). Cf. **Ordo Paenitentiae,** 10.

141. Pius XII, **ibid.**, 23 mart. 1949: "And, in speaking of the care of souls, we have in mind particularly the sacrament of Penance, which demands in the priest an absolutely exemplary life, combined with a sense of responsibility, judgment that is clear

own weaknesses and sins and that, but for divine grace, he might be worse than his penitents. Purity is an indispensable safeguard at all times lest the confessional in any way should become a danger to chastity through thought, desire, or action. Meditation on the teachings of the Church and of holy and learned writers concerning the apostolate of penance will, together with constant prayer for assistance and guidance, help to keep alive and to foster the devotion of the priest to this important part of his ministry.

2. *Knowledge*

The confessor is gravely bound, outside a case of necessity, to have the knowledge which is required for the proper and competent exercise of his office. He must possess at least the average or ordinary knowledge which is necessary in the circumstances and with regard to the penitents of this day and age; such knowledge must vary also with different confessors as their status and particular ministry varies. Every confessor, however, must know what will secure the substance, validity and lawfulness, integrity and effect of the sacrament both on his and the penitent's part, the common and particular obligations of the states of life of the penitents, the species and changing circumstances of sins, the manner of discernment of serious from slight sins both objectively and subjectively and their numerical distinction, the validity and lawfulness of acts, the principles of justice with the obligations of reparation and restitution, reserved sins and censures, matrimonial impediments dispensable in the confessional, sinful occasions, remedies for sins,

> and sure, self-control, prudence, and tact. . . . All this is the ordinary ministry. It is less ostentatious than extraordinary acts and great displays; it is everyday work; it is performed in silence and frequently passes unnoticed. But even so, it should at all times be carried out in the most perfect manner possible, and particularly at the present time, because all the souls whom extraordinary activities win for Christ, or who are led to him by formidable happenings, must ultimately, like others, come within that ordinary care of souls which is continuous and deep. The ordinary care of souls should give to all the assurance of being taken to the bosom of the Church; it is through it principally that the Church fulfills her duty of proclaiming Christ and of teaching and guiding every man, in order to bring all to perfection in Christ Jesus."

fitting and salutary penances and obligations to impose, the main teachings of ascetical theology and of spiritual direction.

A confessor need not have perfect knowledge whereby he can always and immediately and personally solve all cases. It suffices that he can solve the cases that commonly occur and doubt prudently about the more difficult cases, so as, if necessary, to consult books and those more learned or experienced (in the meantime a penitent may be absolved who is willing to return and to abide by the decisions of the confessor). Otherwise he courts the proximate danger of a bad administration of the sacrament and injury to the penitent. If a case must be solved without delay, e.g., with the dying, the confessor will invoke the Holy Spirit and make the best judgment he can, later checking on his solution. It is worthwhile in practice, especially for neo-confessors, to review their solutions, repair their defects, and thus be fore-armed for the future. A priest sins seriously if he certainly knows he lacks competent knowledge and yet attempts to hear confessions, even out of charity or obedience. The approbation of the bishop or the regular superior does not supply for but rather presupposes requisite knowledge. If a priest *prudently* fears that his lack of knowledge risks nullity of the sacrament, he can absolve only conditionally. However, those who have diligently pursued their seminary studies and have successfully passed the prescribed examinations are presumed to be competent as described (and they ought to exercise their ministry in this conviction), until it becomes otherwise evident and certain.

Alumni of seminaries, both secular and religious, are seriously held to maintain a continual study of the sacred sciences, so that they might exercise the office of confessor with fitness, as is required of other professional men.[142] The natural qualities of good sense and good judgment, most advantageous and necessary in a good

---

142. Pius XI, Encyclical **Ad Catholici Sacerdotii**; Pius XII, **Discourse to the Seminarians of the Roman Colleges,** 24 iunii 1939: "But it is no less true that zealous priests, intimately convinced of the truths of faith and full of the Spirit of God, are today winning greater and more wonderful success in the conquest of souls for Christ than perhaps ever before. If you are to become priests such as these, with the help and after the example of St. Paul, nothing must come before study of

confessor, do not substitute for the benefit of theological study and the fruit of the wisdom of others; nor does it provide knowledge of the development of positive legislation in the Church and its interpretation. Experience is no substitute for requisite knowledge, but it is an aid in giving greater insights into human nature, the interior solutions, and a facility in the application of principles and laws. Longstanding experience without study and knowledge has been termed nothing but intimacy with error. A regular review of moral and ascetical theology, canon law, an acquaintance with available ecclesiastical literature, in other words, a continuing education in some form, is strongly recommended for the retention and development of knowledge already acquired. The confessor, moreover, should expound the common teaching of approved authors in accord with the magisterium of the Church and not his own peculiar viewpoint.

3. *Prudence*

Prudence, the practical wisdom which directs the best means to the end, is exceedingly necessary for the confessor, who must apply principles and precepts, remedies and obligations to the conditions of individual persons and circumstances, avoiding excess

> theology, biblical and positive as well as speculative. Let the conviction be stamped deeply on your minds that today the faithful are seeking earnestly for good pastors of souls and learned confessors. Devote yourselves then with pious enthusiasm to the study of moral theology and canon law. Even canon law is directed to the salvation of souls, and by means of all its regulations, and through its laws, it tends primarily to that one purpose, that men may live and die sanctified by the grace of God." Vatican II, **Optatam Totius**, n. 22: "Especially because of the circumstances of modern society, priestly training should be pursued and perfected even after the seminary course of studies has been completed. Hence, Episcopal Conferences ought to make use in their individual countries of the more effective means to this end, such as pastoral institutes involving aptly chosen parishes, conferences held at set times, and fitting projects designed to afford the younger clergy a gradual introduction into the priestly life and apostolic activity under their spiritual, intellectual, and pastoral aspect, and calculated to help young priests renew and develop this life and activity more intensely every day."

and defect, laxity and rigorism. Prudence will direct his ministry in safeguarding the sacrament, leading penitents to the path of Christian living and perfection, and in procuring the common good. Purity of intention, prayer (especially before confessions), docility and earnest industry are means for growing in this prudence.

The confessor must try to adapt his remarks to the concise problem, difficulty, or need of the penitent, i.e., to what the penitent needs and can use, and to refrain from giving a whole course of instructions or long sermons. He ought not to be too hasty in solving difficult cases but give attentive and mature consideration to all the factors, remembering that after all he hears but one side of a situation. He should not guess at an answer nor shirk an evident responsibility to give a definite answer. He should not, unless necessary, send penitents to another confessor or to the pastor, but try to treat the case as satisfactorily as possible. In perplexing cases he should follow a safe and sane norm, doing what, under God, he believes ought to be done in the case, seeking above all to apply solidly probable teaching that is apt to accomplish what the spiritual good of the penitent here and now demands. He should leave the penitent free to go to another confessor; the penitent also must be allowed to abide by a solidly probable opinion that is legitimately applicable in his case. The confessor should never show penitents that he knows them or recognizes them, ask for a name or address, or accept money for Masses in the confessional.

Confidence in other confessors (as well as in parents, teachers, physicians, etc.) must be preserved and not in any way lessened, if this can be avoided. Oftentimes a penitent has misunderstood or misinterpreted the advice or requirements of a previous confessor, or has not explained the case to him in the same way as to the present confessor. Where it is clear or it is suspected that a previous confessor has given wrong advice or made an error, it suffices for the priest to state his lack of understanding of what happened in the previous confession, and that, as the case stands presently before his judgment, his answer is such and such. It is always preferable (and even necessary with an habitual sinner) to find out if the penitent has previously received advice and followed it. The penitent should be encouraged to continue or to renew his efforts, if the previous advice still appears advantageous to the penitent; otherwise new counsel is in order.[143]

E. Duties in the Celebration of Penance

1. Hearing of Confessions

a. *With the care of souls*

Pastors and others to whom in virtue of their office the care of souls has been entrusted are bound by a serious obligation *in justice* to hear, either in person or through another, the confessions of those entrusted to them whenever the latter reasonably request it.[144] This obligation in justice derives from the tacit contract with those from whom they receive sustenance and honor under the condition that they celebrate or administer the sacraments, and with their ecclesiastical superior who appoints them with the understanding that they faithfully discharge their office, of which the celebration of Penance is a part.

In a penitent's *extreme* spiritual *necessity*, i.e., in his extremely great difficulty of escaping the danger of eternal loss, a priest must hear his confession, even at the risk of his own life and although the penitent has not made the request, e.g., a dying sinner who cannot elicit an act of perfect contrition for his serious sins. The priest is likewise bound when the penitent is in probable danger of loss of salvation, e.g., when a dying sinner in serious sin could elicit an act of perfect contrition but only with great difficulty.

---

143. For some norms on the conduct of confessors in dealing with the sixth commandment, cf. S. Off. Instr. 16 maii 1943.
144. c. 892, 1, in which are included assistants (**vicarii cooperatores**) and religious superiors in clerical institutes. "Pastors should also be mindful of how much the sacrament of Penance contributes to developing the Christian life, and, therefore, should make themselves available to hear the confessions of the faithful" (Vatican II, Decree **Christus Dominus**, n. 30). "They are joined with the intention and love of Christ when they administer the sacraments. Such is especially the case when they show themselves entirely and always ready to perform the office of the sacrament of Penance as often as the faithful reasonably request it" (**ibid.**, Decree, **Presbyterorum Ordinis**, n. 13). Cf. **Ordo Paenitentiae**, 10b.

In a penitent's *grave* spiritual *necessity*, i.e., in a serious danger which the penitent strictly can overcome himself, a priest must hear his confession, even at great inconvenience but without risking his life, e.g., if a sinner has a serious disease which is not endangering his life, or if he has serious temptations which he can overcome only with difficulty without the sacrament. The priest need not risk his own life, since such sinners can sufficiently provide for themselves.

A priest is seriously bound to hear the confession of a penitent in *common* spiritual *necessity*, i.e., when the sacrament is reasonably requested. It would be no sin for the confessor to put off the confession for a short time because of a legitimate impediment or because the penitent was merely vexatious or wished to confess too frequently without special reason. A pastor would sin seriously if he would hear confessions only rarely or only on assigned days, or if he made the sacrament distasteful or discouraged the faithful by his attitude. The pastor's own obligation is less strict when he has assistants, unless he is requested personally or the penitent's need requires the pastor's administration. Nevertheless, the pastor should lead by his example as a good confessor.

b. *Without the care of souls*

All confessors in a case of urgent necessity are bound by an obligation *in charity* to hear the confessions of the faithful and, in danger of death, all priests are bound by this obligation.[145] *Every priest* has a serious obligation to provide for *extreme* spiritual *necessity* of his neighbor, even with great inconvenience extending to risking his own life. Such a risk requires that the spiritual need of the penitent is morally certain, there is probable hope of absolving, no other confessor is available, and greater evils will not result from the death of the priest, e.g., many others will perish for lack of a priest.

When a sinner is in *grave necessity* whereby he can free himself from serious sin or from the danger of lapsing into such only with great difficulty, every *confessor* has a serious duty to hear his con-

---

145. c. 892, 2.

fession. This obliges with great inconvenience if there is a general lack of confessors, but not to the extent of endangering life. The common obligation of the priesthood and of the office of confessor obliges in the *common necessity* of the penitent, i.e., when he reasonably requests the sacrament, as long as there is no inconvenience and no other confessor is opportunely available. Even light inconvenience excuses the confessor from obligation and sin, especially grave sin.

2. *Attitude of the Confessor*

The sacrament of Penance was instituted after the manner of a judgment and thus the absolution or retention of sins is a judicial sentence.[146] By the nature, then, of this sacrament the minister is a *spiritual judge*.

As a judge the minister must know the penitent's case and thus he has an obligation to question about those things concerning the penitent which are necessary to form a prudent judgment, primarily to insure the integrity of the confession and less frequently to discover the penitent's dispositions. A penitent may fail, culpably or not, to make a complete confession, e.g., because of lack of examination, shame, ignorance of the obligation, etc.; if he has a reasonable doubt, the confessor must ask questions. Clerics, religious, devout persons usually need no questioning, as they habitually make integral and complete confessions. The primary obligation of integrity is on the penitent but, when necessary to procure the validity and reverence of the sacrament, it may even seriously bind the confessor. In a long session of hearing confessions, for the confessor to omit to question one or another on the species and number of sins is a slight sin or none at all.

The confessor must be always prudent in his interrogation of penitents, especially regarding the sixth commandment. Ordinarily he should not interrupt the penitent until the confession is completed; in lengthy confessions this may be expedient in order not to forget necessary matter. Questions should be clear and understandable to the penitent; ordinarily they should not be negative (e.g., you didn't consent, did you? but rather: did you give consent?)

---

146. Cf. c. 870; Denz.-Schön. 1709.

Nor disjunctive (e.g., did you sin with yourself or with another? but rather: did you commit the sin with yourself?). The confessor should be gentle, benign, and gentlemanly in his questions, aiding and encouraging penitents who are timid or embarrassed.

The confessor, who as judge is bound by office to form his prudent judgment on the sins committed and the penitent's dispositions, must believe a penitent when he accuses, affirms, or denies his sinfulness, unless it is certain he has been lying. If he doubts the penitent's sincerity and despite his efforts for more candor the penitent persists in his confession, the confessor must absolve. If the confessor certainly knows by personal knowledge outside the confessional that the penitent is in serious sin, which he denies, he should not absolve, unless he can assume that the penitent has forgotten it, already confessed it, or has sufficient reason for omitting it. If this knowledge comes from others outside the confessional, the confessor may refuse absolution only if he is morally certain of the truth of their assertion even though the penitent denies it, because the penitent is to be believed over others. If the knowledge comes from the confession of another, the seal must be kept and confessional knowledge not used; the confessor can question the penitent only in general terms, as customary with other penitents, and absolve at least conditionally.

It suffices that the confessor make a *prudent* and *probable* judgment regarding the penitent's confession and dispositions; complete certitude is not always possible nor required in dealing with internal dispositions. The confessor must employ ordinary diligence; if because of noise, distraction, singing, etc., he does not hear certain sins, he must question the penitent when there is probably serious matter present. He is not bound to recall distinctly at the moment of absolution every sin confessed, but at least generally the state of the penitent. The penitent should not be permitted to gloss over his serious sins, especially in matters of justice and marital relations. The confessor will positively doubt about the penitent's dispositions for absolution if, e.g., he is reluctant or very remiss in confessing all his sins or in admitting guilt, or if he as a recidivist does not evidence genuine sorrow or preparedness to accept remedies and penances, etc.

To absolve a certainly well-disposed penitent guilty of serious sin obliges the confessor seriously in justice. If the confessor can have no doubt regarding the dispositions of the penitent and if the latter seeks absolution, absolution cannot be denied or deferred.[147] The general rule is to impart absolution. Trustworthy signs of sufficient dispositions are: a spontaneous, sincere, and humble confession and contrition; a confession made despite great difficulties; a positive reversal of former sinful practices; a sincere resolution to follow the confessor's counsel; great sorrow clearly shown in a habitual sinner; etc.

The confessor must impart absolution even though the penitent holds a different legitimate opinion, as long as he is otherwise properly disposed. The opinion insisted upon by the penitent must be truly probable, either intrinsically or extrinsically, and not a non-probable or false opinion. The confessor is the judge of the penitent's dispositions and not of his moral opinions as long as they are reputable and safe.

To deny absolution to those who are judged incapable or unworthy is likewise a serious duty.[148] Otherwise the absolution would be invalid or at least fruitless and a sacrilege, if administered knowingly and willingly. The confessor should do his best to dispose the penitent for absolution.[149] Absolution should be denied, e.g.,

147. c. 886.
148. "60. The penitent who has the habit of sinning against the law of God, of nature, or of the Church, even if there appears no hope of amendment, is not to be denied absolution or to be put off, provided he professes orally that he is sorry and proposes amendment. 61. He can sometimes be absolved, who remains in a proximate occasion of sinning, which he can and does not wish to omit, but rather directly and professedly seeks or enters into." Propositions condemned by Innocent XI, S. Off. 4 mart. 1679. Denz.-Schön. 2160-2161.
149. "The confessor is to beware lest anyone leave this sacrament of reconciliation offended. Wherefore, if there is a just cause why absolution should be deferred, it is necessary that those who have confessed be persuaded in the most kind words possible that both duty and office and their salvation demand this; and they are most persuadingly to be enticed to return as quickly as possible, so that having faithfully accomplished what has been profitably prescribed, and released from the bonds of sin, they may be refreshed with the sweetness of divine grace." Leo XII, Const. **Caritate Christi**, 25 dec. 1825.

to those who give no signs of sorrow; to those who are unwilling to reform their lives by abandoning the proximate occasions of sin or removing hatreds or enmities or restoring what is possible to rightful possessors, etc. The confessor must be firm in his denial of absolution, especially with priests and those aspiring to Orders or religious profession. He should inform the penitent of the reason in a kind and fatherly manner, urging him to search his soul again and pointing out that the penitent himself is the cause of the confessor's unfortunate inability to impart the divine graces of this sacrament.

To defer absolution is a duty of the confessor, if the disposition of the penitent is clearly doubtful and there is no urgent and proportionately serious cause for absolving conditionally. In practice this is rarely advised today, except for a brief time for the obvious good of the penitent, e.g., to step back into the church for further examination and prayer and then to return to confession, or if the confessor prudently judges a delay useful and the rightly-disposed penitent consents. At times it is very difficult in practice to judge the sufficiency of the penitent's dispositions. If both danger of nullity to the sacrament and of notable detriment to the penitent cannot at the same time be avoided, the latter danger should be avoided and the absolution given conditionally. The doubtfully disposed are to be conditionally absolved, e.g., in danger of death, when marriage is about to be celebrated or Confirmation received, when there is no other opportunity to confess, in danger of grave scandal or infamy to the penitent, etc.

The confessor receives his role as *spiritual physician* from the purpose of the sacrament; it pertains to its integrity. Penance not only binds up the wounds and infirmities of sin but also fosters the health and strength of the soul for the future. For this reason the confessor searches the causes and occasions of sins and the dispositions of the penitent and indicates apt remedies. These consist in the general remedies of love of God, prayer, mortification, frequentation of the sacraments, awareness of the presence of God, frequent examination, etc., and also in particular remedies to eradicate and to ward off sinful habits in the future in respect to the individual penitent. The confessor should make clear what is of obligation and what is of counsel and employ with due caution and adequate understanding those things which can be profitably used from psychology and psychiatry by an expert confessor.

The confessor as *spiritual father* is held in charity more or less, depending on the spiritual state of the penitent and the confessor's possibilities, to propose motives for contrition to those less disposed and thus to prepare them for absolution, e.g., the deformity of sin, the danger of damnation, the shortness and vanity of life, the goodness of God and the gifts of Christ, etc. All penitents, and notably the more needy, should be treated with fatherly love; this love should be signalized by patience, perseverance, and kindness, especially with difficult cases and vexing penitents. Corrections and exhortations must be in the same spirit, avoiding whatever would either terrify or exasperate the penitent. The confessor should not overly spend time with the devout and permit useless conversations. His paternal concern for the penitent should be tempered with caution in the case of women, lest a natural and dangerous affection be aroused on either side.

The confessor as *spiritual doctor* is bound as far as possible to instruct the penitent, in a simple and not prolix but sufficient manner, in those things necessary for a valid and fruitful reception of the sacrament and in the Christian truths and precepts the penitent ought to know, whether the ignorance is culpable or not. By his office the confessor is obliged only to instruct in what is necessary for the administration of the sacrament; by charity he is held to other things.

If a penitent is in bad faith or in seriously culpable vincible ignorance, the confessor must always instruct him, even though no correction is anticipated, as he is in sin and can be harmful to others. Also if the ignorance is invincible and the confessor foresees that the instruction will be profitable now or later on. If the penitent is in good faith or inculpably ignorant, even though vincible, he is to be instructed in the necessary truths, as long as at least future benefit is anticipated. A penitent should not be left in material sin, which is an evil in itself, may lead to formal sin, is harmful to individuals and detrimental to the common good. Penitents with an erroneous conscience must be instructed, especially when they cannot long remain in ignorance of the sinful character of the action, e.g., voluntary pollution, contraception, etc. Often when a penitent asks questions it is an indication that he is no longer in good faith. However, he may be in good faith in asking a question due merely to a scruple or because he considers some action slightly sinful. The confessor should not appear to approve error because of his silence. Sometimes the confessor should answer only precisely what he has been asked, e.g., that the marital debt may be lawfully *given* by one with a private vow, saying nothing about the unlawfulness of *requesting* it.

If no harm will result to the penitent or the common good, instruction may be omitted due to the penitent's invincible ignorance and when no benefit from an instruction is expected, e.g., it is foreseen that a material sin would then become a formal sin whereas it is also seen that the present good faith will perdure. Thus the confessor may omit to instruct if the harm resulting would outweigh the benefit, e.g., if the penitent were informed of the altogether unsuspected invalidity of his marriage, the children would suffer greatly. In doubt whether the instruction would be more harmful than beneficial, it is ordinarily not given, as the penitent is in good faith and formal sin is certainly avoided. If the good anticipated is greater than the harm feared, or it is very probable, the instruction can be given even in doubt. If the public welfare would suffer by the confessor's silence or if scandal could not be avoided, the public good is to be favored over that of the penitent and the instruction given. Thus the practice of conjugal onanism cannot be tolerated, since others would think that what is not corrected is lawful; also the commonly known invalidity of a marriage must be made known to a penitent heretofore in good faith and even if it is foreseen he will not heed the information.

3. *Correction of Defects and Errors*

A confessor is seriously bound in justice to rectify his error, culpable or not, affecting the *validity* of the sacrament, even though he agreed to hear the confession only out of charity. The confessor must repair his own culpable defect even at great inconvenience, if otherwise the penitent would suffer serious damage and it is not known if the penitent will confess again soon, e.g., in the case of the dying. He need not remedy an inculpable defect at great inconvenience, e.g., at the risk of infamy to himself, unless there is danger of the penitent dying in serious sin. The confessor does not have this obligation if only free matter was confessed or if it is prudently judged that the penitent has already confessed again to another priest.

The confessor should correct his own error as soon as possible, even without permission of the penitent; if the latter must be informed, it would not be using knowledge gained from the penitent. If the invalidity is due to the penitent, the confessor must request his permission to speak of the matter. It may be necessary to give absolution again, requiring another confession; this may be summary if the confessor remembers the previous confession and there is no new sin committed.

If the confessor has made an error, culpable or not, affecting the *integrity* of the confession, he is bound to correct it. If he positively misleads a penitent, e.g., by saying that the species or number of sins need not be confessed, he must correct the mistake when the penitent confesses again, or outside the confessional with the penitent's express permission. Serious inconvenience would usually excuse, if there is no damage to a third party, since such a procedure is usually quite disagreeable to penitent or confessor. If the confessor merely negatively misleads the penitent, e.g., by not inquiring about number and species when he could have done so, he need not correct the mistake outside of confession but in the penitent's next confession. The obligation of integrity belongs principally to the penitent and only indirectly to the confessor.

The confessor is bound to rectify his mistake, when he has positively erred with serious culpability in his advice concerning the penitent's obligations in justice. He must withdraw his wrong advice and repair the damage done to the penitent or to a third party. This must be done even outside of confession, saving the seal, as he is the unjust and efficacious cause of damage to another and thus obliged to restitution, e.g., if fearing to displease the penitent, he dispenses the obligation of restitution to which the penitent is obliged in strict justice; or if he obliges the penitent to restitution to which he is not bound. This also applies when a confessor's silence can be reasonably construed by a penitent as positive approval.

If the confessor has negatively erred by failing to instruct when he should have, his obligation of restitution is only one of charity. Restitution obliges in justice when the damage done another is not impeded when *ex officio* one is bound to do so. Confession of itself is not directed to avoiding damage to or procuring the welfare of a third party but to the spiritual welfare of the penitent. If the confessor has inculpably made a mistake, e.g., by declaring in good faith that the penitent is not bound to restitution when he is or bound when he is not, he is not himself obliged to restitution, being free from true sin. If he discovers his mistake after confession, he is obliged to rectify it in charity, but not at great inconvenience. If the confession is not over, he is bound in justice to correct his advice if it involves damage to the penitent, and probably only in charity if it involves only a third party.

Wrong advice given the penitent concerning his obligations in matters other than justice must be corrected by the confessor as best he can, lest a material sin or violation of a law be permitted without sufficient cause. This should be done in the confessional. The confessor is easily excused from repairing this defect, especially if he is not seriously at fault.

4. *Preservation of the Sacramental Seal*

a. *Obligation of the seal*

The seal of sacramental confession is the most strict obligation of observing secrecy about those things which have been declared by the penitent in sacramental confession or for the purpose of sacramental absolution, and whose revelation would in some way identify the sin and the sinner. Every and only a sacramental confession, made for the purpose of confessing to a minister of the Church as such and of obtaining absolution, is the root of the obligation of the seal. This is true whether the confession was valid or invalid, merely begun or completed or sacrilegious, whether absolution was deferred or denied. The sacramental seal is inviolable; therefore the confessor shall take scrupulous care lest by word or sign or in any way or for any reason he betray the sinner.[150]

There is no more serious obligation of secrecy than that of the sacramental seal. It allows of no exception whatsoever, no dispensation, no use of extra-legal equity.[151] It does not permit the use of probabilism, i.e., that a confessor adopt a line of action on the ground that in doing so he will probably not violate the seal or give offense to penitents. This is true both when there is a probability of law, i.e., a division among theologians on a given point whether it is or not a matter of the seal or an offense to penitents, or a probability of fact, i.e., a doubt that this or that fact was confessional matter or known only from confession. The confessor cannot use a probable opinion to the detriment of a certain right of another; the penitent has a right to be free from all injury, burden, and grievance on the occasion of his confession of his sins. Thus the confessor is bound to the seal even if he doubts whether something said by the penitent is directed to confession or absolution, because he must judge on the safer side, i.e., on the side of the obligation of the seal. Even under oath the confessor must state that he knows nothing or has heard nothing,—which means that he has no *communicable* knowledge.

The sacramental seal is implicit in the institution of Penance by Christ and in the purpose for which he established the sacrament. The obligation arises from the natural law of secrecy and of a quasi contract, from the divine law of reverence for the sacrament which should be made as easy of approach as possible and free from injury to the recipient, and from ecclesiastical law. The obligation binds even after the death of the penitent. Every direct violation of the seal, no matter how slight, is a grievous sin and admits of no lightness of matter. It is a most serious injury to the

---

150. c. 889, 1; Lateran IV, 1215, c. 21, Denz.-Schön. 814; cf. Clement VIII, 26 maii 1593; Innocent XI, 18 nov. 1682. Cf. **Ordo Paenitentiae,** 10d.

151. It thus differs from a purely natural secret. The violation of a natural secret, unlike the seal, is not a sacrilege, and it admits of lightness of matter; the obligation even of a committed secret can cease in certain instances, but the seal allows of no exception whatsoever; the obligation of the seal, unlike that of the secret, binds even toward the **penitent or** person who committed the sin.

sacrament, and the faithful are deterred from approaching it when they feel they do not have full security. An indirect violation is a serious sin, but it allows of lightness of matter.

The confessor (who is truly such or even an imposter) is primarily bound by the seal of confession, both in the confessional and outside, when there is question of speaking of things told to him in the confessional. Secondarily, the obligation of preserving the sacramental seal is binding also on an interpreter and on all others to whom knowledge of the confession shall have come in any way,[152] whether by chance or design, lawfully or otherwise, immediately or mediately. The following are thus bound by the seal: a superior requested by a confessor or a penitent for the faculty to absolve in a reserved case, or when approached by an already absolved penitent for his mandate; one who reads a letter to or from a competent authority in a reserved case; a consultor whose advice is sought by a confessor even with permission of the penitent; a priest requested before confession how to make a confession to him, which is subsequently made; all who accidentally or deliberately overhear a penitent confessing or to whom confessional matter is communicated in any way; all who read the written confession of another when it serves as the actual confession or as a means of actually confessing or which has been left in the confessional or been lost by the confessor, but not if the penitent has lost it or is in possession of it outside the confessional; if there is doubt whether the penitent or the confessor left the script in the confessional, it must be considered as under the seal.

The penitent is not bound by the seal but rather by the obligation of a natural and committed secret concerning the things spoken of or done by the confessor in confession, if their revelation would harm the confessor or bring injury or contempt to the sacrament. It is sometimes necessary for a penitent to speak about a confessor, e.g., when he wishes to have his penance commuted by another confessor, or when he is justified in complaining about a confessor. Confessors on their part should employ great discretion in the confessional, since they cannot defend themselves from the tongues of their penitents.

152. c. 889, 2.

Outside the confessional even the priest may not lawfully speak to the penitent about a confessional matter without receiving first the free, express, and certain consent of the penitent. The priest should be very slow to request this permission and then only rarely and for serious reasons. In the confession itself the confessor can speak even of the sins confessed in previous confessions, since the past confessions constitute one and the same judgment and tribunal with the present confession. When the penitent of his own initiative speaks of his sins outside of confession, implicitly he is giving the confessor permission to speak of these sins alone and not of previously declared sins. The penitent then can give a more or less ample permission. In any case the confessor is always bound by a natural and committed secret and must avoid scandal and the suspicion of violating the seal. The confessor may not speak of any sins as long as he knows of them only from confession, even though he is convinced that they are commonly known. He may speak of sins of which he is aware from sources outside of confession but cautiously; he must beware of representing something as certain which previous to the confession he knew only as probable, and refrain from later correcting inaccuracies in view of his confessional knowledge.

b. *Material under the seal*

Subject to the seal *directly* and *of themselves* are all and only those things which have been revealed for the purpose of sacramental confession and not exclusively for another purpose, e.g., for derision, deception, solicitation to sin of the confessor. In this way are contained under the seal:

1) all sins which are confessed, however slight, and even material sins; sins even though only thought of or proposed but not accomplished or fulfilled; internal or external sins, whether of the past or those to take place in the future; all serious sins whether generically or specifically confessed; all slight sins specifically or numerically confessed; secret sins and also public sins insofar as they have been confessed;

2) the objects of sins inasmuch as these are the sins of another, e.g., to confess sinful speech about the sinful pregnancy of a certain girl, to confess hatred of one's father because of his adultery, etc.; the circumstances of sins as such which are thought to be or are necessary or useful in clarifying the case, e.g., certain specific books that have been read, the amount of a theft, the accomplices in a sin whether lawfully or imprudently confessed.

Of themselves and *indirectly* under the seal are all those things which of themselves can lead to a knowledge of the sin as declared by the sinner or to an identification of the penitent. Included in this way are: the deferral or denial of absolution; a sacrilegious confession, since the sacramental confession is present in the penitential judgment and not merely in the sacramental absolution;[153] the lack of dispositions of the penitent; the penance imposed, unless it was very light; the confessional advice requested or given.

Sometimes things may *accidentally* fall under the seal which in themselves are *in no way* material of the obligation. Such things are:

1) sins known to the confessor otherwise than from confessional knowledge; slight sins generically confessed, since there is no confession made without at least free and sufficient matter (however, penitents are usually unwilling that they be revealed); a very light penance inasmuch as this is at least necessary in every confession; sins committed by the penitent in confession, e.g., impatience, attempted theft from the confessor, etc., unless a suspicion may arise that something serious incited them; the confession itself or the bestowal of absolution, although this is ordinarily not to be revealed and may become a matter of the seal, e.g., a confession secretly made or made under unusual conditions. If a person tells a priest something outside of confession for the sake of direction or seeking advice and does so "under the seal," as they say, this does not fall under the sacramental seal if it is in no way referred to confession, but it is a natural and committed secret;

2) the virtue, gifts and good works of the penitent, although they are often under a natural secret, and there may be danger of

---

153. Lateran IV, **loc. cit.**

an indirect violation if the penitent revealed them in order to manifest some sins; merely natural defects of soul or body, although the penitent is usually unwilling that they be made known, e.g., age, hardness of hearing, stubbornness, illegitimacy, scrupulosity (the scruples themselves confessed as sins fall under the seal); poverty; etc.

c. *Violation of the seal*

For a *direct violation* of this obligation there must be an express revelation of the matter under the seal and at the same time a sufficient identification of the sinner or penitent. It is the identification of a particular and specific sin with a particular penitent, or of generically stated grave sins with a designated individual who can be known with certainty by the hearer, even in other ways than by name, e.g., by circumstances. It is not necessary that the hearer be or ever has been acquainted with the penitent in any way or know that confessional matter is being revealed. Since a direct violation does not admit of lightness of matter, the revelation even of a slight sin alone is a serious sin.

The seal must be preserved no matter what effect or harm may befall any individual or the common good;[154] it excuses the priest from material integrity in his own confession. Civil laws in the U.S.A. more or less explicitly protect confessional knowledge from judicial inquiry. Anyone to whom confessional knowledge has come may reply on the witness stand and under oath that he knows nothing of the matters involved in such a source of information.

For an *indirect violation* there must be revelation or other use of confessional knowledge from which there arises the proximate danger of betraying the penitent who has confessed such and such a sin, or of revealing the sin as confessed by this penitent, even if this occurs unintentionally. This may take place because of what the confessor says or does or omits inasmuch as it can lead to the knowledge of or the probable and prudent (and not merely possible) suspicion of the matter of the seal and the party involved. An

---

154. Cf. c. 890, 2. Cf. Clement VIII, Decretum **Sanctissimus Dominus,** 26 maii 1593; Innocent XI, S. Off. 18 nov. 1682.

indirect violation is a serious sin, which sometimes admits of lightness of matter.

The sacramental seal may be indirectly broken in several ways, e.g.: by mentioning the sin of a penitent in such circumstances that he can probably be identified; by stating that a certain penitent by name was not absolved until after some probing; by warning the parents or superiors of a penitent to heed certain occasions or places; by reprimanding a penitent in a loud voice and thus indicating serious confessional material to the bystanders; by singling out one penitent above others for praise in matters of chastity; by announcing that a certain vice known only from confession, e.g., sodomy, is prevalent in a certain institution or in a parish (unless the latter is larger than 3,000 souls); by speaking to another confessor about a certain sin which the penitent has confessed to both; by showing a change of attitude toward the penitent or others, e.g., accomplices, after confession; by using confessional knowledge in external government; by refusing to hear a penitent because of lack of dispositions known from previous confessions; by avoiding a place where the confessor knows only from confession he will suffer harm; etc.

It may happen that a penitent is given a card or certificate (*schedula confessionis*) after confession as evidence that the confession has been made. If the penitent makes such a request, it must be acceded to, even though he did not receive absolution. If the card expressly mentions that absolution has been given these words may not be deleted. The card should be given if a refusal would betray the penitent in any way or entail a violation of the seal or cause scandal. It suffices in any case for the confessor to state that so-and-so came to him for confession and mention nothing of absolution. Where the practice still exists, it should be promptly discontinued.[155]

155. "The practice is to be reprobated of giving in the tribunal of Penance a signed card to those faithful to whom Communion is permitted, with which on the following day they may be permitted to the sacred table." S.C.P.F. 14 ian 1806, and also (1836) to the Vicar Apostolic of Nanking reproving the practice of missionaries counting the penitents to be admitted to Holy Communion in the confessional and consecrating as many hosts as there were penitents. Cf. also S.C. Sac. 8 dec. 1938.

d. *Penalties*

A *confessor* (priest) who *presumes* to violate *directly* the sacramental seal incurs automatically (*latae sententiae*) an excommunication reserved in a most special way to the Holy See.[156] There must be truly a matter of the seal, which is directly revealed, and with full advertence and will, i.e., with deliberation. Therefore, ignorance (even if crass or supine), slight fear, imperfect advertence, not fully deliberate consent, slightly culpable imprudence, will excuse from this penalty.[157]

A *confessor* (priest) who *rashly* violates the seal *indirectly* is liable to the following penalties which may be imposed (*ferendae sententiae*): suspension from celebrating Mass and from hearing confessions (if the offense is serious, the incapacity to hear confessions ever again); deprivation of all benefices, dignities, of active and passive voice (even the incapacity of ever possessing either); degradation in graver offenses.[158] An indirect violation must be interpreted strictly; it does not include the unlawful use of confessional knowledge without a violation of the seal. *Others* besides the confessor who *rashly* violate the seal are to be punished by salutary penalties (*ferendae sententiae*) according to the gravity of their offense, even including excommunication.[159]

5. *Proper Respect for Confessional Knowledge*

It is entirely forbidden to confessors to use, to the detriment of the penitent, knowledge acquired from confession, even though there is no danger that the penitent and his sin will be known.[160] The situation here is the free use of knowledge which the confessor has gained through confession, as long as there is no danger of

---

156. c. 2369, 1. The sanctions of this canon apply to the Oriental Church, S. Off. 21 iul. 1934. A violator will also be suspended from hearing confessions "ad nutum S. Officii."
157. c. 2229, 2.
158. cc. 2369, 1; 2368, 1.
159. cc. 2369, 2; 2233, 2.
160. c. 890, 1.

direct or indirect revelation. No penalties are specified in the law for a violation of this canon.

a. *Unlawful use*

The use of sacramental knowledge is always unlawful when it entails a direct or indirect revelation of confession. Apart from all danger of revelation the confessor is not free to use such knowledge where there may be detriment to the penitent or to penitents in general (even outside the advertence of the latter), or where the faithful generally would be aggrieved or offended, confidence in the sacrament lessened and its frequentation rendered more difficult, or scandal given. Without the penitent's permission such use is unlawful[161] and a serious sin, although admitting of lightness of matter. Moreover, both those who are superiors at the time of confession, and confessors who later become superiors, cannot in any way, for the exterior government of the institute, make use of knowledge which they have had of sins revealed in confessions.[162]

b. *Lawful use*

The use of sacramental knowledge can be lawful if there can result no danger of revelation of confessional matter or detriment to the penitent or to others. Thus by knowledge gained from confession the confessor can better his own spiritual life, avoid the occasions of sin, improve his manner of questioning and of instructing penitents and his general celebration of administration of the sacrament, study his problems and consult lawfully with others, pray for his penitents, act more benignly toward them, etc. Preachers may speak of those things which would not have occurred to them if they had not heard confessions, but they must be careful not to speak in a way to render the sacrament disagreeable or to indi-

---

161. Cf. n. 154 above. Cf. also S. Poen. 1 feb. 1935.
162. c. 890, 2. An Instruction of the Holy Office (9 iun. 1915) laid down norms for confessors in these matters. Although not officially published in the **AAS**, it is agreed that in practice it is an interpretation of the divine law.

cate that confessional knowledge is being used, or to mention particular sins in a small community of people.

Parents, teachers, etc., should not question confessors about their children's confessions; superiors should not inquire of confessors whether their subjects are worthy, for example, of profession or Orders. If queried whether or not a penitent is going to Communion, the confessor should reply normally only with permission of the penitent or refer the inquirer to the penitent. Great discretion is required in the case of a person indisposed to receive Viaticum. Preliminary conversation with a public sinner will sometimes demonstrate his disposition, e.g., if he is prepared to repair public scandal. If the penitent's indisposition is discovered only in confession, he should be dissuaded from communicating; with his consent the fact can be dissimulated from others, e.g., by stating that everything necessary has been done. If the penitent insists on receiving the Eucharist, he must be communicated. If he explains that he has called for the priest only for the sake of respectability or some such reason, there is no sacramental confession and thus no obligation of the seal. However, the natural law obliges the priest to observe all possible secrecy in such matters.

The confessor must solve his confessional problems with all his diligence by applying good judgment to the knowledge he has acquired, by personal study, prayer, and reflection. Consultation with others on confessional matters must be an extraordinary procedure; it should be looked upon as generally unwise to request the penitent's permission for this. However, even an experienced and sufficiently learned confessor at times needs to seek the advice of another. He should first try to contact a competent consultant who does not know the penitent at all. If there should be any danger of violation of the seal, permission should be first requested of the penitent to seek such counsel. If the request is not granted or if it is judged unwise to make it, the confessor should propose his problem to the consultant as a hypothetical case, revealing only what is necessary in the case and changing the case in other ways so that the penitent cannot be identified and yet the substance of the problem is not changed. In an unusual or complicated case the confessor may request the penitent's consent to handle it outside of confession, e.g., in certain marriage cases or problems of justice.

6. *Assistance to Penitents*

a. *The dying*

Catholics

A dying Catholic *must* be absolved as often as this is *certainly* permissible. He must be absolved *absolutely* when he is certainly disposed and has manifested this in some way himself or by the testimony of those about him, at least before becoming unconscious. He *must* be absolved *conditionally* if he gives no sign of contrition or has given none before becoming unconscious, as long as he has lived a Christian life. It is reasonably presumed that such a person wished to die a Christian. Catholic objects, such as medals, rosaries, etc., are probable evidence of this desire.

Absolution *may* be given, but there is no obligation to do so, in the case where it is probably lawful and probably not. Thus a dying person *may* be absolved *conditionally* (*if you are capable*) even though he has led an evil life before becoming unconscious, or even if death overtakes him in the act of sinning. It is considered probable that such a Catholic wishes at least to die with the sacraments.

As often as it is *certainly* evident that a dying person is incapable or unworthy of absolution, it *may not* be given. Thus a confessor must not absolve a person who refuses his ministrations up to the very last moment of consciousness. According to some it is possible that such an unrepentant sinner may during unconsciousness receive the grace to change his attitude and to acquire dispositions sufficient for the sacrament, and thus he can be absolved conditionally. Because of the extrinsic authority of those favoring this position a confessor would not sin in absolving in such a case, but he has no obligation to do so, and he must always guard against irreverence and scandal. A person who knowingly refuses at least to promise seriously to fulfill the grave obligations incumbent upon him as a penitent, after admonition by the confessor, e.g., to restore another's goods, to retract errors, to give up the occasions of sin or an evil practice such as birth prevention, etc., must be refused absolution.[163]

In positive doubt whether a dying person is Catholic or not, absolution may be given conditionally. The priest should try to speak to the unconscious, in case the condition is only apparent or not total, and to mention the sacraments he is about to administer, suggesting to him acts of faith, hope, love, contrition. Absolution must not be given to those who are certainly dead. The naturally certain sign of death is the beginning of corruption or putrefaction, and to a lesser extent rigor mortis. Otherwise, in the absence of certain evidence or of medical certification, it must be judged a case of *apparent death,* since it is not known at what moment life itself ceases to exist. In the case of sudden death the person can as a rule be absolved conditionally up to about two or three hours after apparent demise; if death ensues after a long illness, absolution may be given conditionally up to about a half hour. A conscious dying person may be absolved frequently, even on the same day, as long as the confessor cannot doubt about his sufficient dispositions. Absolution may be given to the unconscious conditionally as often as there is probable reason of more certain disposition or of new necessity.

Non-Catholics

Those Eastern Christians who, in the absence of sufficient confessors of their own church, spontaneously desire to do so may go to a Catholic confessor. In similar circumstances a Catholic may approach a confessor of an Eastern Church which is separated from the Apostolic Roman See.[164] Thus the Catholic confessor may impart absolution also to the dying separated Eastern Christian who requests

---

163. The sacraments cannot be given to those who join or favor the Communist party, who publish, propagate or read books, periodicals, daily papers or sheets which promote the doctrine or action of Communists, or who allow their children to be trained by Communist-influenced associations, and the young people themselves, as long as they have part in these associations. (S. Off. 1 iul. 1949; 28 iul. 1950).
164. **Directorium, Secr. ad unitatem Christianorum fovendam, n. 46, 14 iun. 1967.**

it. The dying who are unconscious may also be absolved as in the case of Catholics.

Since the celebration of the sacraments is an action of the celebrating community, carried out within the community, signifying oneness in faith, worship, and life of the community, where this unity of sacramental faith is deficient, as in the case of non-Catholics who are not Eastern Orthodox, the participation of the separated brethren with Catholics, especially in the sacraments of the Eucharist, Penance, and the Anointing of the Sick, is forbidden. The prohibition, then, is because of the usual lack of same faith in these sacraments and not because these persons are unworthy, since in the individual lives by their response to the graces offered them they may be more worthy than some Catholics. Nor can the giving of scandal and the fostering of religious indifferentism be ruled out. However, the Church can for adequate reasons allow access to these sacraments to a separated brother. They may be permitted in danger of death or in urgent need (persecution, in prisons), if the separated brother has no access to a minister of his own communion and spontaneously asks a Catholic priest for the sacraments—so long as he declares a faith in these sacraments in harmony with that of the Church and is rightly disposed.[165] In the case of these separated brethren who have not requested sacramental absolution and are unconscious, the priest may in practice, but without obligation, confer conditional absolution, since it is not morally certain that there exists an adequate intention to receive this sacrament.

b. *Occasionists*

A circumstance of person, place, or thing may offer an opportunity and an inducement to sin. A person who is influenced by such a circumstance is said to be living in the occasion of sin (*occasionarius*). This differs from merely a danger of sin, which may be from an internal source such as the natural inclinations to sin, and from inordinate passion or frailty. Thus there must be the object which from without affords the opportunity and enticement to sin and the internal inclination to sin. Very often an occasion

---

165. **Ibid.**, n. 55.

of sin is associated with a habit of action on the part of the penitent.

Because of its influence upon the person an occasion is *remote* or *proximate* in the measure in which it exposes him to slight or serious danger of committing sin, if not very often, at least frequently. How serious the danger is must be estimated by the personal experience of the penitent, i.e., by the frequency of his lapses into sin in the same circumstance or condition, e.g., too much to drink two or three times a week in the same favorite bar; by the common experience of other people, since what is generally an occasion of sin to others under the same circumstances is assumed to be such for everyone, until the contrary is evident, e.g., types of pornographic literature, pictures, or films, for adolescents; by the circumstances and character of the penitent, whose particular strong passions or evident frailty are affected in certain conditions or circumstances, and which is a very personal element in judging a case.

An *absolute* occasion is a circumstance that of itself commonly induces man to sin, e.g., a truly obscene representation of a nude woman; a *relative* occasion attracts only this individual, e.g., this boy for this girl. A proximate occasion is *present* or continuous when it is always or habitually at hand and does not need to be sought out, e.g., the possession of foul pictures or living with a mistress; it is *non-present* or interrupted when it is not at hand but can be easily sought out, e.g., a bar or a prostitute. The occasion is *free* or voluntary when it can be avoided or removed with slight difficulty, e.g., forbidden embraces between young people; it is *necessary* or involuntary when the difficulty is great, either physically, e.g., a prisoner in the same cell with a pervert, or morally, i.e., serious spiritual damage or great detriment to life, fortune, or reputation, e.g., wife with an onanist husband, mutual sins of youngsters in the same family, great sacrifice in loss of employment, etc. A penitent alleging serious difficulty of damage in removing a proximate occasion of sin must be prudently questioned by the confessor before confirming the judgment.

Absolution must be given to one living in the remote occasion of sin, since this is the condition of human existence. Any reasonable cause justifies. Absolution must be given if there is doubt whether a given circumstance is a proximate occasion, although the penitent should be warned to take all steps to avoid such danger. The warning to abandon a proximate occasion can at times be omitted if the penitent is ignorant of such an obligation and it is foreseen that the warning would be harmful, as he would commit lesser sins in good faith than if warned. This presupposes first that good faith prudently appears to exist, e.g., the retention of a mistress would belie such a presumption, and second that irreparable perversion would not result, e.g., as in the reading of obscene literature, and finally that there is no scandal.

Absolution may not regularly be imparted to a penitent in the proximate, free, and present occasion of sin, unless there is first a serious resolve to remove the occasion, and in some cases before it is actually removed, e.g., living with a mistress. Otherwise it reveals a will to remain in sin.[166] Mere prayer for the removal of the occasion is not enough. If the penitent gives clear signs of contrition, amendment, and resolve to make the occasion remote, he should be absolved; also if there exists a grave urgency, such as danger of death, lack of further opportunity to confess, etc. The penitent should be warned that failure to stand by his resolve risks denial of absolution in a subsequent confession.

A penitent affected by a proximate, free, and non-continuous or interrupted occasion of sin is usually absolved when there is a firm purpose to desist from seeking the occasion, e.g., bad company, obscene movies, etc. He is thus regularly considered disposed, unless there are signs to the contrary. Repeated failure to keep his resolve may make him a recidivist. One who almost, for example, steals or gets drunk or fornicates with a certain person or persons cannot be absolved unless he at least promises seriously not to see the person or persons again. Because of the penitent's frailty or strong attachments and in order to strengthen his dispositions, the confessor may have to preface his insistence upon this break by strong persuasion.

166. "He can sometimes be absolved who remains in a proximate occasion of sin which he can and does not wish to omit, but rather directly and professedly seeks or enters into." Prop. condemned by Innocent XI, S. Off. 4 mart. 1679. Denz.-Schön. 2161.

In some cases one further meeting may be reluctantly allowed when there is solid reason to judge that sin will not likely result in the instance and when special precautions are taken by the penitent; it cannot be allowed when there are special elements involved, such as vow, marriage bond, scandal, etc.

A sinner in a proximate and necessary occasion of sin can be absolved as a rule, as long as he is truly disposed to render the occasion as remote as possible by opportune and effective means, e.g., prayer, frequent reception of the sacraments, vigilance at all times, avoidance of familiarity with dangerous persons or of being alone with them. The occasion itself is not a sin and does not necessarily lead to sin; with divine help the difficulty can be overcome, as no one is bound to the impossible. If, however, the occasion is evil in itself, e.g., active participation in non-Catholic religious services, prostitution, and it is not avoided, or if there is no improvement or probable hope of the same after repeated warning, absolution must be denied.

A confessor should not be quick to judge an occasion to be proximate. If the sin would probably be eliminated or greatly reduced by the penitent's removal of the circumstance, it can be judged to be truly an occasion. On the other hand, he should not readily excuse the penitent when the occasion can easily be avoided. He must judge in each case the difficulty in abandoning a proximate occasion. It need not be a moral impossibility, but it should be more than a serious difficulty that would excuse from observing a merely ecclesiastical precept.

c. *Habitual sinners*

An habitual sinner (*consuetudinarius*) is one who by frequent repetition of acts of a particular sin has contracted an habitual inclination to commit the *same* sin. The habit is something internal and deliberately acquired; it differs from passion, occasion of sin, and habitual affection which can remain involuntarily after sin has been renounced, although they are not mutually exclusive conditions. How many acts are required before a sinful habit is acquired will depend on the weakness of the will of the individual in failing to resist the sin, on the nature of the sin committed and the manner of its commission, and on the interval between the individual sins. Some sins are of a more alluring type, e.g., insobriety, impurity, etc.; some are more or less easy to commit, and thus the easier it is to commit the sins, the more acts are needed to form a habit, e.g., internal sins over external, sins of the tongue over those of deed, etc.; some are committed more than once in a day but then not for a long time and thus do not constitute a habit, whereas a constant frequency will habituate a sinner in his sin.

The source of failure for some habitual sinners is frailty or a passing surge of a passion, seemingly from outside their will. This is often the case with those who consent to carnal passion (especially pollution), intemperance, and forms of expressions of anger. Such penitents have a general desire to be rid of the habit, albeit hazy, faltering, and inefficacious. Their will is generally set against sin, which they abhor when once committed, and they are almost immediately contrite and desire to be freed from the bad habit. With other habitual sinners the condition has been very deliberately achieved and the habit acquired through malice of will and deep affection for the forbidden object, e.g., in cases of illicit love, of compromise with religious obligations out of human respect or ambition, conjugal onanism, theft, hatred, etc. Such sinners do not easily move away from sin and toward penitence.

A bad habit is not in itself a sin but a bent toward sinful action; it can exist with a present good disposition of repentance. Habitual sinners are thus as a rule to be absolved, as long as they are truly contrite and sincerely prepared to amend their ways (i.e., when they are not also recidivists). It is left to the confessor's prudent judgment to estimate the dispositions of the penitent in the individual case in the normal way. One sign of proper disposition for absolution is correction of sinful acts or strenuous efforts to do so. Extraordinary signs of contrition are not necessary; emotional outbursts do not always indicate contrition. Absolution may not be denied an habitual sinner simply because he will not make more than his annual confession.

The habitual sinner cannot restore himself to a life of habitual grace and charity unless he has a will to help himself, is convinced that the habit must be rooted out and that it can be done by him.

He must avoid dangerous occasions of his sin and employ the indispensable means of prayer, the sacraments, self-discipline by mortification in other areas as well, and avoid idleness. Natural and especially supernatural motivations must be positive so as to carry through the times of temptation when the will tends to "drag its feet." A counter-balance must be developed through the promotion of good habits and practices. With some bad habits, especially impurity (notably self-abuse), frequent confession and even daily Communion are principal aids in conquering the problem. When the penitent refuses to employ the only means of success, absolution must be denied. Habitual sinners often require considerable patience and counselling on the part of the confessor, who may experience a feeling of frustration in his efforts to aid them even to reduce the number and frequency of these lapses. Some habitual sinners may have need of—and need to have recommended to them—outside professional help. When indicated and accepted, this (with other factors) will indicate sufficient disposition for absolution.

d. *Recidivists*

A recidivist in the strict and formal theological meaning is one who, after repeated confessions (on three or four occasions) of certain sins, often relapses into the same sins without making any deliberate effort towards improvement. He is a relapsed sinner, a backslider. In practice a recidivist is most often an habitual sinner, but not necessarily so.[167]

A formal recidivist is one whose relapse is due to bad will or depraved affection with the result that he makes no earnest effort to amend or improve. This condition requires frequent relapses into the same sins after repeated confessions and warnings by the confessor of the gravity of the sins and the means necessary to avoid them, and an entire lack of amendment, even attempted, so that after confession in about the same way and with the same

---

167. There can be an habitual sinner who has not confessed his sinful actions before, and also a recidivist who is not an habitual sinner, since he falls into sin after confession only once in a while and thus not from habit.

case the relapses occur. There is no serious attempt to repel the temptations or to employ means of improvement—an incorrigible sinner.

A material recidivist relapses into the same sins after warnings by the confessor, but more from vehemence of passion, inconstancy, or frailty of will. He is generally opposed to sinning, resists temptation and detests his sin shortly after committing it, even to being disgusted with himself (as often in cases of self-abuse). Moreover, a material recidivist may be one who was not seriously admonished by a confessor, or if admonished relapsed not into the same but different sins, or if warned and yet having fallen has shown some amendment or reduction of sin.

Material recidivists are always to be absolved, as long as they give the ordinary signs of sincere contrition and purpose of amendment. The confessor may estimate the extent of the habit of sin by inquiring how often the penitent has given way to the temptation and how often he has overcome it. The penitent should be encouraged in his efforts to remove the habit, and in a case of impurity, advised to seek out a regular confessor,—which is a means of great value in conquering impure habits.

Formal recidivists are regularly not to be absolved unless they show more evident signs of proper dispositions for absolution. The presumption of sincerity ordinarily favoring the penitent does not normally prevail in their case, as their condition leads their dispositions here and now to be suspect. In practice it is difficult to form a judgment of their dispositions for absolution. The confessor must use the greatest prudence to avoid both laxism and rigorism, trying patiently to incite satisfactory dispositions.

More evident signs of contrition usually sought from a formal recidivist do not necessarily mean extraordinary dispositions, since simple attrition suffices for the sacrament, but signs which are to the confessor more demonstrative of sufficiency of dispositions relative to the character of the penitent, the nature of the temptations or habit, and other circumstances. They vary with penitents and cannot be predetermined in particular, but noteworthy signs are tears in a strong man, a spontaneous confession sought out of accustomed time, the penitent's spontaneous removal of occasions, the attendance at a weekend retreat, etc. Deferral of absolution is seldom advantageous in present-day conditions; in a case of necessity a doubtfully disposed recidivist should be conditionally absolved (*if you are capable*).

e. *Scrupulous*

Scruple, from the word "*scrupulus*" or little stone which when it gets into a shoe tortures the foot of the wearer, is taken to stand for a disturbance of the soul which vexes man and hinders his steps to God. In the moral sense scrupulosity is a fear of sinning where there is no sin or of serious sin where there is slight sin, all arising from unreasonable motives. Scrupulous persons are usually categorized as types of psychasthenics or individuals unable to cope with problems which are truly those of the soul,—a lack of psychic energy. True scrupulosity is commonly considered psychosomatic. Some severe cases may also be accompanied by manifestations of hysteria.

The inordinate preoccupation of the scrupulous person with the moral and religious order, his special type of worry, may center on his entire moral life or on only one sphere, such as matters of faith or of purity, interior actions or external manifestations. The condition may be temporary as at a time of great stress or upset, or constitutional where physical dispositions for most of life incline the individual to scrupulosity. Various symptoms appear in this condition. There is the inability to decide, irresoluteness; decision when made is with great difficulty or under the duress of necessity, with subsequent doubt about the decision or action. A basic insufficiency in the ability to judge and to act is felt. This is usually accompanied by an inordinate fear, even fear of failure itself, with undue anxiety or worry and a sadness because of a realization of the inability to cope with the situation. Involved also may be various obsessions, phobias, and compulsions.

The causes of scruples are difficult to discern, particularly in the individual. Outside of supernatural causes which may intervene in some cases, e.g., God allowing a soul to be thus purified and grow in merit, or the devil disturbing the lower faculties and especially the imagination, many natural and moral causes are assigned and may be present in varied combinations. Some of these are: bodily constitution, temperament, illness and misfortune, nervous ailment and overwrought imagination, excessive work or strain and lack of adequate rest or recreation, religious practices which weaken the body and lower the strength of the spirit, a morbid and self-centered introspection and an inversion or self-centeredness which is characteristic of the scrupulous, deficient moral and religious education, over-rigorist home training, difficulties at the stage of puberty, exaggerated fear of divine justice to the detriment of divine mercy, hidden pride through tenacity of personal judgment, and a spiritual egoism which places more trust ultimately in self rather than in God and his representatives.

The confessor must first distinguish scrupulosity from the delicate conscience. The latter tries to avoid all sin, even the slightest imperfection, which is not in fullest accord with the divine will toward the devout soul and not inducive to the perfection of virtue. This concern is always consonant with the rules of prudence and with realization of the true nature of sins. Moreover, the confessor must be prepared to face the problem of deciding how much help he can give and how much outside assistance the penitent needs from medical and psychiatric sources. It is evident that a confessor can help a scrupulous penitent only for the purposes of present absolution if he is not the penitent's regular confessor or spiritual director. Oftentimes a scrupulous person is aware of his condition but tries to hide it from confessors, consulting different ones without informing them of his state. The confessor must be very prudent in his advice and questioning lest he aggravate the condition.

The confessor must do his best to discern the area of scrupulosity and to fathom its causes, to suggest opportune natural and supernatural remedies. The penitent should be urged to recognize his affliction and to pray for the grace to bear it patiently. He should not judge anything to be a sin unless it is evidently clear to him or to be an obligation which is not certain to him. Avoidance of idleness, of the company of other scrupulous persons or of the reading of literature on the subject should be the rule. Only the briefest examination of conscience should be made, doubtful sins should not be confessed nor anything repeated from past confessions unless the penitent knows for certain that it is serious and has certainly not been confessed. A general confession must not be allowed, unless perhaps only once, if it has never been made before. A scrupulous person must not be allowed to enter a religious institute or a seminary before the scrupulous condition is adequately remedied.

Kindness, patience, and perseverance will be required of the confessor in handling scrupulous cases. He must try to enkindle in the penitent confidence in self, in God, and in the confessor himself. The confessor must play the dominant role at all times, while trying to restore initiative to the penitent so accustomed to depend upon others. He must gradually assert his authority and require strict obedience to his directives, but this will be difficult, since the penitent usually has sought out many confessors. At times the confessor must be stern in his requirements and also propose the sterner truths of religion. He must not vacillate in his advice or responses, being brief and positive, giving no reasons; otherwise the penitent will be confirmed in his anxiety by the authority or hesitation of the confessor, and any reasons given may become the cause of further scruples. The penitent should be reminded that sin is not in the bad thought or feeling but in consent, and so such thoughts about faith, chastity, right intentions, etc., may be confessed only if the penitent can swear to having consented to them, which for the most part will not be the case unless external sin has been committed. The penitent should not undertake to correct others; it is seldom that he would have a certain obligation to do so. Prudence will direct the confessor in imparting the sacramental penance, lest the penitent think that his sins have been serious because of the type of penance imposed.

f. *Children*

The confessor must always be paternal and kind with children, lest they become frightened and turned away from the sacrament. At times they will need to be instructed or drawn out if they are reticent. The confessor should wait until they have stated their sins in their own way, as usually this has been prepared from memory. Sometimes children include under "bad" actions disobedience, immodesty, or impoliteness, and thus the confessor must ask what they mean and not presume that impurity is being confessed. The confessor must be very discreet in his questions and instructions, lest he suggest sins or incite curiosity. He must, however, correct false notions, especially when what is only slight is considered to be serious (sometimes due to great stress put on certain matters at home or in school). The obligation of restitution is usually not urged, unless the object is still in the youngster's possession, but he should be counselled regarding the dangers in even such small thefts.

It may be necessary for the confessor to prompt the youngster in the act of contrition or to recite it with him (where this is the practice of reciting it in the confessional). Usually a light penance is given to children, at least one lighter than adults. Youngsters, however, who are steeped in serious sin are treated as adults. Those who appear to be doubtfully contrite or to have only doubtful sins may be absolved conditionally. The childish actions of young penitents that may occur around the confessional do not necessarily indicate lack of proper dispositions for the sacrament. The confessor must give sound advice in the circumstances to young people who ask about choosing a state in life or a particular position, but he must not determine their decision for them. He should not allow private vows, especially of perpetual virginity by girls, without adequate proof of the penitent's realization of the obligation and ability to observe the vow.

g. *Religious and clerics*

It frequently falls to the role of the confessor to advise or to judge an individual regarding entrance into the religious life or the seminary or regarding continuance in it. He must judge the penitent's physical and moral equipment or lack thereof in accordance with the law and the mind of the Church and of a particular institute or seminary, as well as the circumstances of the individual. Under ordinary circumstances the vice of impurity is generally known only to the confessor and cannot be divulged; in fact, with those discussing their aspirations to the religious or clerical life, he should inquire about chastity so that the unworthy may be deterred from a life which demands a pursuit of sanctity and an excellence in the matter of chastity far beyond any lay state. An addiction to drink or to drugs is to be treated with regard to the religious or clerical life in a manner similar to unchastity.

An aspirant to the religious life or seminary who has a habit of impurity, even though there are periods or desistance, should be firmly deterred from entering the novitiate or seminary. Great prudence, moreover, must be exercised in judging those who have fallen and still retain the inclination to such sins, as well as those who have not fallen but possess a soft and sensual nature given to emotional and particular friendships, since they generally are considered to offer no guarantee for the future. A period of probation of at least several months should be required to demonstrate the effort and the success of the aspirant in developing the virtue of chastity and remaining free from sin. No novice should be permitted to make profession or clerical aspirant to advance who has any habit of impurity. At least two or three months probation are commonly expected, even though the sin is committed only once or twice a month. If the novice or seminarian, in the atmosphere of the aids to grace and protection from sin of the religious novitiate or seminary, cannot maintain purity, there is great reason to fear that the condition will not improve in the subsequent years of training or of the apostolate. A confessor, who is convinced of the individual's unworthiness or of his unlikelihood of keeping chastity as befits the dedication to a more excellent purity, must inform the penitent and even refuse absolution if this would be the only deterrent.

With regard to admission to perpetual or to solemn vows the confessor will judge a religious by the norms of receiving major orders (treated in *The Celebration of Holy Orders*). The term of probation may be shorter than that required of a candidate for major orders. The confessor will also follow the norms of judgment affecting clerical candidates, if the penitent pertains to a clerical religious institute. Where there is a case of consummated sin with another person, especially of the same sex, or of sinful familiarity, a much stricter judgment than in the above instances must be made, whether it is an aspirant, novice, or professed.[168]

168. "Since, then, the state of religious persons is so excellent, it is no wonder that the enemy of our salvation leaves nothing undone to throw them down from that sublime height, by evil suggestion, by the allurements of worldly pleasures, and finally by the excitement of the passions. . . . But in the first place Superiors must use the greatest care, even from the first entrance of the candidates, to see that the youths be not admitted in crowds or hastily, but that those only be received who show signs of a divine vocation and give reason to hope that they may be permanently employed with fruit in the ecclesiastical ministry. . . . Certainly in candidates who are destined for the priesthood the ordinary signs of a religious vocation are by no means sufficient, but the special signs of fitness for the clerical state are also required. . . . Superiors must be watchful and must consider whether in the interval between the conferral of one sacred order and the next, anything new has occurred which raises a doubt as to the candidate's vocation to the priesthood, or shows that he has none." S. C. Rel. 1 dec. 1931, **Instruction to the Supreme Moderators of religious and clerical societies.** "14. . . . We can say, and all Superiors should repeat: Let us seek out quality first of all, because then, if we may use such an expression, quantity will automatically follow. . . . 17. . . . All the individuals [superiors, spiritual directors, confessors] accept a burden in conscience in the choice of priests and religious and in their admission to profession and preparation for ordination, and through their ignorance or negligence they may have a share in the sins of others. . . . 18. . . . Confessors have the grave duty of warning, urging, and ordering unfit subjects, privately and in conscience, with no regard for human respect, to withdraw from the religious and clerical life. Although they may appear to have all the dispositions required for sacramental absolution, they are nevertheless not for that reason to be regarded as worthy of profession or ordination. The principles governing the sacramental forum are different from the criteria whereby, according to the mind of the Church, judgment is formed on fitness for the priesthood and the religious life. Consequently, penitents who are certainly unworthy of profession and ordination can be absolved if they show proof of true sorrow for their sins and seriously promise to drop the idea of going on to the religious or clerical state, but they are to be effectively barred from profession and ordination. Likewise spiritual directors are under obligation, in the non-

The confessor should not delay a religious in confession or allow the penitent to prolong it. He should be brief and concise in his advice, encourage the religious to greater intensification of motivation, especially of charity, and never attempt to interfere in the affairs of the community. On the other hand, he must not be too hasty or discourage the religious from securing all available benefit from the sacramental forum; female religious in particular frequently have no other opportunity to present their queries to a priest or to discuss with him their problems relating to their interior and religious life. The confessor should warn religious penitents especially to guard against lukewarmness and habits of slight sin. The confessor should strive to encourage finally professed religious and priests to seek the fullest perfection of their state and to counsel them in their difficulties.

F. *Abuses*

1. *Solicitation*

In accordance with the norms of law a penitent is obliged to report within a month to the local Ordinary or to the Sacred Congregation of the Holy Office a priest who has been guilty of the crime of solicitation in confession; and the confessor is bound by a serious obligation in conscience to warn the penitent of this duty.[169] The sin of solicitation is committed when a priest in connection with confession attempts to seduce a penitent to some grave sin against chastity, or holds unlawful or unchaste conversation with the penitent, or arranges to commit such a sin. Since a penalty is involved,

> sacramental internal forum, to judge of the divine vocation of those entrusted to them and the obligation of warning, and privately urging, those who are unfit, to withdraw voluntarily from the life they have embraced. . . . 29. . . . Among the proofs and signs of a divine vocation the virtue of chastity is regarded as absolutely necessary, 'because it is largely for this reason that candidates for the ranks of the clergy choose this type of life for themselves and persevere in it'." S. C. Rel. 2 feb. 1961, **Instruction to the Superiors of Religious Communities.** Detailed directives for judging and acting in matters of chastity and in psychopathic cases are contained here.

169. c. 904.

a restrictive view must be taken of the terms of the crime and the penalty.

There must be a sin against the sixth commandment (*peccatum turpe*). It makes no difference whether the confessor solicited a male or female penitent (either before or after the latter's attainment of puberty) to sin with him or with another or solitarily, or whether he solicited the penitent immediately or a third party by means of the penitent. It does not matter who the person is or what type of sin against chastity is involved. The solicitation may be made by words, gestures, signs, touches, looks, deeds, or by a letter or note to be read at the time or later. The crime is likewise committed if the confessor gives indecent advice to the penitent or confirms the latter in an impure practice, e.g., that the wife can directly procure an orgasm as long as it is referred to her absent husband, or that conjugal onanism is not a grave sin in difficult family conditions, etc.[170] Unchaste talk or appointments made constitute solicitation insofar as the confessor thereby wishes to gratify his evil inclinations.

The crime must be serious both objectively and subjectively. Thus the act must be of itself libidinous or provocative of the same, or it must of itself or from the circumstances demonstrate a libidinous affection or evil intention. The confessor must be himself conscious of serious sin or of being the grave cause of it. Unless otherwise evident, the specific malice of the sin is presumed, if the external act is performed by the confessor.[171] Acts which are lightly sinful, or the inducement to them, are not by themselves to be denounced, unless from the circumstances it is certain that there is an evil intention to proceed to or to solicit serious sins.[172] This intention is presumed if the confessor is known to be prone to such evil passion. If the confessor does or says something unbecoming out of innocent simplicity and not from malice, there is no obligation to denounce.

It must be *certain* that there has been an act of *solicitation* to *impurity* which was serious and *related to confession*.[173] Any doubt

170. Cf. S. Poen. 2 sept. 1904.
171. c. 2200, 2.
172. S. Off. 20 feb. 1867.
173. A similar offense related to sacraments other than Penance

of law or of fact will excuse from the penalty. Some things which occur in confession may be good or indifferent, e.g., to inquire about the penitent's place of residence or to make an appointment to meet there. If no other plausible reason can be given for the confessor's action, e.g., he really had some important matters to discuss, he is to be denounced.

The solicitation must be *connected with confession*, either:

a) *in the very act of confession*, i.e., from the preliminary blessing or introductory words until the absolution, even if the latter is not imparted. It may become evident only later that the action of the confessor was prompted by a seriously sinful motive, e.g., the penitent is given a letter to read later, which letter is of a solicitous nature.

b) or *immediately before or after confession*, i.e., as long as no interval of time or no action intervenes which is not referred as a means to the solicitation, e.g., to hear someone else's confession. Merely to be among the bystanders around the confessional is not sufficient.

c) or *on the occasion of confession,* i.e., when the confessor invites the penitent to make a true confession here and now, or when the penitent comes to confession and the confessor uses the opportunity to solicit, even though the confession does not follow, e.g., the penitent indignantly leaves. This is not the case if confession is requested by the penitent for a later date and the solicitation is made on the occasion of the request. An opinion held by many is that there is no obligation to denounce if the confessor uses his confessional knowledge of the penitent's weakness to solicit the penitent later, in no way revealing his evil intention in the confession. This is not the practice of the Sacred Penitentiary.

d) or *under the pretext of confession*, i.e., for the confessor falsely to allege confession or to give the appearance of confession

is not subject to the penalties of solicitation. (S. Off. 11 feb. 1661 ad 10) at least in order to deceive the penitent (and even if only to deceive others, according to the opinion of some). Thus, for example, if a confessor calls a boy to his room for confession which he does not intend to hear and solicits him, or if he visits a sick person on the plea of hearing her confession and solicits her. This is not the case, however, if the sick person should summon the priest under a pretext of confession as a means of seeking to seduce him, or should allege confession as a means for the priest's visit as a means of shielding him in the eyes of others. Likewise, if both confessor and penitent agree to pretend confession in order to hide their sin from others.

e) or, *outside the occasion of confession, in the confessional or in a place permanently designated for hearing confessions or where confessions are heard temporarily, provided that in all three instances both participants act as though confession was being made,* e.g., to place positive acts of simulation, such as to give a blessing as at the beginning of a confession, or to incline the head as though hearing a penitent, etc. It is sufficient that witnesses could be present.

Only the person solicited is obliged by law to make a denunciation, even if below the age of puberty. Anyone else who knows definitely of the solicitation is bound to report it though not under penalty, unless the information itself comes from unreliable sources,[174] or it is known that the one solicited has already denounced.

The denunciation is to be made of every *priest,* and only such, who solicits as a confessor, even if he lacked jurisdiction.[175] It makes no difference whether the confessor solicited a long time ago and his crime is occult or he has gone away; or whether the initiative to sin came from the penitent, or whether the penitent resisted or

---

174. S. Off. 11 feb. 1661; 20 feb. 1867. The soliciting priest is not bound to denounce himself, but if he does so, he will be treated more leniently (**ibid.,** 17 nov. 1626; 20 feb. 1867)
175. Excluded is a priest who is acting as an interpreter in a confession (S. Off. 11 feb. 1661 ad 16), and a priest who commands, persuades, or counsels a confessor to solicit a penitent. (**ibid.,** ad 617)

consented, was aware that solicitation was attempted or realized the malice of the sin or became aware only later that it was true solicitation,[176] or whether the impure action was delayed or the confessor remained passive in the action, as long as truly and positively he manifested consent,[177] or whether a third person was solicited through the penitent as an agent.

There is a serious obligation to make the denunciation within one month reckoned from the time one becomes conscious of the obligation; failing this, as soon as possible. The denunciation is made to the Sacred Congregation for the Doctrine of the Faith or more usually to the local Ordinary of the place of solicitation,[178] or if this is impossible, to that of the penitent or of the soliciting confessor.

The denunciation is made ordinarily by the person solicited (or others who know the fact), in person and by word of mouth, before the bishop or his delegate, in the presence of a notary and under signed oath. The "secrecy of the Holy Office" binds all parties.[179] The one solicited may first orally or in writing informally report to the superior the facts of the case, giving the name of the soliciting confessor and signing the penitent's own name and address. The penitent then awaits the further action of the Ordinary, even if the time goes beyond thirty days, without falling under penalty.[180]

Very great hardship, great danger to life or health or livelihood, the fact that the priest is a close relative or close friend of the victim, will excuse from this obligation (but not remove it), unless at the same time public scandal or damage to the common good outweighs the excuse. The obligation to denounce does not cease with the spontaneous confession of the soliciting priest, nor by his removal, promotion, condemnation, presumed change of life and morals, or for any such causes.[181] Only the death of the soliciting

---

176. S. Off. 11 iun 1707.
177. Cf. **ibid.**, 11 feb. 1661; 20 feb. 1867.
178. **Ibid.**, 9 iun. 1922. It may be made to the delegate of the local Ordinary but not to the Vicar General without special mandate. (**ibid.**, 14 iul. 1753) The religious Ordinary is also excluded.
179. **Ibid.**, 20 feb. 1886. Only in an extraordinary case will a priest alone or a confessor be delegated to receive the denunciation.
180. Cf. **ibid.**, 29 feb. 1886 ad 7.
181. **Ibid.**, 9 iun. 1922.

priest removes the obligation, unless the natural law in a particular case perhaps dispenses; the Holy See will not regularly dispense from the obligation.[182]

A confessor is seriously obliged to warn a penitent who confesses having been solicited of the duty of making a denunciation.[183] He must never ask a penitent about solicitation, unless the latter confesses sins of impurity committed with a confessor or that he knows of such a case. The penitent's good faith does not excuse the confessor from warning him, even if he foresees the denunciation will be refused.[184] The warning may be deferred if the penitent confessing is in even remote danger of death and it is thought the penitent may not agree to the denunciation. The confessor is not obliged to instruct the solicited penitent on the malice of the crime of which he is clearly ignorant. Nor does he incur the penalty of excommunication if he fails to warn the penitent as prescribed by the law.

The confessor must be *certain* that it is a *true case* of solicitation and that the party is bound to denounce by ecclesiastical precept or, lacking any of the conditions for this, by charity. If he cannot form a judgment at the time, he should warn the penitent to return to him at some definite time, and if opportune, request permission of the penitent to consult someone else. He must be wary of female penitents who accuse their confessors of solicitation, being on his guard against both malice and exaggeration on the part of a penitent, especially the emotionally or psychologically disturbed. Penitents who are quite prepared to make a denunciation can be prudently suspected, since the ordinary penitent finds the obligation difficult to observe.

The confessor must be prudent with those in danger of death, lest their passing from life in the state of grace be endangered by an insistence upon denunciation. Outside of this danger of death, if no legitimate excuses can be found, the penitent who persists in refusing to denounce must be dismissed as one indisposed for

---

182. S. Poen., 24 apr. 1884; Paul VI, motu proprio **de episcoporum muneribus**, 15 iun. 1966, IX, 5.
183. c. 904.
184. S. Off. 20 feb. 1867.

absolution. The fear of a penitent that the one denounced will then know who the penitent is can be refuted by its unlikelihood or impossibility, and the argument that the one denounced will suffer great harm may be countered by the greater harm done to souls and by the abuse and profanation of a sacred thing. However, the confessor may in his prudence petition the Sacred Penitentiary for a dispensation from the obligation of denunciation.

A confessor guilty of solicitation is to be punished by being suspended from saying Mass and hearing confessions, and also according to the seriousness of the offence declared incapable of hearing confessions, deprived of all benefices, dignities, active and passive voice, declared incapable of these, and in more serious cases degraded.[185] These penalties are to be imposed (*ferendae sententiae*). A soliciting priest who is truly contrite can be absolved immediately by any confessor, since his crime is reserved neither by censure nor by sin in the common law. He must be warned not to hear in the future the confession of any solicited party, even though not his own victim.

If the person solicited disregards the law of denunciation within a month, he incurs an excommunication, which is not reserved, and he cannot be absolved until he has done so or made a serious promise to do so.[186] If the promise is not kept, the obligation still remains. Those under the age of puberty do not incur the penalty for failure to report,[187] but they are obliged within thirty days after coming to an understanding that solicitation actually took place. All others, besides the one solicited, who are bound to denounce, do not incur this censure.

Anyone who *falsely* denounces a confessor of solicitation incurs an automatic excommunication reserved in a special manner to the Holy See.[188] False denunciation is also the only *sin* reserved as sin to the Holy See.[189]

---

185. c. 2368, 1.
186. **Ibid.**, 2. Even if the solicitation has been mutual, the penitent is bound to denounce, without mentioning his own consent or sin.
187. **Ibid.**; c. 2230.
188. c. 2363.
189. c. 894.

2. Absolution of an Accomplice in Sin

The absolution of one who has been an accomplice in a sin of impurity is invalid, except in danger of death; and even in danger of death, it is unlawful on the part of the confessor, in accordance with the norms of law.[190] Complicity is present when there is the perpetration with another of the same sin of impurity. Complicity must be immediate in the impure act itself[191] and external, i.e., with external consent mutually manifested on both sides to the same sin. One who does not externally resist is considered to consent externally. It is not necessary that the sin committed was on the occasion of or connected with confession,—which would be also solicitation.

The crime embraces any sin against the sixth commandment which is on the part of *both* parties certain, external, and serious by reason of both internal and external act.[192] A sin is serious by reason of external act when it is of itself libidinous, i.e., of its nature tends to excite veneral motion and is placed without proportionate cause, e.g., touches in the private parts. Likewise an act not in itself libidinous but placed with the evident intention of exciting this motion and as a means of provoking such excitement, e.g., touches and kisses in decent parts placed with the evil intention made clear (although it is not easy in such cases to recognize mutual participation). Obscene language and looks are included;[193] in such cases there should be a slowness to judge complicity and in case of doubt the language, etc., should be seen as thoroughly obscene and no motive present to explain it otherwise.

The accomplice of the confessor in the sin of impurity can be

---

190. c. 884.
191. Thus excluded is a connection with another to sin with a third party. However, where cooperation is in effect complicity, the precise sin is present, e.g., the priest conspires with another man for their mutual effort to seduce a certain woman. Even if the seduction does not result, the complicity in a sin of impurity is present.
192. There is no formal complicity within the sense of the law if the other party is asleep, drunk, insane, etc., and thus the absolution is valid.
193. S. Off. 28 mai 1873.

any person, whether man or woman, before or after the age of puberty, as well as a person with whom the priest sinned in this manner before assuming the priesthood.[194]

Absolution outside the case of danger of death is *invalid*, even if the priest accomplice in good faith absolves from the sin of complicity, e.g., he did not advert to the fact that this was his accomplice, or he was ignorant of his lack of jurisdiction.[195] Although it is a matter of disagreement, it may be safely held that the privation of jurisdiction in a sin of complicity is not perpetual but only until such time as this sin is directly remitted by another confessor, when it then becomes not necessary but free matter. As free matter it can thus be confessed to the accomplice priest and absolved. But in practice this should never be done. Thus, when the Sacred Penitentiary gives faculties to absolve a priest under censure for this sin, it customarily demands that he abstain from hearing the confession of his accomplice whenever this can be done without scandal.[196]

It seems that in an extraordinary situation, e.g., in some mission places, where another priest cannot be found and there is little hope of another becoming available, the accomplice priest may lawfully and even directly absolve the sin of complicity outside of danger of death. Nevertheless, if a penitent needs to go to Communion or to celebrate Mass and there is no priest available except the accomplice priest, it is better in practice to elicit an act of perfect contrition and communicate or celebrate than to approach the accomplice priest.

Absolution *in danger of death* is *valid* but unlawful on the part of the confessor, unless it is a case of necessity. The law itself[197]

---

194. S. Poen. 22 maii 1879.
195. c. 16, 1. According to some the invalidity is at least with respect to the sin of complicity alone. It should be noted that, if a penitent is in good faith and inculpably has failed to confess a sin of complicity, the confessor validly absolves from the sins confessed. The sin of complicity, however, which has been removed by the infusion of sanctifying grace rather than precisely by absolution, remains as necessary matter for confession.
196. S. Poen. 29 feb. 1904.
197. c. 2367, 1.

indicates what necessity is meant: 1) if no other priest, even one not approved for hearing confessions, is present or can be summoned; 2) if one is present but he refuses to hear the confession; 3) if one cannot be summoned without grave scandal or infamy to the priest accomplice, but the latter is seriously bound to do what he can to avoid this danger, e.g., by leaving under some pretext, by forewarning the penitent to summon spontaneously another priest, etc.; if he fails to do this he validly but unlawfully absolves and thus incurs the censure; 4) if the dying accomplice refuses to confess to another priest.

To incur the *penalty* of the automatic excommunication reserved in a most special way to the Holy See the confessor must be conscious of a serious formal sin, i.e., conscious of the serious prohibition forbidding him to absolve here and now.[198] The confessor can validly and lawfully absolve, e.g., if the penitent will die before another confessor arrives, or if he is bound *ex officio* to hear confessions and he cannot call in another confessor, especially a non-approved one, without causing great wonder or even scandal. A schismatic or heretical priest is not to be preferred to the accomplice priest. If a confession has been *lawfully* begun by an accomplice priest, it can be completed by him, even if another priest becomes available in the meantime.

The excommunication is also incurred if the accomplice confessor absolves or pretends to absolve his accomplice, when the latter omits to confess the sin of complicity, which has not yet been absolved, induced thereto, whether directly or indirectly, by the said confessor.[199] Thus the confessor who persuades his accomplice that the sin they are about to commit together is not a sin at all, or not a serious sin (whereas it is such), and so absolves or pretends to absolve the accomplice who confessed other sins but not the mutual sin committed, incurs the excommunication.[200]

198. Cf. cc. 2218, 2; 2242, 1.
199. c. 2367, 2. The penalty of this canon applies also to the Oriental Church. (S. Off. 21 iul, 1934) In the internal forum absolution is reserved to the Sacred Penitentiary, in the external forum to the S. Congregation for the Doctrine of the Faith.
200. S. Off. 16 nov. 1934. It should also be ascertained if there has been the crime of solicitation by the confessor.

Pretending to absolve is to simulate the sacrament. Directly to induce the penitent is to forewarn him positively and explicitly not to mention the sin, since the confessor knows it and thus it would be useless. Indirectly to induce the penitent is to persuade him that the shameful act already committed is not a sin or not a serious sin, and thus the penitent concludes that it cannot be mentioned and is not mentioned.[201] When a confessor is inculpably ignorant of the identity of the penitent and absolves a sin of complicity confessed as necessary matter, he does not commit a crime (he is not formally guilty of imparting a forbidden absolution) and thus incurs no censure.[202]

The Sacred Penitentiary absolves from the *penalty* for the internal forum. In danger of death[203] and in a more urgent case,[204] a confessor may absolve and at the same time impose the obligation of recourse to the Holy See within a month. Moral impossibility of recourse within the time does not dispense from the obligation.[205] If present circumstances prevent the penitent from making the recourse, the confessor may allow the penitent to defer the obligation of recourse for a period. When the obstacle ceases he will then have a month in which to make recourse. In an exceptional case, e.g., the penitent priest has an incurable disease, is unable to write and will not see the confessor again, the confessor can absolve from the censure and terminate the obligation of recourse. Besides the sacramental penance, he must impose the mandates usually given by the Sacred Penitentiary, namely, never to hear the accomplice again and to require the latter to seek another confessor, if the accomplice is again approached; to give up hearing confessions for not more than three months, if a simple confessor, and not more than six, if a pastor, if he has absolved an accomplice (the same or different ones) three or more times; to mention the previous absolution when there is a relapse.

201. S. Poen. 19 feb. 1896.
202. Cf. cc. 2195, 1; 2242, 1.
203. c. 2252.
204. c. 2254, 1.
205. **Ibid.**, 3.

IV Candidates for the Sacrament of Penance

A. Frequency of Sacramental Confession

Over and above the abiding obligation of doing penance in this life and of receiving the sacrament of Penance[206] all the faithful (including those of the Oriental rites) are seriously bound to an annual confession of sins in the sacrament of Penance by the positive precept of ecclesiastical law which further determines the divine precept. Thus, each and every member of the faithful of both sexes, on reaching the age of discretion, that is, the use of reason, and conscious of mortal sin, is obliged to make an exact confession of all his sins at least once a year.[207]

This precept is not satisfied by a sacrilegious confession or by one that is deliberately invalid,[208] since the purpose of the precept—reconciliation with God, is not achieved. Every member of the faithful has the right to confess his sins to the confessor whom he chooses, even though the latter belongs to another rite, provided that he is lawfully approved.[209] Thus, the precept of annual confession may be fulfilled in any place where the confessor whom the penitent approaches may hear the confession.

All the baptized (laymen, clerics, religious of any state or condition) who are conscious of serious sin that has not yet been declared in valid confession are bound by this precept. Children are bound even before the age of seven, if they have already reached the age of discretion or the use of reason, i.e., if they can discern between what is morally good and evil and are capable of serious sin. The practice of not absolving children before their First Communion is not approved.[210] If the confessor doubts whether this age of discretion has been reached, he should prefer to absolve conditionally rather than not at all. However, a child who reaches

---

206. Cf. I above.
207. c. 906. Cf. Denz.-Schön. 1708.
208. c. 907.
209. c. 905. Catholics in certain circumstances may approach an Orthodox priest, cf. note 164 above.
210. S. C. Sac. 8 aug. 1910; cf. PCI 3 ian. 1918.

the age of reason need not confess immediately but may wait until the next Paschal season, all things being equal.

The divine precept obliges only to the confession of *serious* sins not yet directly remitted in the sacrament of Penance.[211] The ecclesiastical determination obliges no more strictly. Even if slight sins are present and no serious sins have been committed in the course of the year, the obligation does not bind, since the purpose of the law—reconciliation with God, is factually realized.[212] The precept, however, is satisfied even by the confession of slight sins. Thus, if one has confessed only venial sins and subsequently within the same year has committed a serious sin, he is not obliged by the precept to confess again that year. This is the understanding and practice of the faithful and a safe norm in practice for the judgment of the confessor.

The precept of annual confession may be variously computed (*tempus utile*), e.g., by the civil year from Jan. 1 to Dec. 31, by the liturgical year from one Advent to the next. The common method is from one Easter to another, or as extended by indult in the U.S.A., from one Trinity Sunday to the next. The obligation commences with the beginning of the year and circumstances may add urgency to its fulfillment, e.g., if a person in serious sin foresees that he will not be able later to go to confession before the period expires, he is bound to satisfy his obligation presently. If a person in serious sin has not confessed during the course of the year (or for several years), he should do so as soon as possible, since the period of a year prescribed does not terminate but rather urges the obligation. However, if in this following year he again falls into serious sin, he is not obliged by the precept to confess again, since one and the same confession satisfies the end of the precept of both years—reconciliation with God. The faithful usually associate as one the obligation to confess at least once a year and the precept to receive the Eucharist during the Paschal season.

211. Denz.-Schön. 1679-1682, 1706-1707.
212. The confession of slight sins is most expedient and to be encouraged. The practice of the faithful is not to be disturbed by emphasis on the obligation of confession only in the case of the presence of serious sin.

This practice should not be disapproved, as confession may also be necessary by reason of the sacrament of the Eucharist itself.[213]

B. *Devout and Frequent Confession*

The practice of frequent confession out of devotion with only slight faults has often been praised as most beneficial to spiritual progress. "It is true indeed that there are many ways, all most praiseworthy, of wiping out these faults. But to advance with increasing fervor on the path of virtue We earnestly recommend the pious practice of frequent confession, introduced by the Church under the inspiration of the Holy Spirit. By it genuine self-knowledge is increased, Christian humility grows, bad habits are corrected, spiritual neglect and tepidity are countered, the conscience is purified, the will strengthened, a salutary self-control attained and grace increased by reason of the sacrament itself."[214] For those who communicate daily or almost daily frequent confession suffices to produce these fruits. The frequency should be prudently estimated so that the confessor may not be greatly burdened or the penitent lose the fervor or even the sufficiency of his dispositions through habituation or familiarity with the sacrament.

C. *First Confession*

The suitable age for the first reception of the Sacrament of Penance is deemed to be that which in the documents of the Church is called the age of reason or of discretion, that is, about the seventh year, more or less.[215] It has been the common and general practice of the Church of putting first Confession before first Communion. Moreover, it is the repeated judgment of the Holy See that this practice is to be retained and observed. The introduction

---

213. Cf. c. 856.
214. Pius XII, ency. **Mystici Corporis,** 29 iun. 1943. "This sacrament, prepared for a daily examination of conscience, greatly fosters the necessary turning of the heart toward the love of the Father of mercies" (Vatican II, Decree **Presbyterorum Ordinis,** n. 18). Cf. **Ordo Paenitentiae,** 7b.
215. Pius X, Decree **Quam singulari,** 7 aug. 1910.

to first Confession may be carried out in various ways for catechetical and pastoral reasons, e.g., by having a communal penitential celebration precede or follow the reception of the Sacrament of Penance.[216]

D. *Material for Sacramental Confession*

The material about which contrition, confession, and absolution are concerned for the purpose of forgiveness is sins committed after Baptism. This material is related in various ways to the formula of absolution.

1. *Necessary material*

Those sins which by divine precept must necessarily be subjected to sacramental absolution in order to obtain remission are called necessary material for absolution. Thus a person who has committed serious sins after Baptism which have not been directly remitted through the keys of the Church (no matter how they may otherwise have been remitted) must, after a careful examination of conscience, confess all those of which he is aware and explain the circumstances which make a specific change in the sin.[217] Necessary material is always sufficient for receiving absolution.

Sins are said to be directly remitted when they are rightly submitted in species and number to the absolution of a confessor. Sins are only indirectly remitted by absolution when they are removed by the infusion of sanctifying grace in the soul by reason of the absolution immediately of sins directly submitted, since serious sin and sanctifying grace cannot coexist in the soul. Such sins, then,

---

216. S. C. Clero, 11 aug. 1971, **Directorium Catechisticum Generale, Addendum.** "Going to the sacrament of Penance from the beginning of the use of reason does not in itself harm the minds of the children, provided it is preceded, as it should be, by a kind and prudent catechetical preparation. The spirit of penance can be developed more fully by continuing catechetical instruction after first Communion; likewise, there can be growth in knowledge and appreciation of the great gift that Christ has given to sinful men in the sacrament of the pardon they will receive and of reconciliation with the Church" **(ibid.).**

217. c. 901. Cf. Trent, Denz.-Schön 1706-1707.

omitted in confession through inculpable forgetfulness or from any legitimate cause are remitted indirectly with the direct remission of the other sins confessed. They, however, (as well as sins already remitted through an act of perfect contrition with the desire of the sacrament) must be explicitly submitted in kind and number to the keys, not in order to be taken away but in order to satisfy the precept of Christ and the Church.

Sins confessed but not absolved because of the unworthiness of the penitent or because of lack of jurisdiction on the part of the confessor must be confessed again. It is not certain whether serious sin committed in the very reception of Baptism is necessary or doubtful material, but in practice it seems that it should be confessed to insure the full effect of Baptism and the spiritual welfare of the faithful. An adult Catholic whose first Baptism is called into doubt is rebaptized conditionally; he confesses only the sins he has committed and not directly confessed since his last worthy confession, since the previous confessions or the second Baptism remits the others. An adult non-Catholic who is conditionally baptized upon conversion must immediately confess all the sins of his past life and be conditionally absolved.[218]

2. *Sufficient material*

It is required and it suffices for the sacrament of Penance that sins, as long as they are truly such and regardless of being necessary or free material, be confessed with sincere sorrow and with a desire of absolution. Thus, sufficient, though not necessary, material of the sacrament of Penance are sins committed after Baptism, whether they are serious sins already directly remitted by the power of the keys or slight sins.[219] The confessor cannot absolve a penitent who cannot recall any sins since the last confession. If no sins of the past can be recalled, the penitent should be instructed on the requirements of the sacrament and the proper way to make an examination of conscience.

Insufficient material includes mere imperfections devoid of sinfulness, such as entirely indeliberate acts, involuntary distractions

---

218. Cf. **The Celebration of Baptism,** X C.
219. c. 902. Cf. Trent, Denz.-Schön. 1679-1680, 1707.

in prayer, the omission of a good or a better thing that is not of precept; also deliberate imperfections or transgressions of a counsel unless they arise from slight sin (e.g., levity, sloth, negligence, vanity, inordinate affection), and doubtful sins. In practice, the confessor must judge that, on account of imperfections alone, sacramental absolution cannot be given and that some certain and sufficient material should be evoked from the penitent. The confessor should ask the penitent to express sorrow for some past sin or sins of which he is certain. On the other hand, penitents are not to be discouraged from confessing their imperfections, since slight sin is easily connected with them; likewise from confessing their doubtful sins and daily light sins. The confessor can thus often aid in directing them, especially when they have been encouraged to state the motivations of these imperfect acts.

3. *Free material*

Those sins which can but not necessarily must be submitted in confession for absolution are considered free material. Thus free (but sufficient) material is all slight sins committed after Baptism and not yet remitted, and all sins both serious and slight which have already been directly remitted.[220] Even though a sin has already been remitted, it always remains a sin committed in the past and thus the object of the penitent's renewed sorrow; the absolution increases grace, which is of itself destructive of sin.

Since there is no obligation to confess free material, the confession of the lowest species, the number, and any changing circumstance is likewise not of obligation. It suffices to confess these sins in general. Moreover, although no obligation exists to confess slight sins, they are rightly and beneficially confessed, since many penitents are not able to judge the lightness or seriousness of a sin, and by this confession also virtue is promoted and spiritual guidance is aided. The confession of a certain sin already remitted insures

---

220. **Ibid.;** cf. Benedict XI, **Inter cunctas sollicitudines,** n. 18, Denz.-Schön. 880.

sufficient material for the sacrament when there is no new matter to confess and more surely true sorrow for them.[221]

4. Certain material

Sins for which there is certain culpability and for which absolution would be valid, all else being presupposed, are considered certain material for the sacrament.

5. *Doubtful material*

Sins for which absolution, all else being presupposed, would be doubtfully valid are doubtfully sufficient material for the sacrament and thus unlawful material in the administration of the sacrament of Penance, except in grave necessity.[222] The doubt may arise from any source, such as doubt as to the commission of the sin, as to full knowledge or consent, as to the sinfulness of an imperfection, etc.

A penitent who confesses only doubtful material must be induced to accuse himself of some certain sin of his past life which is already remitted, in order to be lawfully absolved. Thus he may say, for example, "I accuse myself of all my past sins against chastity, or charity, etc." Or the confessor may ask, for example, "Have you been certainly angry in your past life for which you are sorry?" to which the penitent answers in the affirmative. If the penitent has committed no certain sins or for some reason cannot recall any, as long as the sins confessed are of themselves serious and the doubt refers only to the consent, he is to be absolved conditionally (if you are capable) lest he be deprived of absolution to his great spiritual harm, if he has truly committed them. However, if the doubtful sins are only slight, conditional absolution is to be rarely imparted, since in fact the penitent suffers no serious

---

221. **Summa Theol., Suppl.,** q. 18, a. 2, ad 4: "when absolution is given a second time grace is increased, and the greater the grace received, the less there remains of the blemish of the previous sin, and the less punishment is required to remove that blemish."
222. Cf. **The Celebration of Baptism,** III 3.

spiritual damage and the sacrament ought not to be exposed to nullity.

Sometimes a penitent will confess a sin about which he has a doubt, saying in some form the following: "I wish to accuse myself of this as it stands in the sight of God." This is often the case in matters of chastity. The confessor ought not to absolve, at least absolutely, unless the penitent also confesses some certain material.

E. *General Accusation of Sins*

1. *In case of necessity*

A general accusation of sins certainly suffices and is valid in a case of necessity, when a specific accusation is not possible, e.g., "I accuse myself of all my sins." This is clear from the constant practice of the Church, e.g., absolution is imparted absolutely to soldiers when battle is imminent, in the case of shipwreck or other serious accident or danger, when any sign of confession is given by the dying, when, e.g., in mission lands, penitents would inculpably be deprived for a long time, etc.[223] Likewise the deaf and the dumb, and those whose language is unknown to the confessor are absolved validly and lawfully after only a general accusation made in some way. The sacrament is a judgment of reconciliation and not of condemnation, and thus perfect knowledge is not of the essence of the penitential judgment.

2. *Outside of necessity*

Serious sins not yet directly remitted must, at least by the precept of Christ, be confessed in species and number and changing circumstances. A general accusation against a certain virtue or precept without mentioning the lowest species and number in necessary matter does not suffice. Free material which is confessed generically in conjunction with other sins (serious or slight) distinctly and specifically confessed is unquestionably sufficient for absolution. This is laudably done at the end of the confession for greater sorrow and amendment and in order to extend the absolution to these sins. When free material is confessed only generically and

---

223. S. Poen. 25 mart. 1944; S. C. D. F. 16 iun. 1972.

there are no certain serious or slight sins since the last confession, the confessor may in practice absolve validly and lawfully, since a general accusation is valid in time of necessity and the positive precept of Christ and of the Church for individual accusation embraces only necessary and not free material. However, it is desirable (and it is the common practice of the faithful) to confess slight sins or free material specifically. The confessor must keep in mind that the penitent who makes a general confession need not confess in detail any free material.

When sins which are confessed specifically are not certain, the confessor will ask for some certain sin of the past. In practice, the confessor should ask the penitent to mention some specific sin of the past whenever there is a generic confession of sins already absolved or of slight sins; otherwise penitents are apt to become perfunctory in confessing and to forfeit the value of a devout and humble confession. Sorrow for specific and individual sins is more easily elicited and more effective than for sins in general. Unless required for sufficiency of the material, penitents ought not to be greatly disturbed in an effort to elicit a specific accusation of at least one sin in the past.

F. *Acts of the Penitent*

Faith teaches[224] that the acts of the penitent, namely, contrition, confession, and satisfaction, so pertain to the sacrament of Penance that without them there cannot be a perfect and integral remission of sins; and also that these three acts are the quasi material and parts of this sacrament. Theological discussion has centered on the way in which these three acts pertain to the nature of the sacrament and their necessity for the existence of a valid sacrament. The Thomistic and common teaching holds that it is not permitted to administer Penance without these three acts being present and in some way sensibly expressed, since the material of the sacraments must be sensible. Some reputable moralists teach opinions that

---

224. Trent, Denz.-Schön. 1673, 1675, 1704; 1685, 1462, 1709. Cf. **Summa Theol.**, III, q. 84, a. 1, ad 1; a. 2; q. 86, a. 6; q. 90, a. 1; a. 2, ad 2.

require merely internal dispositions of the penitent as pertaining to the essence or validity of the sacrament; the external acts of the penitent are not absolutely necessary but only at best conditions or dispositions. Thus the dispositions of sorrowing for sins and of a purpose of satisfying for them can be presumed in all the dying, even the unconscious, and absolution can be lawfully imparted to them under a condition (if you are capable). The sacraments are for men, but the non-Thomistic and not common opinion of some, as well as the practice of absolving the unconscious with no signs of repentance in any way manifested, do not prove the certainty or validity of the absolution.

1. *Contrition*

Perfect contrition or contrition in the proper sense is sorrow of soul and detestation for sin committed with the purpose of sinning no more.[225] As an act of penance it justifies with the implicit desire of the sacrament. It arises from a motive of charity, of the love of God above all things (and can remit slight sins even without the sacrament).

Imperfect contrition or *attrition* is sorrow for sins committed which springs, not from the perfect motive of charity but from some less exalted but supernatural motive, namely, the baseness of sin or the fear of hell and of the eternal and temporal punishments inflicted by God. These two, to which all other inferior motives are reduced, spring from supernatural faith and actual grace, i.e., they are referred to God. Faith teaches[226] that such attrition, although it cannot of itself lead to justification, disposes the sinner to seek the grace of God in the sacrament of Penance. It is commonly taught that attrition with the actual reception of the sacrament justifies.

For the valid reception of the sacrament any contrition must be *true* and *internal*, that is, not only expressed in words or signs but embraced principally by the heart and soul. It is an act of the will detesting sin committed. It need not be sensibly "felt," as it can be present together with dryness, tedium, etc. Lack of intensity

---

225. Trent, Denz.-Schön. 1676.
226. **Ibid.**, Denz.-Schön. 1678, 1705.

in the act or of an accompanying sensibility does not necessarily affect the penitent's resolution to abandon sin and to fulfill his obligations. The contrition must precede absolution and not be recalled if the latter is to be valid; normally it should exist before confession begins. In some cases the confessor may need to arouse proper dispositions.

Contrition should be *supernatural*, that is, elicited under the movement of actual grace and motivated or referred to God, as noted for perfect and imperfect contrition. The act of penitence should be *formal* and *explicit*, or a positive act by which the will truly and explicitly sorrows for and detests a sin committed as an offense against God. In practice most penitents are not to be greatly disturbed, since in their desire for absolution or in eliciting an act of love there is scarcely lacking a formal act of sorrow. Penitents usually terminate the recounting of their sins with a formula such as "I am sorry for these and all my past sins."

The penitent's contrition must be *universal*, extending to all his serious sins not yet directly remitted, even those which are forgotten or unknown. Although it is far better, nevertheless it is not necessary to have sorrow for each serious sin individually and distinctly (although they must be so confessed) but at least implicitly. It is not required to have contrition for all slight sins or even for certain ones. Since they are free material, one can confess and have sorrow for one and not for another. The frequency of slight sins is itself a deformity subject to contrition. True sorrow for slight sins also must be internal, supernatural, and appreciatively supreme, although not always universal. The devout penitent will normally express a sorrow which is universal for all slight sins.

Contrition should be at least *appreciatively supreme*, i.e., the penitent appreciates that no other evil is as great as sin, and he is so displeased over the sin committed that he is generally prepared to forego any good or to risk any harm than to fall into sin again. There is no need for the confessor to compare evils, as the penitent may become disturbed and confused. It suffices for the latter to be prepared to do what he can in the future with God's help. Likewise the contrition need not be intensively supreme or more vehement or more poignantly felt than any other sorrow. Some expressions of sorrow, such as tears, sighs, striking of the breast, etc., are not necessary, but yet not to be frowned on. No particular degree or duration of sorrow is necessary. Perfunctory acts of contrition should be cautioned against and formulas expressing true motives for sorrow taught and promoted.

Contrition is to be elicited with a view to *sacramental* confession and absolution and renewed every time a new serious sin is committed. In practice, whenever a penitent immediately after absolution remembers a serious sin he had forgotten and confesses it, he should make another act of contrition; the same penance or preferably a new one should be imposed.

The contrition necessary for forgiveness, besides sorrow for and detestation of sin committed, must also include a *purpose of amendment*, that is, the resolution (*propositum*) or fixed and firm determination not to sin again.[227] It is explicit and formal, if formulated as a distinct act; implicit and virtual, if included in the act of sorrow (which is the minimum necessary). This resolution is the best indicator of true contrition. It should be *firm*, whereby the penitent here and now seriously and deliberately purposes to sin no more, to amend his life, and to endure with God's help any evil or fear rather than to offend God. The penitent may be aware of his own inconstancy and frailty and judge that he will fall again in the same manner. However, in most cases this does not affect his actual resolution of amendment here and now. With children it is often necessary for the confessor to get them to agree to try to do better in the future. When an adult's disposition is doubtful, e.g., in some cases of birth prevention practice, the confessor will seek an explicit purpose of amendment.

The resolution must be *efficacious*, i.e., the penitent must intend to use the means necessary to avoid sin and its occasions, e.g., prayer and vigilance, to repair as far as he is able any damage done, etc. Such a resolution is efficacious if some means are adopted, but if no means are taken when they easily could be, it is suspect. There can be a doubt of the penitent's resolution if there is a fall immediately after confession. However, relapse into sin is not neces-

---

227. **Ibid.**, Denz.-Schön. 1676.

sarily a sign of want of true resolution, as habits of sin are not easily nor at once rooted out or frailty quickly overcome.

The will to exclude all serious sins in the future should be *universal,* although the sins need not be thought of individually. It is not required for absolution from slight sins that the purpose of amendment be universal; if only slight sins are confessed, there must be a resolve at least to avoid some definite sin confessed or group of slight sins or the most pernicious of them or those which are fully deliberate or to lessen the number of them, i.e., a will to improve. Confessors should try to arouse penitents who frequently fall into the same sins through negligence, etc., to a more fervent contrition and a firmer resolve to amend.

2. *Confession*

a. *Characteristics of sacramental confession*

Sacramental confession is the accusation of one's own sins committed after Baptism, made to an authorized priest for the purpose of obtaining absolution, which confession is necessary by divine precept.[228] *Personal* actual sins, and not merely imperfections, are to be confessed to a spiritual judge who is authorized to judge them for the purpose of absolution. A confession made for some other reason, such as counsel, consolation, or mockery, is not sacramental (and thus not under the seal).

By the ancient custom of the Church confession should be *vocal.*[229] The obligation is grave to confess one's sins orally, unless a just cause in case of necessity requires nods, signs, or writing. Such a just cause is present if the penitent is dumb, or because of illness or some other reason is able to speak only with great difficulty, or he cannot make an integral declaration of sins because of extreme embarrassment, anxiety, or scruples, or if the confessor is hard of hearing and cannot hear the penitent without bystanders also hearing. The deaf and dumb are obliged to confess in signs and nods according to their ability. Those who do not know the

---

228. **Ibid.**, Denz.-Schön. 1679, 1706-1707. Cf. **Ordo Paenitentiae 11.**
229. Cf. Benedict XI, Bull **Inter cunctas.**

language of the confessor should confess by signs and nods as best they can.[230]

A *secret* and *auricular* confession has always been recommended and in use in the Church.[231] Public confession or manifestation of sins is not obligatory. Moreover, a penitent is not bound to choose an interpreter, but such a person when employed is bound by the law of the seal.[232] It can be so arranged that the interpreter does not know the responses of the penitent, e.g., by not facing the penitent who then answers the confessor's questions by nods and by showing a number of fingers.

The penitent should make a confession that is *simple* and *discreet*, being prohibited from narrating what does not pertain to it. He should not list the sins of others nor reveal the name of an accomplice. Sins against the sixth commandment should be told in modest and succinct language, which, however, is sufficiently clear and exact. The penitent should be *humble* in words and gestures and make the confession kneeling, unless just reason excuses. There must be a disposition to accept and to obey the just commands of the confessor as well as to receive humbly his rebukes. The same one who has not been ashamed to commit the sin ought not to be ashamed to confess the sin committed.

Perfect *truthfulness* and *sincerity* ought to be present in every confession so that the penitent manifests his sins as they are in his conscience, as certain or doubtful, mortal or venial, etc., neither denying, lessening, or exaggerating the sins committed. The penitent is bound to reply sincerely to the legitimate questions of the confessor,[233] e.g., about habits of sin, occasions and circumstances of sin, the dispositions of the penitent, etc., without which information the confessor cannot form a prudent judgment as his office requires. If the questions are manifestly indiscreet, the penitent

---

230. Missionaries would exhort penitents whose language they do not know to confess at least one slight sin through an interpreter. Cf. S. Off. 28 feb. 1633; S. C. P. F. 6 sept. 1630.
231. Trent, Denz.-Schön. 1683.
232. c. 903.
233. Cf. proposition 58 condemned by Innocent XI, 4 mart. 1679: "We are not bound to confess to a confessor who asks us about the habit of some sin." Denz.-Schön. 2158.

is not bound to reply, and for a just cause he can use a mental restriction in his replies.

To *lie* in confession about a *serious* and necessary matter is a grave pernicious lie and a sacrilege. It perverts the judgment of the confessor; the confession is not integral and the absolution not valid. Of itself it is a serious sin to confess a grave sin that has not been committed or to exaggerate the number of serious sins or to confess as light a serious sin. However, penitents sometimes do this out of scrupulosity, disturbance of soul, simplicity, or ignorance, and they are excused from all or from at least serious sin. To *lie* about *light* matter or serious free matter is in itself a slight sacrilege, e.g., to confess a light sin that was never committed, to deny one already committed or a serious sin already properly absolved. This does not render the penitential judgment perverted in serious matter nor invalidate the sacrament or impede its effect. It can be a serious sin if only serious matters are confessed. In making a general confession it is not forbidden of itself to include sins committed since the last confession indistinguishably with past sins already forgiven, but the truth must be told to the confessor who interrogates about recent sins.

To *lie* about *non-confessional* matter is not for that reason a sacrilege, as it in no way perverts the penitential judgment. It takes on the sinfulness of the lie in question; as a serious sin it renders the penitent indisposed for absolution. Moreover a penitent does not sin because he confesses his slight sins to one confessor (such as his ordinary confessor) and his serious sins to another, as long as he confesses the serious sins first and the procedure is due to an honest motive. If he intends to deceive his ordinary confessor out of vainglory or some other inordinate motive, he sins slightly. But the sin is serious if grave danger is present, e.g., if this is done in order to sin more freely or to remain in the proximate occasion of sin, or in order to be admitted to religious profession or clerical orders, which admission would otherwise be restrained because of the type or habit of sin.

b. *Integrity or completeness of confession*

Confession must be integral, that is, complete and entire, so that to one and the same confessor is subjected at the same time the whole necessary matter which has not yet been duly submitted to the keys. *Material* or objective *integrity* embraces absolutely all the serious sins which in reality have been committed since Baptism and not yet duly confessed. *Formal* or subjective integrity consists in the accusation of all the serious sins which, all things considered, the penitent here and now, according to his capacity and after a careful examination, morally can and must confess according to his conscience, although for a just cause he omits some. All sins must be declared, since the minister is the judge of them all; this sacrament has been instituted in the form of a special judgment in which at the same time all or none of the sins are remitted. Thus integrity is necessary by divine precept for the validity of the sacrament, formal integrity actually and by a necessity of means and precept, material integrity at least *in desire* by a necessity of means, and regularly by precept from which there can be excusing causes. Of itself confession should be materially integral, but formal integrity alone sometimes suffices. It is a serious sin and a sacrilege to omit a sin which one can and must declare here and now in confession.[235]

Each and every serious sin committed after Baptism and not directly remitted must be confessed in species or kind, in number, and in circumstances which change the species,[236] as a generic accusation outside of necessity is insufficient. The *lowest theological species* must be confessed, inasmuch as some sins are more serious than others, and also the *lowest moral species,* inasmuch as sins are distinguished by their formal malices, e.g., justice is differently violated by theft, detraction, homicide. In the event that the penitent does not confess the lowest species, e.g., due to ignorance or forgetfulness, the confessor and penitent must try to determine it as best

234. Trent, Denz.-Schön. 1679.
235. A confessor cannot excuse from the integrity of confession because of the great number of penitents. Cf. prop. 59 condemned by Innocent XI: "It is permitted to absolve sacramentally those who have only half confessed, by reason of a great crowd of penitents, such as for example can happen on a day of great festival or indulgence." Denz-Schön. 2159; also cf. S. C. D. F., 16 iun. 1972, on general absolution.
236. Trent, Denz.-Schön. 1679, 1707.

possible. The next higher species must be confessed. When later recalled, it should be confessed in its lowest species.

The precise and certain *number* of serious sins should be confessed as far as morally possible. If a careful examination does not yield this, the penitent should confess the approximate number. If this is not possible, he should confess the approximate number of times he has committed such a sin or sins each day or week or month or year, or whether in a certain period he has very often, often, or sometimes committed these sins. Some theologians hold that the sins confessed in an approximate number by the penitent according to his knowledge at the time are all directly remitted as being sufficiently contained in the more or less determined number declared; thus there is no obligation to confess later the precise number. This is safe to follow in practice. Others hold that the penitent need not later confess his error made in good faith if he declared a greater number than were actually committed, since the greater includes the lesser, but he must if a notably lesser number were declared. It should be noted that if a very definite and precise number were given and later even one serious sin is recalled, it must be directly declared.

Circumstances which *change* the nature, i.e., multiply the kinds of species, of sin must be confessed: grave circumstances which are so realized by the sinner, e.g., fornication with a married person. It should be observed that sins are to be confessed in their integrity, not according to the greater knowledge or theological science later acquired by the penitent but according to the knowledge (and thus the voluntariety) possessed at the time they were committed. Of themselves *circumstances* which *aggravate* or increase the malice of sin need not be confessed, e.g., the amount of serious theft, the number of persons, the dignity of the person, etc. (unless it also multiplies the malice). In practice, however, the faithful are accustomed to confess notably aggravating circumstances (and are so to be encouraged) for greater peace of conscience, greater humility and penitence, and to secure richer graces. Exception is made in the case of the scrupulous and ordinarily in matters of chastity. In cases where reservations or censures are incurred when a sin is committed in this or that circumstance, the latter, even if only aggravating, must be confessed, e.g., the place of solicitation. Both changing and aggravating circumstances are the legitimate object of the confessor's interrogation of the penitent.[237]

Although the *external act* does not differ specifically from the internal act, it is the ultimate element of integrity of the sin and completes it in its kind or species. It is likewise forbidden by God and should be declared in confession. The confessor judges differently about the state of the penitent with internal and with external sins, e.g., concerning occasions, the obligation of restitution, etc. This is the understanding of the Church and the practice of the faithful.[238] *Foreseen consequences* must be confessed as being voluntary in cause and thus sinful, e.g, pollution resulting from obscene reading, to miss Sunday Mass due to drunkenness. Evil effects foreseen but retracted or not foreseen at all need not be confessed as not being voluntary and thus sinful (although damage must be repaired).

Doubtful sins may regard any of three situations: 1) doubt as to the *existence* of a serious sin, i.e., that it was committed at all. There is no obligation of itself to confess these sins, since a doubtfully committed sin is not sufficient (and thus not necessary) material for absolution; we are bound to confess sins which are on our conscience after a careful examination. They may be confessed, and frequently it is recommended that they be made known, in order to form one's conscience, and especially at the hour of death when the confessor's presence is usually a more secure safeguard than an act of perfect contrition. If a penitent confesses a sin as doubtfully committed, he is not held to confess it as certain if he later recalls it as such. Implicitly the confessor has directly absolved it on the condition that it was committed. 2) doubt as to the *seriousness* of a certainly committed sin. There is no certain obligation to confess these sins, as there is no consciousness of their gravity. In doubt as to full consent or perfect advertence, the favor or presumption

---

237. Cf. n. 233 above.
238. Cf. Alexander VII, prop. 25 condemned 24 sept. 1665: "He who has had intercourse with an unmarried woman satisfies the precept of confession by saying: I committed a grievous sin against chastity with an unmarried woman, without mentioning the intercourse." Denz.-Schön. 2045.

is to follow the condition of the penitent: a penitent of tender conscience and unaccustomed to sinning seriously would not be held to confess them, whereas the lax and frequent sinner is to confess them. It is the practice for those who are neither lax nor scrupulous to confess a doubtfully serious sin. The uninstructed should declare them, as it is very difficult for the penitent alone to rightly form his conscience. 3) doubt as to the *confession* of a certainly committed serious sin. If the doubt is merely negative, such sins should be confessed, since there is a certain obligation to confess certainly committed serious sins, and this obligation cannot be satisfied by a doubtful fullfillment. If there are positive indications that the sins have already been confessed, e.g., in the case of one who frequently goes to confession and regularly makes a careful examination, the confession need not be made.

c. *Excusing causes*

General norms

No precept can or is intended to oblige to what is *physically* impossible, since no one is obliged to the impossible; therefore, in such a case one is not obliged to material integrity. For *moral* inability to excuse from material integrity these conditions must be present at the same time: 1) another confessor cannot be found to whom without inconvenience the sins can be integrally confessed: 2) the confession is here and now necessary, e.g., before paschal Communion, before celebrating or communicating the Eucharist, because otherwise scandal or infamy is risked, because the sinner would have to remain in serious sin in danger of death and loss of salvation for some time (beyond three days or even one day); 3) only those sins and circumstances are omitted which cannot be declared without grave inconvenience. This moral inability must be extrinsic to the confession itself and only accidentally connected with it here and now. Great repugnance, shame, fear of reprimand by or loss of reputation with the confessor, etc., are intrinsic to confession and insufficient causes for excusing. It must be impossible for the penitent to make a materially integral confession without serious spiritual or temporal damage to himself, the confessor, or to another. Prudent fear of this harm suffices.

The sins thus not directly accused and forgiven must be confessed in the next confession after the cessation of the excusing causes. These causes suspend but do not remove the obligation of material integrity. The penitent, moreover, should confess as clearly and distinctly as he can. He must repeat if he perceives that the confessor has not heard or understood, e.g., because the latter is hard of hearing or sleepy, or because of singing or music playing in the place. If he intentionally tries to confess so that he will not be understood, he commits a sacrilege and must repeat the confession. A known incomplete confession must be completed in the next confession to be integral.[239] If the confession is known to be invalid for any reason or sacrilegious, it must be repeated.

Physical inability

Lack of strength or power suffices to excuse, e.g., the penitent is so infirm or near to death that it is very difficult or impossible for him to think or speak or go on with the confession. The confessor must be more concerned to elicit an act of true contrition from the penitent. A similar case exists when the confessor himself probably may die before hearing the full confession.

Defect of speech excuses, i.e., a mute is excused if he cannot confess integrally by sign language. He should manifest his sins to the confessor at least by nods. Writing is recommendable but not obligatory, and the confessor should see to it that a written confession is destroyed immediately. A penitent who is ignorant of the language of the confessor is excused when no confessor who understands him is available and the obligation to confess urges. He should express his sins and his sorrow in the best way he can;[240] he is free to employ an interpreter.[241]

Lack of time sometimes excuses. This applies only to imminent

---

239. **Ibid.**, prop. 11: "We are not bound to express in a subsequent confession sins omitted in confession or forgotten because of the imminent danger of death or for some other reason." Denz.-Schön. 2031.
240. Cf. S. Off. 28 feb. 1633.
241. c. 903.

danger of death, e.g., at the time of shipwreck, battle, fire, accident, disastrous and contagious disease, etc. It does not apply to the delay involved in hearing a large number of penitents, since devotion and ecclesiastical precept must yield to the divine law of material integrity.[242]

Ignorance or forgetfulness suffices to excuse. The penitent is obliged to make a serious examination of conscience. If as a matter of fact he, culpably or not, cannot remember a sin or inadvertently omits it, he is validly and lawfully absolved. If a serious sin is recalled before Communion, it is better to confess it if convenient; but there is no obligation, and it suffices to declare it in the next confession. Neither is there an obligation to write down one's sins to avoid forgetting them.

Moral inability

Great scrupulosity in confessing and explaining his sins suffices to excuse a penitent who finds considerable difficulty with confession and the confessor fears that it will become odious. When the confessor prudently judges it to be necessary, he may terminate the confession for the good of the penitent and absolve.

Danger to one's life will excuse from integrity, e.g., if the confessor prudently fears infection at the time of plague or contagious disease; if the penitent fears spies, etc., during a persecution. In such cases the confessor may hear one or another sin and absolve.

The risk of giving scandal or of lapsing into sin which is feared will arise for the penitent, the confessor or both from the confession, is an excusing cause. The penitent because of his own known and experienced weakness strongly fears that he will consent again to carnal sins if he makes a careful confession of them. The penitent has a grave fear that, if he or she confesses certain carnal sins, solicitation to commit them will be made by the confessor (this must not be a presumption but a well-grounded fear, e.g., based on previous incidence of this attempt regarding the penitent or others). The penitent seriously and with sure foundation fears that by an integral confession the confessor, of whose weakness

242. Cf. n. 235 above.

he has knowledge, will be induced to sin, e.g., by a confession of evil desires of sinning with him. Also the rare instance when the confessor fears that very probably he will scandalize himself or the penitent by a diligent questioning, due to his own or to the penitent's weakness.

Danger of breaking the seal is an adequate excuse. The priest judges he cannot make an integral confession without manifesting the sins already confessed to him by a penitent and the latter's identity becoming known or surmised. The penitent seriously and reasonably fears that the confessor will violate the seal either directly (which is most rare) or indirectly, e.g., by raising his voice at serious sins in the hearing of others. There is not sufficient excuse if the penitent fears that the confessor will oblige him to manifest his sins to another outside of confession, e.g., to avoid damage to a third party.

Danger of infamy of the penitent or a third party: The infamy or loss of reputation is not before the confessor but before others, e.g., a patient in a ward cannot make an integral confession without others close by hearing, such as doctors, nurses, patients. Penitents who are deaf or hard of hearing should use any hearing aids provided in the confessional box. If their condition is learned during the confession, they should be taken to the sacristy, if this can be done without causing suspicion. They should be required to use the sacristy at least in subsequent confessions. In the confessional box it may be necessary to impose only a light penance so that the bystanders will not know that a serious sin has been confessed. In the case where, from the length of time required to make an integral confession, the bystanders very probably will necessarily conclude that the penitent has many serious sins, the penitent may be excused from material integrity. However, the length of a confession is not normally or necessarily a sign of the gravity of sin; even a vague suspicion of this will not excuse from integrity.

The obligation of integrity sometimes involves confessing a sin which cannot be explained without danger of defaming a third party or of revealing an accomplice in sin. Divine law requires an integral confession, whereas the natural law forbids injury to another's reputation without grave cause. A confessor must prohibit a penitent from naming an accomplice or a third party when unnecessary. The penitent must conceal the crime of another insofar as he can and go to another confessor who does not know the accomplice or the third party, if this is possible without serious inconvenience and no just and proportionate cause excuses. Otherwise, the penitent can, and most probably must, confess integrally, even with the grave risk of revealing another's sin. It is lawful to reveal the crime of another for a just and proportionate reason, especially as no harm results; due to the sacramental seal there is no danger of further divulgation. An accomplice by sinning implicitly permits the revelation, knowing that the other party must confess the sin. This is the practice of the faithful in confessing, e.g., husband and wife. Those, however, who hold differently cannot be refused absolution for that reason.

Since the confessor can never oblige the penitent under penalty of denial of absolution to reveal to him as confessor the name of an accomplice,[243] neither can he ordinarily directly inquire about him. It would be a serious sin which renders the sacrament odious and induces the penitent to defame another without cause. For a proportionate cause the confessor can make indirect inquiries, e.g, by asking if the accomplice is married, a relative, a cleric or religious, a proximate occasion of sin, lives in the same house, etc., in other words, by inquiring about the qualities of the accomplice necessary for the confessional integrity and for detecting the nature of the proximate occasion, even if indirectly the accomplice becomes known.

For only the *gravest* cause and for the sake of the *common good*, the confessor can, under penalty of denial of absolution, oblige the penitent to denounce his accomplice outside of confession to a competent authority (even to the confessor himself, if he is also the superior), e.g., to reveal the promotor of heresy or homosexuality in an institution. This is more an obligation in charity than of confessional integrity. The revelation should always be made to one who is not the confessor. However, if the penitent will make the denunciation only through the confessor, the name of the accomplice

---

243. c. 888, 2.

must be declared; this should be done very rarely and the name should be given again outside of confession.

Some theologians cautiously admit as a probable excuse from material integrity (or even from the obligation of confessing here and now) the case of a penitent who experiences extraordinary shame and insuperable difficulty or repugnance in declaring certain sins to a particular confessor. They hold that, although this arises by reason of confession, it strictly and absolutely is not intrinsic to confession, e.g., an especially disgraceful sin to be confessed by a parent to son, sister to brother, venerable old pastor to young curate, religious superior to subject. The excuse is held to be allowable to certain individual cases but not in all cases, as though a general moral principle would apply.

d. *Examination of conscience*

The precept of integrity necessitates some examination of conscience.[244] The obligation is grave for those who are in serious sin and can make the examination. The degree of diligence required will depend upon the length of time since the last worthy confession and the condition of the penitent. Those who are not prepared because they have made no examination or made it remissly should be admonished and, if expedient, requested to retire for a time to make a proper examination and then to return to confession. Devout penitents should be urged to make an examination especially of their more frequent deliberate slight sins for the sake of their spiritual improvement. The scrupulous should make a very brief examination or none at all, as the confessor directs.

A method of examination is not prescribed; daily examination of faults is most profitable. A formula of examination is often helpful. The penitent, invoking the guidance of the Holy Spirit, should review his more notable and more frequent sins, the precepts of God and the Church, the duties of his position in life, his obligations toward his neighbor, his thoughts, words, deeds, and omissions against the virtues. Sometimes the confessor will have

244. c. 901.

to help the penitent to examine his conscience when there has been a history of neglect of the sacraments.

e. *General confession*

A general confession will be *necessary* for a penitent who must repeat some or all of his past confessions when it is morally certain that they were invalid or sacrilegious. It will be *harmful*, when new anxieties, scruples, etc., will probably arise or new temptations fostered by reason of a general or an accurate accusation of past serious sins of impurity. In such cases a general confession should not be allowed. For proper motives it may be *useful*, e.g., before embracing a new state or role in life, during a serious illness, at the hour of death, for more fervent contrition and amendment, humility, etc.

A general confession is regularly not to be imposed on any one. It should not be used as a standard practice with new penitents. On the other hand, it should not be permitted until the penitent's motives are judged worthy, prudent, and profitable. The confessor must be patient and kind, discreet in his questions, and cautious about interrupting. When requested for help, he should not harry the penitent with useless or involved questions. The penitent must be given sufficient time to prepare and to confess. Unless the confession is necessary he need not confess every sin in lowest species and number. The penitent who makes a careful examination and sincere confession according to his ability should not thenceforth be disturbed about the past; the only material that should be confessed in any subsequent confession is a certain sin not yet directly remitted.

3. *Satisfaction or Penance to be Fulfilled*

Satisfaction is the compensation for the temporal punishment due to sins through the good works and the penalties imposed by the confessor and voluntarily accepted by the penitent. Sacramental satisfaction *in desire* is absolutely necessary and essential for the validity of the sacrament.²⁴⁵ Its actual fulfillment is necessary for sacramental integrity or completeness. By the very fact of being done as it should, it brings about the remission of temporal punishment.

The confessor not only can but he must impose a penance or satisfaction on the penitent.²⁴⁶ He should impose a salutary and suitable penance based on the kind and number of sins and on the character or condition of the penitent; which penance the penitent must be willing to accept and perform in person.²⁴⁷ He, as the minister of Christ's power of binding and loosing, should act in accordance with the ways of God who inflicts temporal punishments not only as acts of vindication but as medicinal remedies. To impose other than remedial penalties (except in certain cases) would be against the divine intention and to deprive the penitent of great benefits. He should be guided by justice, prudence, and love and not act arbitrarily. There should be no public penance as such, except when necessary to repair public scandal.

It is of itself a grave obligation to impose a penance and certainly a serious sin not to impose a penance for necessary material in confession, but a light sin regarding free material. The penance must be regularly given before absolution, since it must be voluntarily accepted by the penitent. It can and must be given after absolution if the confessor has forgotten to impose it. (The penitent should request the penance in this case). Causes which excuse from imposing a penance are: 1) physical or moral inability on the part of the penitent, e.g., he is near to death, unconscious, too weak, etc.; 2) it is divinely revealed that the penitent's temporal punishment has been remitted; 3) if immediately after the absolution the penitent confesses a forgotten sin, at least if it does not change substantially the confession. The confessor may confirm the previous penance, but it is better to impose a new one, even though it is light. The first case is the only certain and proper occasion when the confessor is not held to impose a penance. Even here

---

245. Trent, Denz.-Schön. 1689-1691, 1693, 1712-1715. Some theologians hold it to be a mere disposition or necessary condition.
246. Trent, Denz.-Schön. 1692, 1715.
247. c. 887.

he often can have the penitent speak the Name of God, kiss a crucifix, strike his breast, or something similar.

The penance imposed must be in keeping with the number and nature of the sins confessed. A grave penance is to be given for serious sins; it would be sinful to give a very light penance for such sins without just cause. It seems that a confessor may give a light penance for a serious sin inculpably omitted in one confession and confessed later in another. The more numerous and the more serious the sins, the heavier should be the penance, but not in a mathematical proportion and increase. It is better to impose a lighter penance that will be fulfilled than a heavier one that will be neglected or only partially satisfied. However, the confessor should not permit penitents to take a light or casual view of serious sin, even though he has an obvious reason for giving a light penance for it.

It is left to the prudent judgment of the confessor in the confessional to consider what is a grave or a light penance in an individual case. Long drawn out, involved, useless, too difficult or naturally repugnant penances are normally inexpedient. Penances which are commonly considered as grave are: to hear a Mass, to fast or abstain for a day, to recite a third part of the Rosary, to recite the seven penitential psalms, the Way of the Cross, a quarter hour meditation or spiritual reading, at least six times the Our Father and Hail Mary, some notable action on behalf of a neighbor's welfare, etc. A penance which is light in itself may become grave if it is to be repeated several times or because of some added action, e.g., to be said daily for a week, etc. Penances commonly considered to be light are: one of the common litanies, acts of faith and hope and charity, five times the Our Father and Hail Mary, expression of kindness or service to a neighbor, etc.

The lessening of the amount of penance imposed is to be judged not only by the seriousness of the sins confessed but also by the ability of the penitent, since the confessor is not only judge but physician as well, minister of divine mercy as well as justice.[248] The penance imposed will be suited first to the physical ability of the penitent. In some cases it may be incumbent upon the confessor

---

248. c. 888, 1. Indulgenced prayers and good works can be given as a penance (c. 932).

to help him to make satisfaction by reciting some prayers with him or by encouraging him to bear with his sufferings as a penance. Secondly, it should be suited to his spiritual capacity, e.g., the confessor may impose together with a light penance something that is already of precept, as Sunday Mass, or habitually done by the penitent, as saying the Rosary. Thirdly, it must be suited to the intensity of contrition of the penitent. At times it is evident to the confessor that the sinner has suffered much from the realization of his sins or as a result of these sins; this may be accepted by the confessor as part of the suitable satisfaction. Yet, with such souls there is a willingness to accept grave penances. Indulgenced prayers and works can be given as a penance. The confessor himself may with the penitent's permission assume and satisfy some of the penance imposed. The confessor is not to request or to accept any money from the penitent.

The confessor should try to strike a balance between too great a severity and too great a laxity, so that a light penance is not regularly imposed or a grave penance easily omitted. He should be more concerned over the sinner than the sin, adhering more to mercy than severity, the good of the penitent than the exaction or the vindication of divine justice (which can continue in Purgatory). In doubt as to the necessity or opportuneness of a graver penance, he should favor the more benign judgment. But, never or rarely to impose a heavy penance is a type of laxity that does not sufficiently draw the penitent away from sin, and such indiscreet kindness may serve to confirm a bad habit. Penitents are to be so disposed that they are ready and willing to accept moderately grave penances, which at times can be made more acceptable by specifying an object of impetration in addition to the satisfaction itself, e.g., to pray for deceased relatives or friends, for peace and welfare at home, to certain saints, for the persecuted, etc. The confessor should not habituate himself to the same or stereotyped formulas of prayers, nor should he impose the same penance on all who come to him.

It is certain teaching that the penitent is bound to *accept* the reasonable penance imposed by the confessor.[249] The obligation

---

249. Cf. c. 887.

is serious when the penance given is grave, the material of the confession necessary, and the confessor intends to oblige seriously (which is presumed in such circumstances). The penitent can refuse an unreasonable penance or ask for another from the same or from a different confessor. The confessor should normally acquiesce in the reasonable request of a penitent.

The penitent has a serious obligation to *fulfill* a penance imposed (under the conditions mentioned for acceptance) for serious and necessary material, a light obligation with respect to light or free material (even if the penance given is grave). Culpably to omit the whole or a notable part of a grave penance is itself a serious sin. If the penitent has forgotten his penance, he should ask the confessor what it was; if this is not possible or if the confessor cannot recall it, a new penance can be given on an indication of the penitent's state of soul in the previous confession. Failing this, the penitent can say what he believes the penance was. Unless the confessor makes it otherwise clear, the penance he imposes is to be understood according to the practice in the Church. A penance is satisfied when the same work done out of devotion is performed, e.g., congregational recitation of the rosary. The penitent need have only an habitual intention of satisfying his obligation.

The penance should be fulfilled immediately after confession or when it is morally possible; it need not be done before Communion or before the next confession.[250] The penitent may sin seriously if he foresees that he will not satisfy a grave penance later. A penance to be fulfilled at a stated time must be performed even outside the time since, being accessory to the obligation, time does not terminate but urges the obligation. If a penance is too difficult the penitent can request an easier one, or (without having received absolution) approach another confessor.

Commutation

For a reasonable cause a penance may be commuted, e.g., for

---

250. "They are to be judged sacrilegious who claim the right to receive Communion before they have done worthy penance for their sins." Prop. 22 condemned by Alexander VII, S. Off. 24 aug. 1690. Denz.-Schön. 2322.

the spiritual good of the penitent. Before absolution the commutation is easily made because the sacrament is not perfected. After absolution the commutation can come only from the same confessor (immediately after absolution or even outside of confession) or another (but only in a confession made to him). The penitent need manifest his former confession only generically. Commutation in a reserved case must come solely from one enjoying proper jurisdiction.

Reserved Cases

I. *Ecclesiastical censures*

   A. *Notion of censure*

A censure is a penalty by which a baptized person, who has committed a delict and is contumacious or obstinate, is deprived of certain spiritual goods, or of goods connected with the spiritual, until he gives up his obstinacy and is absolved.[1] A censure, which is one form of ecclesiastical penalty, is by its nature a medicinal punishment; thus it is intended primarily to prohibit the crime and to correct the erring ways of the sinner or withdraw him from his contumacy, and indirectly to repair the public order that has been violated. There must be a delict or crime, i.e., an external and morally imputable violation of a law to which a canonical sanction, which is at least indeterminate, is attached.[2] A censure can be inflicted upon or incurred by only an offender who is contumacious. It can be removed only by absolution, but once the guilty individual has abandoned his obstinacy or contumacy, the absolution cannot be denied him.[3]

As with other penalties, censures are subject to benign interpretation.[4] Unless the terminology of the law and the sanction is literally fulfilled according to a fair meaning of the words contained, the delict is not committed or the censure incurred. Thus, no matter how analogous or parallel cases may seem or how guilty the individuals involved may appear to be, the censure is incurred only when the particular case and the particular individual or individuals fall under the exact wording of the law containing the sanction.[5]

A censure, being an ecclesiastical punishment, deprives the delin-

1. c. 2241, 1.
2. c. 2195, 1.
3. c. 2248, 2.
4. c. 2219, 1. A strict or narrow interpretation is given to laws which entail a penalty (cf. c. 19).
5. Cf. c. 2219, 3.

quent only of those goods which have been committed to the Church as the Body of Christ and over which she has jurisdiction. These are spiritual goods, e.g., the sacraments, sacrifices, divine offices, indulgences, public suffrages and satisfactions, the external communion of the saints; and goods connected with the spiritual, e.g., admission into the Church, ecclesiastical burial, the fruits or revenues of benefices, honors, jurisdiction. All these effects or deprivations need not be incurred at one time, as will be noted later. Censures are of three types: excommunication, suspension, and interdict.

B. *Manner of establishment*

Censures can be established only by those ecclesiastical prelates who enjoy unimpeded jurisdiction in the external forum, i.e., the power to make laws or impose (jurisdictional) precepts.[6]

A censure is called *a iure* (from the law itself) when it is established or laid down in the law itself or in a general precept, whether *latae* or *ferendae sententiae*.[7]

A censure is termed *ab homine* (from the person competent to impose it) when it is inflicted or established in the manner of a particular or personal precept, or by a judicial condemnatory sentence, even if stated or specified in the law. A *ferendae sententiae* censure attached to a law is a penalty *a iure* only before a condemnatory sentence; it is both *a iure* and *ab homine* after sentence, but it is considered as *ab homine*.[8] Thus every *latae sententiae* censure is *a iure* and every *ferendae sententiae* censure after infliction becomes *ab homine*.

C. *Manner of incurrence*

Censures which are incurred *ipso facto* or automatically upon commission of the delict or crime are called *latae sententiae* (the

---

6. c. 2220, 1. Thus those holding only dominative power over subjects cannot impose canonical penalties.
7. c. 2217, 1, 3º.
8. **Ibid.**

sentence contained in the law is passed or takes effect at the moment of the commission of the delict). In other words, sentence upon the delinquent has already been passed by the terms of the law or precept itself without any sentence of ecclesiastical authority being expressed; it is an anticipatory sentence (i.e., no person in authority is required to act in order for the penalty to take its effect). This censure can sometimes be confirmed by a declaratory sentence (*sententia declaratoria*) of ecclesiastical authority[9] declaring that the crime has been committed and thus indirectly that the censure has been incurred. Although a censure binds in both the internal and external fora, the Church does not intend to urge *all* its effects in the external forum, even retroactively, unless she has made a declaratory sentence.[10] Such a declaratory sentence, however, does not make the censure to be *ab homine*.

Censures which are to be inflicted upon a delinquent by a judge or a superior are called *ferendae sententiae* (the sentence contained in the law is to be passed or put into effect by the competent person in authority). The penalties have no effect until the sentence of the superior is passed; it is a sentence subsequent to the crime and is not automatic. The sentence that is subsequently passed or imposed is called condemnatory (*sententia condemnatoria*); the penalty and its effects are binding from the moment the condemnation is rendered and it thus becomes an *ab homine* censure. Unless a law or a precept expressly states that a censure is *latae sententiae*, or *ipso facto* or *ipso iure* contracted, or uses other similar words, a censure must always be considered as *ferendae sententiae*.[11]

D. *Manner of reservation*

Reservation is the restriction of jurisdiction to absolve in cases of special gravity, thus adding an element of severity to the penalty imposed for the delict or crime.[12] The power to absolve from censures

---

9. cc. 2223, 4; 2225.
10. c. 2232.
11. cc. 2217; 2225.
12. c. 2246, 1.

is limited to certain persons or classes of persons. A reservation must be strictly interpreted.[13] Some censures are reserved and others are not reserved.[14] A *latae sententiae* censure is not reserved, unless this is expressly stated in the law or precept; should there be a doubt in this respect either of the law or of a fact under the law, the reservation does not bind.[15]

Absolution of *ab homine* censures is always *reserved* to the one who has inflicted the censure or imposed the sentence, or to his competent superior, successor, or delegate.[16]

Of censures *a iure,* some are *reserved* to the *Ordinary* (local or religious), others are *reserved* to the *Apostolic See* either simply (*simpliciter*) or in a special way (*speciali modo*) or in a very special way (*specialissimo modo*).[17] The difference in the reservations to the Apostolic See consists in this, that anyone who has received general faculties to absolve from censures reserved to the Apostolic See can absolve from those simply reserved, whereas to absolve from the other two classes special or most special faculties need to be obtained.

Some censures are called *reserved to no one* (*nemini reservata*). Any confessor can absolve from them in the internal forum; anyone enjoying jurisdiction in the external forum can absolve in the extrasacramental forum.

E. *Subject of censures*

Only a living and validly baptized person who has the use of reason and the capability of committing a crime and who is subject to the jurisdiction of the one imposing the penalty is liable to censure. Those who have not completed their seventh year (*infantes*), and the insane, are considered to be incapable of sufficient deliberation and freedom to be legally responsible for transgressions liable

13. Ibid., 2.
14. c. 2245, 1.
15. Ibid., 4.
16. Ibid., 2.
17. Ibid., 2, 3.

to ecclesiastical penalties.[18] Those who have not yet attained puberty (*impuberes*), i.e., reached the age of adolescence (in penal law, fourteen years of age), are excused from *latae sententiae* censures and are rather subject to correction by educative measures.[19] Minors (*minores*), i.e., those who have not completed their twenty-first year, are less imputable for crime in proportion as their minority approaches infancy, unless the contrary is evident.[20]

The Holy Father and pontifical law, such as the Code, enjoy jurisdiction over all baptized everywhere, a local Ordinary in his own territory, a regular prelate over his own subjects everywhere. Wanderers (*vagi*) are bound by all the penalties of the common law and also of the particular place where they are staying.[21] Visitors (*peregrini*) are bound by the penalties of the common law, unless they do not bind in the place where they are staying; committing a crime outside the territory of their domicile or quasi domicile, they cannot be punished by the *latae sententiae* censures of the latter, unless the transgression causes harm in their territory or the laws are personal or the censure is *ab homine*. They can be punished by the particular precept of the Ordinary in whose territory they commit a crime, since they become his subjects by reason of the crime, or because the laws transgressed affect the public order or determine the solemnity of acts.[22]

Exempt religious are subject to the censures of the local Ordinary only in those things in which they are expressly subject to his jurisdiction. Jesuits and generally all Mendicants by special privilege can be censured by the local Ordinary only in three cases: 1) if they presume to preach in their own churches or those of others without the local Ordinary's permission, 2) if they presume to hear the confessions of seculars without his approbation, 3) if they expose for public veneration images depicted in an unusual or scandalous manner.[23]

18. cc. 2201, 1, 2; 88, 3.
19. cc. 2230; 88, 2.
20. cc. 2204; 88, 1.
21. c. 14, 2.
22. c. 14, 1; cf. c. 1566, 1.
23. Gregory XV, Const. **Inscrutabili**, 5 feb. 1662; Innocent X,

F. *Material for censures*

Only a crime or delict which is external, grave, consummated, and joined with contumacy is punished by censure; however, a censure may be imposed on delinquents whose identity is unknown.[24] The action must be *external;* thus the notion of sin is of wider application than that of delict or crime, which must be an external and morally imputable violation of a law to which some canonical sanction is attached.

The delict committed must be *grave,* since only moral imputability that involves serious sin is punishable. Thus, whatever excuses from serious sin also excuses from the grave penalty, which is a censure; this includes both *latae* and *ferendae sententiae* censures, even in the external forum, provided the excusing circumstances can be proved in the external forum.[25] The crime also must be *certain,* i.e., certainly committed, certainly grave, and certainly reserved (no doubt of law or of fact in the individual case).

The crime must be *consummated* or complete, i.e., perfect in its kind according to the precise meaning of the words of the law even for an attempted crime.[26] Consummation of the crime should not be confused with its effect.

Joined to the crime must be *contumacy* or obstinacy, i.e., a certain contempt of the penalty. The delinquent must know at least that some legal punishment is incurred by his violation of a law or precept, although he need not know the precise penalty. The contumacy is formal when the person violates the law precisely in contempt of authority, virtual when knowing a thing is in some way forbidden under censure he still violates the law, without intending direct contempt, i.e., the contempt is contained in the violation of the law which he knows has an attached penalty. In the

---

Const. **Cum sicut accepimus,** 14 maii 1653; Urban VIII, Const. **Sacrosancta Tridentina,** 15 mart. 1643.

24. cc. 2242, 1; 2195.
25. cc. 2218, 2; 2199. The imputability of a crime depends on its malice (**dolus**) or its guilt (**culpa**), the latter arising from culpable ignorance or lack of due care.
26. c. 2213, 3; cf. cc. 2212; 2213; 2235.

case of *ferendae sententiae* censures contumacy is considered to be present when the offender, notwithstanding the warnings specified in c. 2233, 2, fails to desist from the crime or refuses to do penance for it and make proper amends for the injury and the scandal; in regard to *latae sententiae* censures, it suffices to transgress the law or precept to which the censure is attached, unless the offender is excused from it by some legitimate reason, which must be adequately established.[27] Contumacy is regarded as terminated when the offender has sincerely repented of the crime committed and has also given satisfaction for the injury and the scandal or has at least seriously promised to do so; the judgment of the sincerity of the repentance, the adequacy of the satisfaction, and the seriousness of the promise is left to the one from whom the absolution is sought.[28]

Associates or cooperators in a crime are liable to censure, i.e., those who have so induced or concurred or cooperated in a crime that otherwise it would not have been perpetrated, and all formal and positive cooperators.[29] For such cooperation, in the juridic sense, the crime must be objectively one, e.g., the murder of one man, and subjectively multiple, i.e., imputable in its integrity to many individuals as accomplices or authors, without dividing or fractioning the responsibility among them.

G. *Binding force and multiplication*

One is excused from observing a censure in the external forum before a declaratory or a condemnatory sentence, or if the crime is not notorious, or if the offender cannot observe the censure without infamy or scandal.[30] Given the sentence or the notoriety, the danger of infamy or of scandal cannot be verified.

Not only different censures but also the same censure can be multiplied in the same individual. *Latae sententiae* censures are multiplied by the same or different actions which transgress several laws carrying censures, or by distinctly repeating the same crime,

27. cc. 2242, 2; 2218, 2.
28. c. 2242, 3.
29. Cf. c. 2209.
30. c. 2232, 1.

or by committing once or repeatedly a crime punished with different censures by different superiors. *Ab homine* censures are multiplied if many precepts or many sentences or their several distinct parts each inflicts its own censure.[31] Absolution from one censure does not include the others.[32]

H. *Causes excusing from incurrence*

1. *Fear*

Grave fear excuses from incurring *latae sententiae* censures, except when the crime involves contempt of the faith or of ecclesiastical authority or involves public harm to souls,[33] even though the act in question is intrinsically evil and gravely culpable.[34] The exceptions do not excuse from but do lessen the imputability.[35]

Light fear excuses from incurring censures, if the law contains the words: *praesumpserit, ausus fuerit, scienter, studiose, temerarie, consulto egerit,* or others requiring full knowledge and deliberation.[36] In other cases it does not excuse from but lessens imputability.

2. *Ignorance*

Ignorance is the lack of due knowledge of something, an habitual and negative state of mind. Ignorance of the *law* exists when the existence, extent, or the meaning of a law is not known; of the *fact* when the conditions or circumstances under which the law is applicable, or whether a certain action or fact comes under the law, are

---

31. c. 2224.
32. c. 2249,1.
33. c. 2229, 3, 3⁰. It can be judged in practice that even fear which is intrinsic will excuse, e.g., fear of infamy. Fear itself is a disturbance of mind arising from present or future danger. It is light when the evil threatening is not serious or the danger is remote and easy to avoid; it is grave when the evil threatening is serious and the danger imminent.
34. PCI 30 dec. 1937.
35. c. 2205, 3. Examples of the exceptions: contempt of faith— public apostasy (c. 2314), of ecclesiastical authority—to sue one's own bishop in court (c. 2341), public harm to souls—to traffic in false relics (c. 2326).
36. c. 2229, 2.

not known; of the *penalty* when the existence of a sanction attached to a law or its reservation is not known. Considered equivalent to ignorance in reckoning imputability are inadvertence, forgetfulness, and error which, in the external forum regarding a law or penalty, are not presumed to exist but must be proved.[37] In law, related to imputability, culpable and inculpable ignorance are the same as vincible and invincible ignorance, but for greater clarity they are separately defined here before stating the influence of ignorance in the penitent or delinquent upon the incurrence of a censure.

Ignorance is *invincible* when it cannot be cured or overcome, either at all (physically) or with the moral diligence due in the circumstances (morally); it is *vincible* when it can be removed by means suitable and adequate in the circumstances. Ignorance is *affected* (*vincible*) when one deliberately maintains the state of knowledge insufficient to act of which he is aware, because he wishes to remain ignorant with the idea of avoiding or extenuating responsibility; this adds up to malice (*dolus*). *Inculpable* ignorance exists when there is no obligation to know a thing or when, despite the use of required diligence, it is not known. When there is insufficient and blameworthy effort to know what is required, the ignorance is *culpable;* it implies guilt (*culpa*) because it is voluntary at least in cause. Ignorance is light or lightly culpable when the negligence in removing the lack of due knowledge is slight; it is *grave* or seriously culpable when the failure to use sufficient means to acquire requisite knowledge is due to serious negligence, although some effort was made; crassly culpable, or *crass* or supine ignorance exists when one, although he seriously suspects the existence of something or realizes the need to acquire knowledge of it, makes absolutely no effort or little effort to find out the facts, due to particularly serious negligence or indifference. It is a more culpable degree of ignorance than seriously culpable ignorance.

Invincible or *inculpable* ignorance of the law (or the fact) or the penalty excuses from censure, since there is no cause or reason for inflicting a medicinal punishment. *Affected* ignorance of the

---

37. c. 2202, 3; cf. cc. 16, 2; 1825.

law (or the fact) or the penalty attached to it does not excuse from *latae sententiae* censures, even those containing the words *praesumpserit, ausus fuerit, scienter, studiose, temerarie, consulto egerit,* or others requiring full knowledge and deliberation.[38] *Lightly culpable* ignorance excuses even in the external forum if it can be proved.[39] *Gravely culpable* ignorance of the law (or the fact) or penalty, although not excusing from vindictive penalties, always excuses from *latae sententiae* censures.[40] *Crass* ignorance of the law (or the fact) or the penalty excuses only from *latae sententiae* censures which demand full knowledge and deliberation.[41]

3. *Other causes.* Intoxication, omission of due care, mental weakness, or the impetus of passion do not excuse from *latae sententiae* censures, if the crime remains gravely culpable, notwithstanding lessening of imputability.[42]

I. *Manner of absolving censures*

A censure once contracted is removed only by legitimate absolution.[43] A censure must be first absolved before absolution from sins is imparted, unless it is a censure that does not impede the reception of the sacraments, e.g., suspension.[44] The form of absolution in the sacramental forum is that contained in the usual form of sacramental absolution of sins. In the non-sacramental internal and external fora absolution from censure is regularly given according to the form in the Roman Ritual or prescribed by competent superiors.[45] If a confessor *presumes* to absolve without faculty from an excommunication *latae sententiae* reserved to the Apostolic See *specialissimo* or *speciali modo*, he incurs *ipso facto* an excommunication reserved *simpliciter* to the Apostolic See.[46]

38. c. 2229, 1.
39. Cf. c. 2218, 2.
40. cc. 2229, 3, 1º; 2218, 2. Some few hold that a penitent, knowing that he incurred a censure but not knowing that it was reserved, probably may be absolved by any confessor, since ignorance of the reservation only excuses from it.
41. c. 2229, 2 and 3, 1º.
42. **Ibid.**, 3, 2º.
43. c. 2248, 1 and 3.
44. Cf. 2250, 1 and 2.
45. Cf. c. 2250, 3.

Absolution from censure in the general external forum removes the effects of the censure in both fora (yet, there must be absolution of the sin in the sacrament of Penance). A delinquent who is absolved in the internal forum only may conduct himself as absolved in his acts of the external forum, as long as there is no scandal. Yet, superiors of the external forum may demand observance of the censure in this forum until absolution is given in this forum, or until there is proof or the legitimate presumption of absolution in the internal forum, e.g., for the internal non-sacramental forum, or the delinquent has made public reparation for his crime. If he wishes, he may obtain a written certificate from his confessor that he has been absolved.[47]

If a confessor, ignorant of a reservation, absolves a penitent from a censure and a sin, the absolution of the censure is valid, provided it is not a censure *ab homine* or *specialissimo modo* reserved to the Apostolic See.[48] The absolution is only in the internal forum. The two censures are excepted, the first lest the authority of the one imposing it be belittled, the second since special penances and instructions are given. In these two exceptions, although the censure is not removed, the sin itself is removed directly.[49] Since the law does not specify, the ignorance of the confessor embraces even crass or supine ignorance. Moreover, forgetfulness, inadvertence, error, are equivalent to ignorance.[50] Absolution is invalid, if there is confessed only the sin reserved by censure and the confessor absolves in bad faith, knowing of the reservation and his lack of jurisdiction in the case. If other matter is confessed, absolution is valid directly for the non-reserved matter and indirectly for the sin with reserved censure; the latter must be submitted subsequently to a confessor with necessary jurisdiction.

---

46. c. 2338, 1.
47. Cf. c. 2251; S. Poenit. **monita** 31 iul. 1924.
48. c. 2247, 3.
49. S. Off. 10 sept. 1556. However, some commentators hold that only in the case when the penitent accuses himself also of other sins besides the one under censure is the absolution valid, directly for the other sins, indirectly for the censured sin.
50. c. 2202, 3.

J. Jurisdiction to absolve

1. In danger of death

When there is danger of death, every priest, even though he is not approved for the hearing of confessions, can validly and lawfully absolve any penitent whatever from all sins and censures no matter how reserved or notorious, even though an approved priest is present, without prejudice to the regulations on the absolution of an accomplice and the obligation of recourse. The danger may be from an internal or external cause, including mobilization. A prudent judgment suffices that at least a probable danger of death exists, even though positive doubt is present.[51]

Penitents, absolved in danger of death from an *ab homine* or a *specialissimo modo* censure or in the case of a priest who has attempted marriage and is unable to separate from his partner, are bound, within a month after their complete recovery from the danger, at least by letter and through the confessor, if this can be done without grave inconvenience, to have recourse to the one who imposed the *ab homine* censure, or to the Sacred Penitentiary or to a bishop or other person having the faculty if it is *a iure*, and to abide by their mandates or orders.[52] The recourse must be made under penalty of falling back into the censure. Unless stated in the mandate, failure to comply with the mandate does not seem as such to reimpose the penalty. The confessor is not always obliged to warn the penitent of the duty of recourse; he can do so and generally should, if he hopes it will be successful and beneficial. If the penitent is *in extremis* or if it is prudently feared that the warning will be harmful, it is omitted.

2. Outside the danger of death

Every confessor can absolve from non-reserved cases, but in the sacramental forum only; outside the sacramental forum only one who has jurisdiction in the external forum.[53] *Ab homine* cen-

---

51. c. 882; S. Poenit. 18 mart. 1912; 29 maii 1915; cf. c. 209.
52. c. 2252; cf. S. Poenit. 18 apr. 1936; 4 maii 1937.
53. c. 2253, 1º.

sures can be absolved only by the one who inflicted them or pronounced sentence, or his superior, successor or delegate, even though the delinquent has transferred his domicile or quasi-domicile elsewhere (but not the superiors of the place of transferred residence).[54] *A iure* censures are absolved by those who imposed them or those to whom they are reserved, their successors or competent superiors or delegates.[55]

Cardinals can absolve in the sacramental forum anyone in any place from all reserved censures, excepting those reserved *specialissimo modo* and those incurred by revealing the secrets of the Holy Office.[56]

All *Bishops,* both residential and titular, may absolve anyone whomsoever of the faithful anywhere, but in the act of sacramental confession, from all censures, even though reserved, with the exception of: a) censures *ab homine;* b) censures most specially reserved to the Apostolic See; c) the excommunication for priests and all others who presume to contract marriage, even civilly, with them and are actually living together. Residential Bishops can use this faculty even in the external forum for their own subjects. Moreover, local Ordinaries may grant this same faculty to confessors of outstanding knowledge and prudence.[57]

Major exempt clerical religious superiors in occult cases can personally or through another remit all *latae sententiae* penalties established by the common law, excepting censures *speciali* or *specialissimo modo* reserved.[58]

A *Regular confessor* can absolve by privilege from the *latae sententiae* censures reserved in the common law to the local Ordinary.[59]

In *more urgent cases,* namely when *latae sententiae* censures cannot be observed externally without danger of grave scandal or of infamy, or when it is a hardship for the penitent to remain in the state of grave sin for such time as may be necessary in order

54. Ibid., 2º.
55. Ibid., 3º.
56. c. 239, 1, 1º.
57. Paul VI motu proprio **Pastorale munus,** 30 nov. 1963, I, 14, II 4.
58. c. 2237, 2.
59. Cf. Confessors who are Regulars.

that the competent superior may provide, then any confessor can, in the *sacramental* forum, absolve from the same no matter how they are reserved, imposing under penalty of falling back into the censure the obligation of having recourse within a month, at least by letter and (or) through the confessor, when it can be done without grave inconvenience, without mentioning the name, to the Sacred Penitentiary or to a bishop or other superior who has the faculty, and of abiding by his mandates.[60] Nothing prevents the penitent, even after he has received absolution as above, or even after he has had recourse to the superior, from going to another confessor who has the special faculty needed for his case, and of obtaining absolution from him, repeating the confession at least of the crime with the censure; and when he has received absolution he is to receive mandates from the same confessor, without being bound afterward to observe the other mandates which may come from the superior.[61]

It suffices and is required that the priest can act as the confessor of the penitent here and now in this place and that the penitent is in a more urgent need. The confessor himself must carefully judge whether all elements necessary for incurring a censure are present or excusing causes apply, and whether he has the faculty to absolve validly and lawfully. He must judge the existence of the requisite urgency; if the estimation is wrong the absolution is valid and licit, provided the judgment was reasonable and with foundation, at least subjectively.

The danger of scandal or of infamy must be at least probable. It will usually be a situation of a censure which is occult at least in the place where its external observance would be an occasion of scandal or of infamy. The danger must be imminent, that is, it will probably be verified before the proper faculties can be obtained, e.g., when another sacrament, such as the Eucharist or Matrimony, must be received immediately or soon after confession, or Mass must be celebrated. On the other hand, the hardship of remaining in serious sin for the time necessary to petition and to receive faculties to absolve must be felt by the penitent. It is not the objective

60. c. 2254, 1.
61. **Ibid.**, 2.

evil of being or remaining in sin but the present actual subjective dispositions of the penitent in this respect that measure the urgency. The confessor should do what he can to bring about such an attitude in the penitent. To be compelled to remain in serious sin for a single day without absolution may be a hardship, or even for a few hours in the case of some penitents. The element of hardship will not apply to the censure of suspension, as urgency in this case can arise only from the danger of scandal or of infamy.

The *conditions* of the more urgent case are applicable to all *latae sententiae* censures of both general and particular law or precept,[62] as well as censures brought to formal trial or declared by a declaratory sentence (as hardship could be felt here). It is a safe although probable opinion that the more urgent case will apply also to *ab homine* and *ferendae sententiae* censures with the obligation of recourse. The only censure certainly excluded from becoming a more urgent case is that of a priest who has attempted marriage and is unable to cease living with his partner; except in danger of death absolution cannot be imparted.[63] Absolution can be given from the *latae sententiae* censure of false denunciation[64] only after the delinquent has made an actual formal retraction of the false accusation and as best a reparation of damages as possible (a mere promise does not suffice); a grave and long penance must be enjoined.

The confessor is bound to impose the obligation of *recourse* to the proper authority in each case; if he fails to do so his absolution will be valid but he will sin seriously. The obligation of recourse falls directly and immediately upon the penitent, who must comply within a month of his becoming aware of the obligation.[65] The least he can do is to make recourse by letter or through the confessor. In practice, in most cases the obligation of recourse will

---

62. S. Poenit. 21 apr. 1921. It is disputed whether **latae sententiae** censures reserved to the Holy Father in person are included.
63. c. 2388, 1; S. Poenit. 18 apr. 1936; 4 maii. 1937
64. c. 2363. The sin itself is reserved **ratione sui** to the Apostolic See (c. 894).
65. The term of one month is to urge but not to terminate the obligation. The excusing causes of ignorance, fear, etc., apply to the reincurrence of the censure for failure to have recourse.

be undertaken by the confessor out of charity, unless he is prevented by some just cause. The confessor in his letter to the proper authority should state briefly the crime committed, the censure incurred, the fact that absolution was given in virtue of c. 2254, and that the penitent is prepared to observe any mandates or commands the superior may give. The mandates are the things enjoined by the superior along with the penance and satisfaction, entailing a serious obligation to abide by the mandates if the penitent is to be in the state of grace. The penitent's name must never be given, but a fictitious one used, and the letter (in double envelope and sent by registered mail) should be signed by the confessor who includes an address to which the reply may be sent. Formulas for presenting such petitions to the bishop or the Sacred Penitentiary are noted in the standard textbooks.

If in some extraordinary case this recourse is morally impossible, then the confessor himself, except in the case of absolution of the censure for absolving an accomplice, can give absolution without the obligation described above, but he must prescribe what should be prescribed in such a case and impose a suitable penance and satisfaction for the censure, so that if the penitent does not perform the penance and make the satisfaction within a suitable time which shall be prescribed by the confessor, he shall fall back into the censure.[66] Moral impossibility exists if neither the penitent nor the confessor can make the recourse by letter, or if the penitent cannot return to the confessor or is unable to make the recourse himself and finds it a hardship to go to another confessor, or if the confessor is merely temporary and does not live nearby and may not return. The confessor's obligation to prescribe what ought to be prescribed in the case refers to the rectification of the condition responsible for the sanction, e.g., an attempted marriage before a non-Catholic minister should be convalidated. Besides the sacramental penance for the crime the confessor must impose a distinct and usually grave penance for the censure.[67] The satisfaction required consists of reparation of any harm (e.g., restitution) or scandal (e.g., convalidation of a marriage in a manner to offset the

---

66. c. 2254, 3.
67. S. Poenit. 10 dec. 1880.

scandal given). The time within which the penance is to be performed and the satisfaction given is to be precisely determined by the confessor; the time prescribed for the satisfaction should not exceed six months. If there is culpable omission of what is enjoined by law, or of the penance or of the satisfaction, a new crime is committed and a censure specifically the same as before is incurred.

The following differences ought to be noted between cases of danger of death and more urgent cases: 1) in danger of death: any *priest* can absolve from all censures; the confessor is not held always to enjoin the obligation of recourse; recourse binds with only certain few censures; in such cases the recourse is to be within a month of complete recovery; 2) in a more urgent case: any *confessor* can absolve from almost all censures; the confessor is bound always to impose recourse where possible; recourse binds with all reserved censures; it must be made within a month of the penitent's awareness of the duty.

K. *Excommunication*

1. *Notion.* Excommunication is a censure by which a person is excluded from the communion of the faithful, with effects specified in the law and which are inseparable one from another.[68] An excommunicate is tolerated (*toleratus*), with whom the faithful may freely communicate, even in sacred functions. He is to be avoided (*vitandus*), with whom the faithful must not associate, especially in divine things; such an excommunicate must be named by the Holy See, publicly denounced, and an express declaration made that he is to be avoided.[69]

2. *Effects.* The common, ordinary, and immediate effects of excommunication[70] are that every and all excommunicants are forbidden:

---

68. c. 2257, 1.
69. Cf. c. 2258.
70. For further effects, when there is a declaratory or condemnatory sentence, cf. cc. 2264; 2261, 3; 2265, 2; 2260, 1; 1240, 1, 2º; 1095, 1, 2º; 765, 2º; 795, 2º; for **vitandi** cf. cc. 2262, 2, 2º; 2259, 2; 2266; 2267.

a. to receive the sacraments.[71] To do so is unlawful but valid.

b. to confect or to administer the sacraments or sacramentals.[72] To do so is unlawful, unless requested by the faithful for any just cause; unlawful after a sentence, except in danger of death.

c. to assist by right at divine offices, except preaching.[73] These are functions belonging to the power of orders.[74]

d. to place legitimate ecclesiastical acts.[75] To do so, e.g., to be a baptismal or confirmation sponsor, or to vote in an election, is unlawful but valid.

e. to exercise ecclesiastical offices or duties.[76] To do so is unlawful but valid.

f. to enjoy privileges.[77] To do so is unlawful but valid.

g. to elect, nominate, present.[78] To do so is unlawful, but after a sentence it is invalid.

h. to acquire dignities, offices, benefices, pensions, etc.[79] To do so is unlawful but valid.

i. to exercise jurisdiction in either forum.[80] To do so is unlawful but valid, unless requested by the faithful; it is invalid after a sentence, except in danger of death.

j. to share in indulgences, suffrages, public prayers of the Church.[81]

k. to receive ecclesiastical burial.[82] This refers to those who are notorious or public and manifest sinners.

3. *Specialissimo modo.* Excommunications which are *most specially* reserved to the Apostolic See[83] and from which faculties

71. c. 2260, 1.
72. c. 2261.
73. c. 2259, 1.
74. c. 2256, 1º.
75. cc. 2263; 2256, 2º.
76. c. 2263.
77. **Ibid.**
78. c. 2265, 1, 1º.
79. **Ibid.**, 2º.
80. c. 2264.
81. c. 2262.
82. c. 1240, 1, 2º, 6º. Public sinners should not be denied burial if before death they give some sign of repentance and no public scandal is given to the faithful (S.C.D.F. 20 sept. 1973).
83. Those which are reserved to the Holy Father in person are

to absolve may be obtained only from the Cardinal Major Penitentiary are:

    a. *Maltreatment of the sacred species*,[84] or to throw away, take away or retain for evil purposes.

    b. *Violent attack on the person of the pope.*[85]

    c. *Absolution attempted or fictitious of an accomplice.*[86] The confessor is always bound to impose the obligation of recourse.

    d. *Direct violation of the seal of confession.*[87] The violation must be direct and done with full advertence and consent, since "*praesumpserit*" is used in the law.

    e. *Unlawful episcopal consecration, even if under grave fear.*[88]

4. *Speciali modo.* Those *specially* reserved to the Apostolic See from which faculties to absolve are enjoyed by all bishops in the act of sacramental confession and by residential bishops (and certain confessors designated by them) in the external forum for their own subjects[89] are:

    a. *Apostasy, heresy, schism.*[90] This censure also includes adherence to an atheistic sect.[91] Those who profess belief in the materialist and anti-Christian doctrine of Communism, and especially those who defend or propagate it, incur this automatic censure;[92] likewise, parents and those holding their place who teach boys and

---

censures attached, for example, to the Apostolic Constitution of Pius XII **Vacantis Apostolicae Sedis**, 8 dec. 1945; cf. also **motu proprio** of John XXIII **Summi Pontificis Electio**, 5 sept. 1962.

---

84. c. 2320.
85. c. 2343.
86. c. 2367.
87. c. 2369, 1.
88. S. Off. 9 apr. 1951.
89. Paul VI, **motu proprio Pastorale munus**, I, 14; II, 4.
90. c. 2314. This canon is only applicable to those who, after culpably giving up the Catholic faith or communion, repent and ask to be reconciled with Mother Church. Secr. ad unitatem Christianorum fovendam, **Directorium,** n. 19, 14 maii 1967.
91. PCI 30 iul. 1934.
92. S. Off. 1 iul. 1949.

girls what is contrary to the faith and Christian morals.[93]

b. *Suspicion of heresy*.[94] This crime is present after juridical warning has been given to remove the cause for the suspicion and no correction has been made after the lapse of six months. The following are suspect: those who maltreat the sacred species;[95] those who appeal from pope to General Council;[96] those who administer or receive the sacraments simoniacly;[97] those who obstinately remain under censure for a year or who spontaneously and deliberately assist the spread of heresy or take active part in non-Catholic religious functions.[98]

c. *Simulating Mass or hearing confessions by one not ordained*.[99]

d. *Appeal from Pope to General Council*.[100]

e. *Publishing laws against the rights of the Church or having recourse to lay authority*.[101]

f. *Impeding Apostolic letters or acts*.[102]

g. *Citing before a lay tribunal Cardinals, etc*.[103] The censure contains the words *"ausus fuerit."*

h. *Laying violent hands on Cardinals, etc*.[104]

i. *Usurping property rights of the Church of Rome*.[105]

j. *Fabrication or forgery of papal decrees or use of the same*.[106]

k. *False charge of solicitation against a confessor*.[107] If any-

93. **Ibid.**, 28 iul. 1950.
94. c. 2315. The penalties of c. 2319 have been abrogated, with retroactive effect, by the motu proprio **Matrimonia mixta**, 31 martii 1970, n. 15.
95. c. 2320.
96. c. 2332.
97. c. 2371.
98. cc. 2340, 1; c. 2316, which is to be viewed in the light of Secr. ad unitatem Christianorum fovendam, **Directorium**, 14 maii 1967.
99. c. 2322.
100. c. 2332.
101. c. 2334.
102. c. 2333.
103. c. 2341.
104. c. 2343, 2, 3.
105. c. 2345.
106. c. 2360.
107. c. 2363.

one personally or through others falsely makes to superiors a *juridical* accusation of solicitation against a *confessor*, he (or she) automatically incurs this censure from which he may *in no case* be absolved unless he shall have formally retracted the false accusation and repaired as far as possible the damage which may have resulted; and moreover a grave and long penance is to be imposed. It is also a reserved sin.[108] In danger of death and in a more urgent case absolution is possible, with recourse necessary.

l. *Clerics who engage in forbidden trade or business.*[109]

m. *Opponents of legitimate ecclesiastical authority, those unlawfully assuming offices, etc., or allowing the same, and all participants.*[110]

5. *Simpliciter.* Those *simply* reserved to the Apostolic See, from which in occult cases the Ordinary can absolve personally or by delegation,[111] and from which faculties to absolve may be obtained as noted in each case are:

a. *Trafficking in indulgences.*[112]

b. *Joining a Masonic sect or similar societies.*[113] The censure is incurred if the society is one which plots against the Church or legitimate civil authority. It is disputed whether such societies must be secret; those which are secret certainly fall under censure. Likewise disputed is the case of those who formally adhere to the Communist party. The Knights of Pythias, Odd Fellows, Sons of Temperance are forbidden as intrinsically wrong but not under censure. The conditions for absolution from this censure are total withdrawal from the society, abjuration of the sect before the confessor with the promise to have nothing to do with it in the future or to pay dues, to repair any scandal as far as possible, to denounce all ecclesiastics and religious known as members, to promise to turn over all books, mss., emblems and insignia pertaining to the

---

108. c. 894.
109. S.C.C. 22 mart. 1950; cf. c. 2380.
110. S.C.C. 29 iun. 1950; cf. cc. 2331, 2; 2334, 1o, 2o; 2394.
111. c. 2237, 2.
112. c. 2327.
113. cc. 2335; 2336. Under certain conditions the Apostolic Delegate may permit to converts passive membership or retention of adscription for purposes of particular financial benefits, etc.

sect to be sent to the Holy Office, or if grave reason prevents, at least to destroy them and take his name off the rolls as soon as possible without grave loss.

 c. *Presuming to absolve without faculty from most specially or specially reserved censures.*[114]

 d. *Aiding or knowingly abetting a vitandus.*[115]

 e. *Daring to cite before a lay tribunal a bishop, prelate or certain religious superiors.*[116]

 f. *Presuming to usurp ecclesiastical property.*[117]

 g. *Dueling or abetting the same.*[118] The censure includes also those who challenge or who accept a challenge, unless it is certain they did not have the intention of dueling.[119]

 h. *Attempted marriage by or with clerics in Sacred Orders or religious of solemn vows.*[120] The censure includes clerics from diaconate onward and all religious with a solemn vow of chastity (thus excluding postulants, novices, simply professed and Jesuits whose simple vow nevertheless invalidates marriage); likewise all who presume to contract marriage with them. Mere concubinage does not suffice, but there must be an appearance of marriage, either canonical or civil, whether consummated or not. All parties embraced by the censure must presume (*"praesumentes"*) to attempt marriage. Absolution of a priest in these circumstances, who for very grave reasons cannot separate from his partner, is reserved exclusively to the Sacred Penitentiary.[121]

 i. *Simony in offices, benefices, dignities.*[122]

 j. *Falsifying, etc., documents of the episcopal curia.*[123]

6. Reserved to the local Ordinary.[124]

114. c. 2338, 1.
115. **Ibid.**, 2.
116. c. 2341.
117. c. 2346.
118. c. 2351.
119. PCI 26 iun. 1947.
120. c. 2388.
121. S. Poenit. 18 apr. 1936; 4 maii 1937. cf. motu proprio **Pastorale munus,** 30 nov. 1963, n. I, 14, II, 4.
122. c. 2392.
123. c. 2405.
124. The automatic excommunication of the III Plenary Council

a. *Violent attacks on clerics or religious.*[124a] Real (as opposed to verbal) injury must be inflicted on the person of clerics of rank inferior to bishops or on the person of religious of either sex, excluding those who do not take public vows in a religious institute, e.g., novices or members of a religious society without vows. Lawful self-defense, accidental injury, blows in jesting, and whatever is lacking for an externally manifest serious sin does not incur the penalty. The object of the injury can be the body, liberty or dignity of the offended, but the act must be of its nature malicious and it must be known that the person attacked is a cleric or religious. If the Ordinary of the injuring party is the local Ordinary, the Regular confessor may absolve, but not if it is the major religious superior in an exempt clerical institute.

b. *Procuring abortion.*[125] The censure is incurred by those procuring an effective abortion, including the mother among them. Abortion here signifies the ejection of a living and immature or nonviable fetus from the womb of the mother (and not craniotomy, embryotomy, etc.). All those cooperators whose help or counsel is necessary for the commission of the crime also incur the censure.[126] The abortion must be a serious sin subjectively and objectively, directly intended as an end in itself or as a means to another end. It must actually take place and result directly from any of the means used and not from some other cause. Grave fear on the part of the woman of losing her good name if the child is born may excuse from the penalty for the sin.

c. *Making false relics, knowingly selling, distributing or publicly exposing them.*[127]

d. *Religious of a simple perpetual vow of chastity presuming to marry or to attempt marriage, and their partners.*[128] The vow

> of Baltimore (n. 124) inflicted upon Catholics who have dared ("ausi fuerint") to attempt marriage after having obtained a civil divorce is still in effect; it includes not only the one who obtained the divorce but also the one who merely marries a divorced person, since this is positive and necessary cooperation (cf. cc. 2231; 2209, 3).

124a. c. 2343, 4.
125. c. 2350, 1.
126. Cf. cc. 2209, 1-3; 2231.
127. c. 2326.

must be taken in a religious Order or Congregation. Even a civil marriage is included. A religious who runs off with a person of the other sex, or who attempts or contracts even civil marriage is *ipso facto* dismissed from the institute; whether the religious is also released from vows or not depends on the constitutions of the particular institute.[129] If released from the vows at the time of the automatic dismissal, the person incurs no censure at the time of a subsequent marriage.

e. *Apostate religious.*[130] An apostate from the religious life is a religious in perpetual vows, whether solemn or simple, who leaves the religious house unlawfully and with the intention of not returning, or who leaves the house lawfully but does not return because he intends to withdraw himself from religious obedience; this intention is presumed in law if the religious does not return within a month and has not at least notified his superior within that time of his intention to return.[131] This censure is reserved to the major superior if it is a clerical exempt institute (the Regular confessor cannot then absolve) and in all other cases to the local Ordinary of the place where the apostate actually is.

7. Reserved to no one.

a. *Daring to force the unlawful Christian burial of the unworthy.*[132]

b. *Knowingly to alienate Church property.*[133]

c. *Compelling another to enter the clerical or the religious state.*[134]

d. *Failure to denounce solicitation.*[135]

L. *Suspension*

1. *Notion.* Suspension is a censure by which a cleric is ex-

128. c. 2388, 2.
129. Cf. cc. 646; 669, 1.
130. c. 2385.
131. Cf. cc. 644; 645.
132. c. 2339. Cf. also S. Off. Instructio **de Cadaverum Crematione**, 8 maii 1963.
133. c. 2347, 3º.
134. c. 2352.
135. c. 2368, 2.

cluded from his office or benefice or both.¹³⁶ It prohibits the use or exercise of office, which will be unlawful, and after sentence in certain respects invalid. It likewise prohibits taking the revenues or fruits of a benefice, but it does not take away the office or benefice itself.¹³⁷ When it is inflicted for a definite time independently of the delinquent's withdrawal from contumacy, it may be a vindictive penalty.¹³⁸

2. *Division.*

A suspension may be *a iure, ab homine, latae sententiae, ferendae sententiae,* reserved, non-reserved, in the same manner as with excommunication.

General or total suspension embraces both office and benefice with all their effects.¹³⁹ *Particular* or partial suspension implies only one species, either wholly or in part.

Suspension *ex informata conscientia*¹⁴⁰ is an extraordinary remedy which is applied only when there is a grave inconvenience in following the norms of law.

3. *Effects of particular suspensions.*

   a. *ab officio.* If it is an unqualified suspension, it forbids every act of orders and of jurisdiction and of even mere administration coming from office (except the administration of one's own benefice.¹⁴¹

   b. *a beneficio.* It deprives one of the fruits of a benefice.¹⁴²

   c. *a iurisdictione.* Every act of both ordinary and delegated jurisdiction as such is forbidden in both fora.¹⁴³

   d. *a divinis.* It forbids every act of the power received through sacred ordination or privilege (but not preaching).¹⁴⁴

   e. *a sacris ordinibus.* (from major Orders); *a certo et*

---

136. c. 2278, 1.
137. c. 2280.
138. Cf. c. 2298, 2.
139. Cf. cc. 2278-2285; cf. c. 2336.
140. Cf. cc. 2186-2194.
141. c. 2279, 1.
142. cc. 2280-2281.
143. c. 2279, 2, 1°.
144. **Ibid.,** 2°.

definito ordine exercendo, conferendo; a certo et definito ministerio; ab ordine pontificali; a pontificalibus.[145] An irregularity *ex delicto* is incurred by a cleric who exercises a *sacred* Order from which he is barred by canonical penalty.[146]

f. A suspension *ab ordine* binds everywhere, *a iurisdictione* binds only in the territory of the one imposing it. One suspended generally, or *ab officio, a divinis, ab ordinibus,* cannot lawfully administer the sacraments and sacramentals. For any just cause the faithful can request these of the one suspended, especially if other ministers are lacking, and the administration is then lawful. In the case of one under sentence, the faithful can request absolution only in danger of death, and lacking other ministers, the other sacraments and sacramentals. If the suspension forbids the act of jurisdiction in the internal or external forum, the act is invalid after a sentence or if the superior expressly revokes the jurisdiction; otherwise it is unlawful only, unless requested by the faithful.[147] Other effects of *general* suspension are as in the case of excommunication.[148] Suspension as a censure is removed only by absolution.

4. Reserved to the Apostolic See.

    a. *Episcopal consecration without Apostolic mandate.*[149]
    b. *Clerics knowingly simoniacal.*[150]
    c. *Presuming to receive Orders from a specially unworthy minister.*[151]
    d. *Dismissed cleric of perpetual vows.*[152]
    e. *Conferring Orders without required documents, title, permissions.*[153]

---

145. **Ibid.**, 3o-9o.
146. Cf. cc. 985, 7o; 986; 2232, 1.
147. c. 2284.
148. c. 2265.
149. c. 2370.
150. c. 2371.
151. c. 2372. In most cases the Sacred Congregation for the Doctrine of the Faith will consider the delinquent as a layman, and thus marriage is possible, all things being equal.
152. c. 671, 1o.
153. c. 2373.

f. *Religious in major Orders admitting a deceitful and invalid profession.*[154]

g. *Unlawful admission to office, benefice, dignity.*[155]

5. Reserved to the Ordinary.

a. *Cleric daring to cite before a lay judge an ecclesiastic inferior to a bishop.*[156]

b. *Fugitive religious.*[157] Flight from religion is the withdrawing of a religious from the religious house without the permission of the superiors with the intention of returning to the institute, but meanwhile of withdrawing from religious obedience. Such a religious *ipso facto* incurs privation of any office he may have held in his institute, and if he is in sacred orders, suspension reserved to his own major superior; and when he returns he is to be punished according to the constitutions, and if these make no provision for such punishment, the major superior shall inflict penalties according to the gravity of the case. In the case where the major superior is the Ordinary of the place where the fugitive resides, a Regular confessor can absolve him in the internal forum.

6. Reserved to no one.

a. *A priest presuming to hear sacramental confessions without required jurisdiction is ipso facto suspended a divinis.*[158]

b. *A priest presuming to absolve from reserved sins is ipso facto suspended from hearing confessions.*[159] This probably refers to sins reserved without censure.

c. *Those maliciously and unlawfully ordained.*[160]

d. *Clerics presuming to resign unlawfully into lay hands an office, benefice, or dignity.*[161]

e. *Omission of blessing of an abbot or prelate nullius.*[162]

154. c. 2387.
155. c. 2394, 3.
156. c. 2341.
157. cc. 2386; cf. 644, 3.
158. c. 2366.
159. **Ibid.**, cf. also c. 2338, 1.
160. c. 2374.
161. c. 2400.
162. c. 2402.

f. *Vicar capitular unlawfully granting dimissorials.*[163]

g. *Religious superiors presuming unlawfully to grant dimissorials.*[164]

M. *Interdict.* An interdict is a censure by which the faithful, while remaining in communion with the Church, are forbidden certain sacred things.[165]

II. *Reserved sins.*

A. *Notion of reserved sin.* The reservation of a sin is the withdrawal of a sin to the judgment of the one making the reservation, so that no one can validly grant absolution in the case, except the superior or his delegate.[166] The sin is said to be reserved as sin (*ratione sui* or *ratione peccati*) and not merely reserved by reason of a reserved censure attached to it (*ratione censurae*).

B. *Manner of establishment.* The Holy See can establish reservations everywhere and for everyone. Actually, only one sin is reserved *ratione sui* by the Code to the Holy See, namely, the sin of false denunciation of a confessor, made before ecclesiastical judges or superiors, of the crime of solicitation.[167] Even though a censure may not have been incurred because of some excusing cause, the sin can be incurred and the reservation remain.

The Ordinary of a diocese can reserve to himself not more than four more heinous sins, external and specifically determined, which have not already been reserved *ratione sui* or *ratione censurae* (even to no one) by the general law of the Church. Only the superior general in an exempt clerical religious institute or the abbot of an independent monastery can do the same for their sub-

---

163. c. 2409.
164. c. 2410.
165. Cf. cc. 2268-2277.
166. c. 893, 1-3.
167. c. 894. It is also a specially reserved censure (c. 2363). The duty to restore the good name of the falsely accused priest still remains (PCI 10 nov. 1925).

jects.[168] Visitors and strangers (*peregrini, vagi*) are bound by the reservations in the place where they confess,[169] since the reservation is the withdrawal or limitation of the jurisdiction of the confessor of the place.

C. *Excusing cause.* Unless the bishop explicitly or implicitly determines otherwise, ignorance of a reserved sin does not excuse from its incurrence. The same is also true of the one sin reserved to the Holy See. If a confessor, ignorant (or in error) of the reservation of a sin *ratione sui*, absolves a penitent, the absolution is invalid, unless the contrary is stated by the one reserving.[170]

D. *Jurisdiction to absolve.*

Any priest can absolve from any reserved sin in danger of death.[171]

Residential and titular *Bishops* can absolve anyone whomsoever of the faithful anywhere from all reserved sins with the exception, however, of the sin of false denunciation whereby an innocent priest is accused of the crime of solicitation before ecclesiastical judges.[172]

During the time in which the Easter duty can be fulfilled, *pastors* and those who come under the category of pastors in the law have the faculty to absolve from episcopal reserved cases.[173]

Vicars forane or rural deans are usually to receive this faculty from the bishop, which they may subdelegate in an urgent case.[174]

Those who give *missions* to the people (and other priests when

---

168. cc. 895-898. Cf. also c. 519 for absolution of religious by a diocesan confessor.
169. PCI 24 nov. 1921, c. 14, 2.
170. Suspension is incurred (c. 2366) for a deliberate violation. A few commentators admit the applicability of an urgent case.
171. c. 882.
172. c. 239, 1, 1º. Paul VI, motu proprio **Pastorale munus**, II, 3 (30 nov. 1963).
173. c. 899, 3.
174. **Ibid.**, 2.

assisting them in confessions) enjoy the same faculty as the pastors above during the time of the missions (and probably also during novenas, retreats, and all such spiritual exercises).[175]

Regulars as confessors cannot absolve in virtue of their papal privilege from a sin reserved *ratione sui* by the bishop to himself, unless the same sin is already reserved *ratione censurae* to the local Ordinary in the common law.

E. *Cessation of reservation.* Any confessor who enjoys faculties to hear confessions in the place can absolve from reserved sins (but not censures), whether episcopal or papal, no recourse being required, in the following cases,[176] because in these cases the sins are not reserved nor his jurisdiction restricted:

1. In the case of the sick who cannot leave the house. This includes the aged and all those impeded by infirmity from going out of their residence, whether it is a home, college, religious house, hospital, etc.

2. In the case of those about to get married. It makes no difference if the marriage is to be convalidated, or subsequently does not take place, or if the confession takes place a few days before the event.

3. Whenever the legitimate superior has refused the faculty requested in a particular case.

4. Whenever the confessor reasonably judges that the faculty to absolve cannot be requested from the proper superior without danger of violating the sacramental seal, or without grave inconvenience to the penitent. Thus, e.g., if there is serious difficulty in returning to the confessor, if the penitent cannot stay away from Communion or refrain from celebrating Mass without injury to his good name, or if it is difficult for him to remain in serious sin until faculties to absolve are granted (or even for a short time). The estimate of the danger or inconvenience is left to the judgment

---

175. Ibid., 3.
176. c. 900; PCI 10 nov. 1925.

of a prudent confessor; in doubt of either the confessor can absolve.

5. Whenever the penitent who has incurred a sin reserved to his bishop goes outside the diocese, even if for no other purpose than to obtain absolution. However, if the same case is reserved also in that other diocese, the confessor there cannot absolve the penitent.

Chastity and Its Violations

CHASTITY

I. *Role of Chastity*

The name "chastity" comes from chastise (*castitas-castigare*). Children are corrected by being chastised, since by being given their own will they become more unruly. In like manner the various concupiscences of man, which are inclined to seek their own satisfaction, need to be chastised by reason, especially the most vehement —but in itself not the most pernicious—concupiscence or drive which is for venereal pleasure. Chastity therefore is antonomastically linked with this concupiscence.[1]

Chastity is a special virtue in the area of temperance which moderates the sexual appetite and its acts by which the human race is propagated, together with the venereal pleasure which is normally joined to such acts and which especially attracts man. Chastity exercises its control in accordance with the demands of right reason enlightened and directed by supernatural faith in the context of the state, condition, and situation of each person.

Although terms are often used interchangeably, chastity in the strict sense differs from:

1. *continency, (continentia)* which is an habitual disposition or inclination of the will to resist evil concupiscences of touch, especially of a venereal kind. It habitually resists and does not consent to these movements, but at the same time it does not dominate them, as does the full virtue of chastity.[2]

2. *virginity*, which is the holy and firm will to abstain perpetually from every voluntary venereal act in one who has never been a partner to a sexual action. It consists materially in bodily integrity

---

1. Cf. **Summa Theol.**, II-II, q. 151, aa. 1-2. The pleasure experienced in the genital organ and of itself ordered to generation is called venereal after the pagan goddess Venus, who presided over this pleasure or love.
2. **Ibid.**, q. 155.

free from every voluntary corruption whether by solitary action or with another, and formally in the firm purpose of perpetual abstinence from every venereal act, even from those allowed in legitimate marriage, because of the goodness of virtue itself and the desire for absorption in God and divine things. Perfect chastity, on the other hand, can be possessed by those who have had previous carnal experience or who simply have the intention of entering marriage.[3]

3. *modesty* (*pudicitia*) or purity is not a virtue distinct from chastity but rather expresses a circumstance of chastity in general. It is concerned mainly with the signs of unchastity or things which not being venereal in themselves are more or less influential in arousing such pleasure, e.g., looks, touches, kisses, words, undress and exposure, etc.[4] The guardian of modesty, as of all innocence and chastity, is the natural endowment of a sense of shame (*verecundia*). On its part modesty strictly differs from decency which relates to the less becoming acts connected with the meaner vegetative functions of the body and its organs offensive to the customs of civilized and cultured peoples. Such actions may concern the genital organs in their less typical generative functions not necessarily connected with impure or venereal experience. The distinction is practical in judging the confessions of youngsters confessing having done "bad things."

Chastity is: *perfect*, which abstains from all carnal pleasure including what is lawful in marriage; *imperfect*, which abstains only from the unlawful pleasures of the flesh outside the married state; *virginal*, which has never experienced carnal pleasure whether in or outside marriage; *conjugal*, which is observed by spouses abstaining from what is forbidden to the married; *vidual*, which abstains from any further carnal pleasure upon the dissolution of a marriage; *common*, which is observed by all the unmarried, even if not virgins, and is also called chaste celibacy.

3. **Ibid.**, q. 152, aa. 3-4; **Suppl.**, q. 96, a. 5; cf. Apoc. 14:4.
4. **Summa Theol.**, II-II, q. 151, a. 4.

Common chastity is commanded by the Sixth and Ninth Commandments for all men.[5] These precepts forbid all sins of unchastity both internal and external; positively they prescribe the preservation of the chastity which corresponds to one's state.

II *Kinds of Pleasures*

Pleasure (*delectatio*) is the rest or sedation, the complacency or satisfaction of the appetite in the presence or possession of its object. Pleasures are usually distinguished by reason of the powers and objects from which they arise.

1. *purely spiritual*. This pleasure follows reason and is contained in the higher faculties of man and usually has no effect upon his sensible part, being morally good or evil as the object itself which pleases, e.g., to discover a truth or an answer after much mental effort or investigation, to consider the beauty of virtue or a new way of injuring another, etc.[6]

2. *spiritual-sensible*. The representation or the presence of an object which is loved spiritually mainly because of its spiritual qualities gives rise to a pleasure or delight with the effect that, beside the spiritual delight, by an overflow from the higher affection, the lower faculties also experience a certain pleasant sensible motion such as the stepping up of the movement of the heart and blood, e.g., the delight accompanying the love between parent and child, husband and wife, friend and friend. In itself it is distinguishable from carnal pleasure and is morally indifferent, although properly handled it is good and commendable.[7]

3. *merely sensible*. Also called organic pleasure or delight, it

---

5. Exodus 20:14, 17.
6. This pleasure is called by St. Thomas (I-II, q. 31, a. 5 et ad 3) "**delectatio intelligibilis**," "**delectatio rationis**," "**delectatio quae consequitur rationem**."
7. Referred to by St. Thomas (ibid.) as "**delectatio spiritualis cum redundantia in appetitum inferiorem**."

arises from the sense being affected by its own object without it normally being apt to stimulate venereal activity, e.g., to smell a field of lavender, to view a beautiful sunset. Such pleasure is in itself indifferent morally; inordinate use usually does not exceed a venial sin, such as to take undue delight in the pleasures of the table.[8]

4. *sensual* or *sensible-carnal*. This pleasure responds to a merely sensible object, but, given human nature as it is, it is apt also to arouse venereal pleasure,[9] e.g., certain looks, touches, kisses, conversation with a person for whom there is a strong sensible attraction, etc. This is the dangerous area involved in company keeping, petting, etc. The entire delight resides in the sensitive appetite and when its vehemence increases, the stimulation more easily than the above-mentioned pleasures excites carnal motion and venereal passion. If there is a proximate danger of consenting to the venereal disturbance by the one experiencing the sensual pleasure, there is in itself serious sin. If this danger is not proximate and if there is sufficient reason to justify the indulgence in the pleasure, e.g., custom among prudent people in the place, lawful friendship, etc., there is no sin or at the most a slight sin.

5. *venereal* or *carnal*. This is a sense pleasure which arises from the motion or activity of the organs and the fluids which pertain to generation: in a man the pleasurable erection of the penis and its agitation which causes seed to flow, in a woman the pleasurable erection of the clitoris and the contraction of the vagina with a distillation. Chastity, as noted, is concerned only with venereal pleasure, which is proper to the genital organs and can be experienced only in them. When the cause of this sexual stimulation is deliberate and outside of wedlock, the pleasure is seriously sinful.[10]

---

8. St. Thomas (ibid., aa. 5-6) calls this **"delectatio sensibilis," "delectatio animalis secundum cognitionem."**
9. Some writers designate pleasure as **sensual** with respect to touch and **sensible** with regard to the other senses.
10. Merely sensible pleasure or agreeableness may arise in the genital organs from causes other than sexual stimuli; thus

Pleasure is said to be *complete* when the action proceeds to its ultimate natural term, satisfies the sexual drive and quiets the faculty; otherwise it is *incomplete*. It is called *voluntary* when there is a participation or intervention of the will in the sexual process or motion; the pleasure is then either *sought* or *procured*, i.e., deliberately intended and brought about, e.g., to initiate self-abuse, or *accepted* or *admitted*, i.e., deliberately consented to or embraced after the pleasure has arisen through no personal effort, e.g., consciously to complete an orgasm by self-abuse when an erection has previously been brought about during sleep by natural causes. Mere agreeableness (*placentia*) experienced in the venereal parts due to physical or physiological causes is neither morally good nor bad in itself; a complacency (*complacentia*), however, is seriously sinful, i.e., if the pleasure is consented to or willed inasmuch as it is approved, desired, accepted, or even procured.

VIOLATIONS OF CHASTITY

I. Inordinate Character of the Violation of Chastity

Unchastity, the violation of chastity or lust (*luxuria*), is the inordinate desire for and use of venereal pleasure; it is the undue use of sexual activity. The physical or venereal pleasure which normally accompanies the sexual function is a sign that sexual activity is going on; it is strictly accessory and is designed to incite, facilitate, and insure the achievement of the divine purpose. Its inordinate desire and use of itself and by intention excludes the primary purpose of the Creator, the procreation and education of offspring in lawful wedlock.

> certain physical or physiological changes or disturbances take place occasionally, such as early morning abundance of blood in the area or the pressures coming from the urinary deposit in the bladder, etc.

Unchastity which is *merely internal* consists in the affection alone for venereal objects and pleasures. These are comprised under morose delectation, sinful desire, and sinful pleasure, all of which are forbidden by the Ninth Commandment.

The Sixth Commandment forbids the *use* of venereal things and the *voluntary* disturbance of the sexual organs. Such external unchastity may be:

1. *completed* or *consummated,* when the external act reaches its natural term or orgasm with the normal accompaniment of the satiation of carnal pleasure and sedation of the sexual impulse. This may be *in conformity with nature,* inasmuch as the act is apt to achieve generation, as in the case of fornication, incest, adultery or *contrary to nature,* whereby the acts are unnatural or generation is impossible of achievement, as in the case of pollution, onanism, sodomy.

2. *uncompleted* or *inchoate,* when the external act falls short of achieving its term or orgasm. Included here are actions which are provocative of venereal motions although not venereal in themselves.

Unchastity is *willed directly* and *in itself* when venereal motions and pleasure are intended and sought or procured for themselves, e.g., to desire to, to intend to, or actually to look at an obscene picture; to deliberately stimulate the sex organs.

When one does not intend or seek venereal pleasure but at the same time does not hinder it, when it involuntarily arises, in the manner and degree he ought to and could, unchastity is said to be *indirectly willed.* The forbidden activity of pleasure in this negative way is accepted, admitted, approved, e.g., to fail to put down a book at the time when, quite accidentally and not by design of the book itself, it happens to arouse venereal disturbance.

A further effect is said to be *willed in cause* when one willingly places a cause which bears some influence upon the further effect that takes place, although the latter is not necessarily intended in itself (there must be a culpable relationship, of course, for sin), e.g., one who is responsible for his state of intoxication could have or should have foreseen (or actually did foresee) the impure actions that would result in the case.

II. Objective Moral Norms

A. *All directly willed venereal action outside of marriage is of its nature seriously sinful and does not admit of any slightness of matter.*

The works of the flesh are clearly forbidden in Scripture and condemned by the Church.[11] The more necessary and important a thing is in the preservation of the order of reason, the more serious is the failure. The venereal function, the activity of the generative faculty, has been instilled by the Creator for the benefit and continuance of the human race; unchastity is opposed to this either by excluding the possibility of procreation or by rendering befitting education uncertain and insecure.

Completed unchaste acts, i.e., completed and consummated venereal actions deliberately and directly willed outside of marriage, as well as uncompleted unchaste acts, i.e., uncompleted and unconsummated activity of a venereal nature, whether internal or external, are always of themselves intrinsically and gravely evil and sinful. No intention or purpose can justify them as regards what is willed. Physiologically the uncompleted or inchoate actions are of the same nature as the completed or fulfilled actions, e.g., the evil desire, the passionate kissing and petting, the fornication itself. To place and to will the beginning is implicitly to desire and will the fulfilment. Regardless of the intention of the agent the inchoate venereal actions are intrinsically connected with and directed to their complete realization, although they do not in every case necessarily or always lead to consummated acts. Because of the vehemence of concupiscence and the common frailty of man, it is morally impossible to contain sexual concupiscence at will within certain limits.[12]

11. Cf. Gen. 13:13; Ex. 22:19; Lev. 18:22; 20:15-16; Rom. 1:26-27; I Cor. 5:1-5; 6:9; 7:9; Gal. 5:19-21; Eph. 5:5 Cf. Denz.-Schön. 835; 897; 1367; 2044-2045; 2148-2150; 2241-2242; 2247-2248; 2252; 3684; 3717. Cf. Pius XII, Address to the Italian Catholic Union of Midwives (29 oct. 1951).
12. Cf. **Summa Theol.**, II-II, q. 153, aa. 2-3; q. 154, a. 4; I-II, q. 1, a. 6: "because the beginning of a thing is always ordered

No matter how slight the action or how brief or insignificant the pleasure, all such actions are deprived of their proper ordination or direction as established by nature; thus in all directly willed venereal action outside of marriage there is no slightness or parvity of matter. (Within marriage, as long as the ends of marriage are not positively excluded, there is no sin or at most venial sin.) There can be slight sin deriving only from the imperfection of the human act itself, i.e., if there is not complete advertence or sufficient reflection, or if there is not proper and full consent. Even though some people may erroneously or out of a form of ignorance think that there is slight and not serious sin in taking pleasure in certain impure thoughts or uncompleted actions, the fact of their essential ordination remains and is not changed by the will of man.[13] In those who are innately highly sexed or suffer abnormal mental aberrations there may be diminution of imputability; in some exceptional cases responsibility and imputability may have disappeared. The diminution or lack of control, however, must be established and not assumed in the particular case.

B. *Indirectly voluntary venereal action is of itself slightly sinful, but sometimes it is seriously sinful due to the danger of consent.*

A man cannot be indifferent to the movement of the lower appetite; he shirks his duty when he does not direct and repress or positively resist such inordinate movement when he can and should. Thus, when an unchaste motion or presentation arises which he has not sought out or procured or intended, he does not sin grieviously if he does not give positive consent, but he sins to some degree by not resisting it positively and by taking only a negative stand through failure to repress it when he can and

to its consummation." **de Malo,** q. 15, a. 2, ad 16 et ad 18; **de Verit.,** q. 15, a. 4.

13. Alexander VII (18 mart. 1666) condemned as at least scandalous the proposition: "It is a probable opinion which states that a kiss is only venial when performed for the sake of the carnal and sensible delight which arises from the kiss, if danger of further consent and pollution is excluded." S. Off. 11 feb. 1661: "Since in venereal matters there is not parvity of matter. . . ." Denz.-Schön. 1140; 2013.

should. If there is a proximate danger in such a case of giving positive consent, there is serious sin. Indirect methods of repression or removal are more practical and profitable in these matters such as to change the direction of one's thoughts or desires, to distract one's attention by praying or stopping what one is presently doing or to take up some other business or activity. Direct methods often tend to keep the unchaste object in the forefront of consciousness and make it more difficult to avoid or remove the temptation, e.g., by chastising the body through squeezing the members, by trying to suppress the image itself, by trying to talk over the dangerous intimacy with the very party involved.

At times, especially with the scrupulous, the concern to avoid or repress temptations rather excites the imagination and continues or increases the motions. This is just cause for showing opposition by simple displeasure and contempt of the motions, and going about one's duty. In such a case positive resistance is implicit. Experience in other situations may also show that this attitude is sufficient, e.g., when the activity engaged in is necessary or useful, such as exercise or daily work in which both sexes are present, or when the motions or temptations are slight and quickly passing, although frequent.

C. *Unchastity which is voluntary in cause is of its nature a serious sin but admits of slightness of matter, and at times even of no sin at all.*

The consent of the will to venereal pleasure which is voluntary or willed in cause is as sinful as the cause placed which provokes this pleasure. In judging whether such an action is sinful or not, besides estimating the influence of the cause on the result, the action must be also justified by a proportionate reason. In matters of chastity it is often difficult in practice to judge when the conditions justifying an action are verified, namely, that the action or cause placed is morally good or indifferent; that the venereal effect, if such follows, is not intended; that there is sufficient and proportionate reason for the action in the first place. Judgment must be made on what is done or about to be done, why it was done or is about to be done, how it has affected or will affect the individual or others, since each one differs in inclination and disposition and dangers affect different people diversely; finally there is the sufficiency and adequacy of the justifying reasons. Charity itself obliges one not to lead or help others to sin and, moreover, to take prudent steps to prevent others from sinning when possible.

Some actions by their nature are apt to arouse motion and excite venereal pleasure as proximate and more or less vehement occasions of sin. Such things or actions which commonly and practically are proximate incitements to unchastity are truly called obscene, e.g., frequent or prolonged gazes or touches upon the forbidden parts of the opposite sex (or, with some individuals, of the same sex), looking at pictures or movies or reading printed matter or attending theatrical presentations when their theme or content is of an unchaste or sexually exciting nature and at the same time their manner of presentation tends to throw an attractive emphasis on the unchaste element. Some actions of themselves only remotely or slightly incite an unchaste result, e.g., to touch one's own genital parts, a passing glance at the female breast or a slight and passing touch of the same, etc. Countless other things and activities have no relationship to venereal matters or generation and serve quite other purposes. Yet incidentally and at times venereal excitement or pleasure may be aroused as a by-product in this or that individual because of some weakness, habit, perversion, or some other factor connected with the particular person. Such incidental influences or causes may be: the study or practice of medicine, the study of physiology or moral theology, decent dancing, a modest kiss or embrace as accepted in the place as a sign of friendship or relationship, bathing, horseback riding, immoderate eating or drinking, a movie or play or book with an occasional suggestive scene or description, etc.

It is a serious sin, without proportionate reason, to place a cause which arouses strong carnal motion and great venereal pleasure which is a proximate occasion for sin, even if the disturbance did not take place, e.g., out of curiosity to look at certain magazines which are obscene. Only if by experience it is known that the individual is not so disturbed is it safe or permissible to place such an action. It is a slight sin to place a cause without just reason which only slightly or remotely or accidentally results in even a strong disturbance, as long as there is no proximate danger of consent. Any reasonable and proportionate cause of necessity, usefulness, or convenience would suffice to act lawfully and without any sin, e.g., a physician who must look at or handle the less decent parts of his patients, a priest who must study about sins against chastity and hear confessions of the unchaste, the need to exercise, etc.

III. *Sins against chastity completed in a manner apt to achieve natural generation*

A. *Fornication*

Fornication is the completed use of the generative faculty by mutual consent between an unmarried man and an unmarried woman. The presence or absence of bodily virginity does not affect the nature of the sin. It is simple fornication if there is no added species of malice in the act, e.g., marriage bond.[14]

Fornication is intrinsically and gravely evil, evidently condemned in Scripture,[15] and by the Church.[16] It cannot be justified for any reason whatsoever. Fornication is forbidden by the natural law as of its nature opposed to the substantial order in carnal intercourse whereby the generation and especially the education of offspring is provided for and demands the actual as well as the juridic lasting association of the parents. The evil nature of the act is not changed by the fact that in certain individual cases (which do not commonly happen) the intercourse remains sterile, e.g., the woman lacks ovaries, or the man can (or even binds himself to)

---

14. The word "fornication" comes from the Latin term for brothel, **"fornex,"** or narrow arched cells in which the Roman whores under distinct trademarks were accustomed to carry on their business.
15. Deut. 23:17; I Cor. 6:9-10, 15-20; Gal. 5:19-21; Eph. 5:5-6.
16. Cf. Denz.-Schön. 2045; 2148; cf. also cc. 133, 3; 2176-2181; 2357; 2359.

support and educate the child and provide for the mother. If fornication were for any reason justifiable, society would certainly suffer,[17] as it presently does from widespread violaters. In cases of fornication the confessor should keep in mind the occasionist, the habitual and the relapsed sinner. Discreet interrogation may be in order as to resulting pregnancy or its prevention, obligations to mother and child, possible abortion, etc.

Prostitution (*meretricium*) is the practice of a woman, for the sake of gain or of pleasure, engaging in fornication with several or all comers, whether this is public (e.g., a civilly registered or professional prostitute) or hidden (carried on behind some front of respectability or accepted position). This practice does not differ specifically from fornication, although the malice is greater because of the readiness to sin and implied willingness to remain in sin, the preparedness to commit adultery, etc., and the frequent effect of becoming sterile. Although of itself not strictly necessary, the penitent, especially if interrogated by the confessor, for the sake of better judgment and advice, should mention the fact of approaching a prostitute or of being a prostitute.

Concubinage (*concubinatus*) is habitual sinning with the same woman, whether the fornicator keeps her at home or not. It is called concubinary fornication since the partners live in a sort of marital manner, in at least a tacit relationship. For this reason it is a form of permanent condition and a will to remain in sin, more serious than prostitution or simple fornication but not specifically distinct from the latter. The circumstance of concubinage should be mentioned in confession for the better judgment and advice of the confessor and because of the scandal or occasion of sin to be removed and the possibly incurred penalty.[18] A penitent confessing concubinage is not to be absolved, however contrite, until the occasion has been removed, e.g., removal of the woman from the house; a serious promise usually suffices only in danger of death when absolution cannot be delayed.

Fornication that is onanistic, i.e., begun in the usual manner but completed in an unnatural fashion, such as withdrawal, or

---

17. Cf. **Summa Theol.**, II-II, q. 154, aa. 1-2.
18. cc. 2357, 2; 2358; 2359, 1.

condomistic, i.e., with the employment of an artificial device to prevent insemination, is an external sin of pollution and an internal sin of fornication. It is objectively more sinful than simple fornication but often subjectively less gravely sinful if the fuller sexual satisfaction is foregone in order to spare the woman and society, but not if only for the sake of pleasure without its attendant burdens and responsibilities. The confessor must insist upon the actual confiscation or destruction of the artificial devices before giving absolution, or at least a serious promise that appears will be efficacious.

B. *Adultery*

Adultery is a carnal act between a man and a woman at least one of whom is married. It is simple or multiple as only one or both parties are married; in the latter case there is double malice against both fidelity and justice as well as mutual unchastity.

Scripture most severely condemns adultery.[19] Consent to the adultery of one's partner does not change the nature of the sin,[20] since besides unchastity injustice is still committed against the indissoluble contract established by divine law and against the right of the sacrament. The offspring of an adulterous union may bring temporal injury to the innocent spouse and the rights of the legitimate children.[21] Under adultery is also included an unnatural act by a married person with himself or with his own partner, since this is also against justice.

C. *Rape*

Rape (*stuprum*) is the oppression of a woman who is unwilling or the deflowering of a virgin who is unwilling. The woman may be a virgin or not, married or not; the virgin is taken in the physical sense. The violence which the rapist employs against the unwilling victim may be physical or moral, e.g., by threats, fear, deceit, fraud, force, during sleep, while inebriated, etc.

---

19. Lev. 18:20; 20:10; Deut. 22:22; Prov. 6:29; Eccli. 23:25-30; I Cor. 7:4.
20. Innocent XI, Denz.-Schön. 2150.
21. Cf. **Summa Theol.**, loc. cit., aa. 1, 8.

Besides chastity, rape is a serious sin against justice, since it violates a grave right of a woman over her own body. Although in certain circumstances justice may be distinctly sinned against by violating the carnal integrity of a virgin, the circumstance of virginity need not be confessed. An oppressed woman who consents may also offend against piety toward her parents. The rapist may also sin against charity in the effect the violent action may have on the one raped, her family, or on her prospects of marriage.[22]

An oppressed woman is gravely bound without qualification to resist internally any venereal pleasure lest there result formal sin. She is bound to resist externally at least to the extent proportionate to her powers and the circumstances of her situation. She may defend her chastity even to the death, as long as death is not intended, although she need not resist to this extent. The lawfulness of the use of a vaginal lotion or douche after rape is controverted. However, in practice the seed may be expelled from the vagina (and even from the uterus) before conception takes place, which is variously estimated, e.g., from one hour to one hour and a half after the attack.

D. *Abduction*

Abduction (*raptus*) is the forceful seizing of a person or the injurious privation of another's liberty which is inflicted for the purpose of committing a sin against chastity with that person. The force used may be physical or moral and directed against the person kidnapped (male or female, married or unmarried, a virgin or not) or against those under whose authority the person lives.

Besides the serious sin against chastity (at least internal, if no external act takes place), there is always serious sin against justice either towards the person abducted or the parents or guardians. Abduction is also a diriment impediment to marriage when the woman is kidnapped for this purpose.[23]

22. Cf. **Summa Theol.**, loc. cit., aa. 1, 6. Penalties may be imposed for rape, cf. cc. 2357, 1-2; 2358; 2359, 2. St. Thomas strictly terms the oppression of a woman abduction or **raptus**, whereas others call it **stuprum**.
23. Cf. c. 1074; cf. **Summa Theol.**, loc. cit., aa. 1, 7.

E. Incest

Incest is sexual intercourse between those who are related by blood or by marriage within the forbidden degrees, and between those legally or spiritually related, i.e., based upon legal adoption or Baptism. Spiritual and legal incest differ specifically from each other and from incest between blood relatives and is at least of graver malice than between in-laws, if not specifically distinct.

Incest is strongly reprobated in Scripture[24] and penalized by the Church (as well as in civil laws).[25] It is a serious sin against chastity and against the piety that is due to those close to us. Venereal union among relatives is especially repugnant (unless dispensed by the power of the Church for proportionate cause) because of the special honor to be mutually shown relatives, the prevention of carnal union among those who must live together, and the fittingness of multiplying friends through marriage.[26]

F. Carnal sacrilege

Carnal sacrilege is the violation by a carnal act of some sacred person, place, or thing. In the strict sense it is a personal sacrilege since the very object is the carnal violation of a sacred person, whereas in a local or real sacrilege the thing or place violated is accessory and a circumstance changing the nature of the sin. The three sacrileges are specifically distinct.

Carnal sacrilege is always a serious sin against chastity; it is also a sin against religion but admits of slightness of matter.[27] A personal carnal sacrilege is committed when a person in sacred orders or with a public vow of chastity is involved. It may be committed by a sacred person alone, either internally or externally, or by a non-sacred person with a sacred person (even when unwilling), or by a sacred person with a non-sacred person (at least cooperating in the sacrilege by voluntarily bearing it). When both persons in an unchaste act are sacred the sacrilege is doubled. A person in sacred orders and public vow commits only one sacri-

24. Lev. 18:6-18; 20:11-17; I Cor. 5:1-5.
25. Cf. cc. 2357, 1; 2358; 2359, 1.
26. Cf. **Summa Theol.**, loc. cit., aa. 1, 9.
27. Cf. ibid., aa. 1, 10.

lege, being obligated by one and the same formal motive, but more gravely. A sacred person who without seeking pleasure for himself induces another to sin against chastity with a third party does not commit a sacrilege.

G. *Obligations in justice*

A fornicator is not bound in justice to restitution toward the woman who willingly fornicates with him unless this is imposed by a judge, or unless the fornicator has damaged her reputation by revealing the crime. Both parents are bound *in solidum et pro rata parte* to provide for the sustenance and education of any offspring, i.e., if either party fails to or cannot contribute a proportionate share of what is needed, then the other party is bound to provide in full.[28] Marriage is not recommended unless all things are prudently judged by the pastor to be present to indicate that the union will be successful and lasting, especially when one party is non-Catholic, even though a civil marriage has already been contracted or most likely will be. The priest should also be satisfied that the woman has not "framed" the man or is not deceiving him as to her condition. Since the bond of a true marriage, especially when it is sacramental, is indissoluble, no priest will be hasty to witness or "fix up" a marriage; if elements of incompatibility or of breakup, whether from the parties themselves or from other factors, are prudently judged to be present, delay at least will be in order until there is more to judge upon.

If a woman has been led into sin through force or fraud, the man alone must repair any damage to the woman, her parents, or to any offspring, being required to bear all the expenses attendant upon the offspring. All things being equal, he has an obligation to marry the woman (which is not grave unless he had promised marriage), or to make it easy for her to marry another. If the

---

28. A prostitute is not bound in justice to restore the price received in plying her trade (cf. **Summa Theol.**, II-II, q. 32, a. 7; q. 62, a. 5, ad 2). S. Poen. 23 aug. 1822: "The woman penitent is not to be forced but to be exhorted to turn over to pious uses the price of her prostitution, according to the judgment of a prudent confessor."

crime is occult and the woman has suffered no damage or has condoned it or has married, died, etc., he has no further obligation.

If a man, whether sincerely or deceitfully, promised marriage in order to achieve intercourse, he is bound in justice to marry the woman as the normal adequate reparation, unless the woman refused or had deceived him also, or the parents are reasonably opposed in the case of a minor, or there is an indispensable impediment, or some other such serious obstacle. Although relieved of the obligation of marriage, he is still bound to repair any damage resulting from the sin, but he is not obligated in strict justice to legitimate the offspring. If a promise of marriage was given in order to engage in impure actions short of intercourse, the man is bound at least in fidelity to the marriage, and in justice if the woman should suffer irreparable damage to her reputation.

If a woman has sinned with two men so that the father of the offspring is uncertain and the woman has concealed her dual sin, neither man has any obligation and the whole obligation toward the offspring rests on the mother. However, if both men were aware of the situation, both are bound, as formal cooperators, to provide along with the mother. The civil law obliges even though it imposes the duty on only one of the men, since its purpose is to provide for the offspring.

If no offspring issues from an act of adultery, the adulterer is not bound in justice to anything beyond seeking pardon of the lawful spouse, when this can be done with a prospect of success. If there is offspring and both parties to the adultery are guilty, both are strictly bound *in solidum* to repair any damage to the innocent spouse or the legitimate children, otherwise only the one who extorted consent to the adultery by force, fear, or fraud. The adulterous woman in every case (and sometimes even the adulterer) is excused from repairing any damage if this can be done only by revealing her crime; the revelation usually results in worse evil than the absence of reparation. In practice in occult cases it is most difficult to urge reparation or restitution without raising greater problems.

Great caution and prudence is required of a pastor and a confessor lest he jeopardize the measure of good faith still actually present in a case by too early an insistence upon restitution or reparation. Before recommending any overt action in any case the pastor or confessor must be morally certain of the obligation in the factual situation in view of all the factors involved. When expedient, advice should be sought from one more expert or experienced, or recourse to such a person is to be recommended. If a woman is unable in practice to make amends, she can always compensate by a more zealous application to her role in the family.

IV. *Sins against chastity completed in a manner precluding the achievement of nature's purpose*

Unnatural sins against chastity are those which are completed in a manner which is opposed to or which frustrates the natural ordination or destination laid down by nature for these acts (*contra naturam*), since they render generation impossible by reason of the ineptness of the acts. Nature itself has established the main purpose for the use of the genital apparatus, thus to frustrate or preclude this purpose is, of itself and other things being equal, the gravest type of violation of chastity. In other sins against chastity, i.e., completed in a way which does not impede generation, the purpose of nature as perceived by reason are frustrated but the natural physical fulfilment of the function of the organs is achieved. The relative gravity of unnatural sins arises from the greater abuse involved than merely from the undue use. In concrete circumstances it sometimes happens that a sin consummated in the natural manner may be more serious than an unnatural sin. This may be due to the fact of many sinful species being involved in one act, or another species than unchastity being incurred (such as injustice in adultery), or the greater malice or boldness of the sinner in sinning, or the future consequences of the action.

A. *Pollution or masturbation*

This sin consists in the separate and complete venereal satisfaction or use of the generative faculty without carnal intercourse. It may be accomplished either alone or with an accomplice; it differs from impure acts and uncompleted acts. Pollution is principally specified by the separate unlawful use of the genital faculty.[29] It is provoked by stimulation of the genital nerves either from physical causes (touches, friction, pressure) or psychical causes (obscene reading or sights, vivid imagination). Pollution differs from distillation which is a subtle, sticky, colorless, non-prolific, urethral and prostratic fluid produced with little or no disturbance or pleasure. Distillation is no sin when there is no sexual satisfaction and no obligation to avoid its cause; when accompanied by venereal pleasure it is judged in gravity and species of unchastity as pollution.

Pollution is *voluntary* when it is freely and deliberately aroused, or when it is freely and deliberately accepted or approved or admitted if it is naturally or spontaneously aroused. It is directly provoked when it is sought for itself, as in self-abuse, or for something else, as producing seed for artificial insemination or medical analysis; it is provoked indirectly or in cause by doing something from which it is foreseen a pollution will result but without precisely intending the latter. Pollution is *involuntary* when it follows from natural causes without the intervention of the will provoking or approving it, e.g., from a physical debility or abnormality, or from natural nocturnal emission, without actual advertence and consent.

The intrinsic and grave malice of direct and perfectly voluntary pollution or masturbation is clearly stated in Scripture[30] and by

29. Pollution is usually accompanied by the effusion of male seed or of the female vulvovaginal fluid and without intercourse. If it takes place deliberately in the course of natural or unnatural sins of unchastity, it is reduced to these sins. It is called: **pollution,** since it as it were stains the subject with this secretion; **softness, (mollities)** since it reveals a weakness or immaturity of spirit; **masturbation (quasi manu-stupratio, manu-turbatio),** since the manual method is the more frequent manner of accomplishing it; **solitary sin** or **self-abuse,** since it is perfectly accomplished by oneself. In a less strict sense it is sometimes called **onanism.**
30. Rom. 1: 24; I Cor. 6:9-10 (**molles** means masturbators); Gal. 5:19; Eph. 5:3.

the Church.[31] Every directly procured or directly consented to pollution is gravely forbidden by the natural law as a serious deordination in the serious matter of the propagation of the race and as frustrative of the natural end for which the generative faculty functions and for which the accompanying pleasure is given. Thus, for no reason, not even to save one's life, can this be allowed. There is no specifically different malice between male or female pollution or masturbation.

The various ways of procuring pollution or of masturbating does not change the formal and specific nature of the sin. There may be an added and specifically different malice involved in one and the same action. Thus, there may be also a sin against justice, e.g., if a married person commits self-abuse or masturbates another or causes pollution in another who is unwilling; against religion, e.g., if the person or place is sacred; against charity, e.g., to masturbate another or cause pollution in another who is willing (which may also easily excite thoughts and desires of fornication, adultery, sodomy, etc.). When only pollution has taken place but the desire or intent was for fornication, adultery, sodomy, etc., the latter must be specifically confessed as well as the masturbation itself.

An indirectly voluntary pollution is seriously or slightly sinful or no sin at all according to the application of the principle of the two-fold effect. It is lawful to do things which are customary in one's condition in life, even though it is foreseen that a pollution will likely follow because of one's excitability, e.g., to wash or bathe, to make a necessary examination of the genital parts, to relieve itching in the area (as long as this is not the result of

---

31. Alexander VII, 24 sept. 1665, condemned the proposition: "Masturbation (**mollities**), sodomy, and bestiality are sins of the same ultimate species; and thus it is enough to say in confession that one has procured a pollution." Denz.-Schön. 2044. Innocent XI, 4 mart. 1679, condemned the proposition: "Masturbation (**mollities**) is not prohibited by the natural law. Wherefore, if God has not forbidden it, it would often be good, and sometimes obligatory under pain of mortal sin." Denz.-Schön. 2149. S. Off. 2 aug. 1929: "Q. Whether directly procured masturbation is allowed in order to obtain sperm by which the contagious disease **blenorragia** (gonorrhea) may be detected and, insofar as it can be done, cured? In the negative." Denz.-Schön. 3684.

The Celebration of Penance 179

passion and there is no consent to any venereal pleasure), to greet another with a handshake or a kiss, to study anatomy, to assist the pregnant, etc. However, when there is proximate danger of consent to a pollution following, although the thing in itself is in no way or only slightly stimulating, it is gravely forbidden.

Passive pollution which takes place in a person involuntarily, either from external causes which cannot or need not be avoided, or from an internal malfunction or ailment, or from a natural excess which the body throws off almost exclusively during a period of sleep, is not sinful at all, even though a dream should spontaneously occur which gives pleasure. For passive pollution occurring during sleep to be voluntary in cause with a grave responsibility or culpability the sources of stimulation, e.g., thoughts, images, reading, etc., must proximately and seriously influence the effect or be fostered for this purpose. If venereal excitement has naturally arisen but then voluntarily sustained or promoted, e.g., by movements, touches, position, etc., it is seriously sinful. There is no strong obligation to restrain by positive methods a pollution which has involuntarily arisen, as long as there is no proximate danger of consent; however, indirect methods are recommended such as prayer, distraction of the mind, change of position or of location, etc. When one adverts to the onslaught or to the instant of orgasm and can do something about it easily and without hardship, there is a slight obligation to resist at least indirectly, lest knowingly and willingly one permit the rebellion of concupiscence and risk some consent. It is not sinful to have an inefficacious desire for or rejoice in the fact of a merely natural pollution which occurs in the normal manner of nature's functioning to relieve itself and to quiet disturbance, as long as the willing of it through aid, approval, or consent is absent. For medical reasons medicines may be taken to regulate natural pollutions, but medicine may not be taken for the purpose of producing a pollution, since this would be to intend it for its own sake.

Masturbation is the most widespread sin of impurity, especially among the youth of both sexes. It is a sin extremely easy to commit, the habit or practice is swiftly acquired. On the other hand, as a temptation it is a hard thing to overcome, and as a habit it disappears only slowly and, as it were, grudgingly, through persevering efforts continued despite failures and setbacks. Pastoral efforts both in and out of the confessional with regard to victims of this sin demand on the part of the priest or confessor great patience, kindness, and understanding, and even a constant struggle against discouragement, if these efforts are to achieve any success. Each individual case must be considered on its own merits and in the context of its problems, history, and the present attitude, understanding, and applied resistance of the sufferer. Mutual masturbation or exhibitionistic masturbation does not usually or necessarily imply homosexual or lesbian affection or desire. There are no hard and fast rules of thumb to be applied to every concrete case. The priest in the busy confessional can at least give his advice on the basis of the commonly recommended supernatural and natural remedies and aids; the more personal attention to the individual he can give in the limited time and circumstances the better. The habitual sinner and those whose masturbatory difficulties are more than transitory should return frequently to the same confessor. The priest will always offer encouragement, as well as help to overcome guilt anxiety or discouragement. It is recommended that wherever possible and prudently expedient both for penitent and priest the confessor's help should be given at least from time to time outside of the confessional (even though the victim may wish it to be under the seal) in order to provide time and even less formal atmosphere for fuller discussion and help. Good will and the desire to struggle for victory despite difficulties and failures are indispensable in the repentant sinner or victim of this habit.

The remedies of the supernatural order that are always to be urged upon every sinner are prayer which is persevering and an unwavering confidence in the grace of God who allows no one to be tempted beyond his strength to resist and overcome.[32] Frequent confession, especially after a fall, cannot be too highly recommended; also frequent Holy Communion, even daily reception; a spirit of mortification of the senses and the imagination in order to control the lower appetites and self-will and to strengthen the

---

32. I Cor. 10:13.

will itself in the pursuit of perfection and holiness in a state of grace; the fostering of a generous will to cultivate chastity and to resist even the remoter stimuli to sin; an appreciation of sex and purity in the plan of salvation and in the context of true love; devotion to one's guardian angel and daily petition for the intercession of the Virgin Mary; and supernatural motivations. In the natural order a better realization of the occasions of temptation and the circumstances which make temptation more influential and acceptable can aid in bringing about the removal of the causes of relapse, based especially on the sinner's history or experience. Various suggestions that may be made depend upon the personality and condition of the sinner in the particular case and his peculiar problem, e.g., avoidance of idleness and of daydreaming, at least of a dangerous type, as well as the tendency or temptation to melancholy; better regulation or organization of one's day and activities; cessation of overdelay in rising from bed or in taking care of the necessities of nature; not retiring before being sufficiently tired to go to sleep reasonably promptly; sufficient physical exercise, fresh air, and rest; adequate emotional and intellectual recreation to avoid or lessen tensions; physical cleanliness, especially genital hygiene; care in the selection and use of protective devices during the menstrual period; greater moderation in eating and drinking, especially alcohol; choice of companions of either sex; diversion of attention to other non-sexual things of interest, or walking away; clothing that is not too binding or covering that is not too warm; etc.

The sin of masturbation must be first judged objectively on the basis of the norms given above. Difficulty often arises in judging the subjective guilt. It must not be assumed that an individual has not committed serious sin; investigation in this complex matter must be made of the sufficient advertence or reflection and understanding and a full consent of the will. With some youths and adolescents there can be a lack of understanding or deliberation of the serious nature of the impure action, although if they confess it, they realize that something is morally wrong. The more deeply engrained the habit or the more vehement the passion the less free will be the consent and responsibility and culpability in the individual act may be lessened. When it is prudently judged that a particular act in the circumstances is not seriously sinful, it is not recommended that the sinner be informed, unless he directly asks (and then the priest explains what serious guilt requires and lets the individual draw the conclusion), but rather he is to be encouraged and exhorted to greater efforts toward rehabilitation in the future. The normal person should be assured that his problem is not an abnormal one or unique, and that it is soluble; the truly abnormal person may be judged (not too readily but with the cautious judgment of prudence) to be in need also of medical or psychiatric advice and help, but even here the priest may be the only person in practice to whom the sinner can or will turn, and thus he must do what he can to help as a theologian and spiritual counselor and not simply as a medical or psychiatric practitioner or amateur.

B. *Sodomy and homosexuality*

This sin, so-called from the vice of the citizens of ancient Sodom, in the strict sense is unnatural carnal copulation with a person of the same sex, and in the wider sense it is rectal intercourse with a person of the opposite sex. Carnal union or copulation differs specifically from an impure touch when some member of one person touches the genitals (or body in general) of another and in turn is usually so touched, e.g., mutual masturbation, etc. Carnal copulation, however, includes an affection for or inclination toward a person of the same sex and in its overt expression includes an application of the genitals of one party to the body of another in the manner of intercourse, although this is unnatural. With persons of the same sex the species of the sin is not changed by the circumstance of age, agent (*pygista*) or patient (*mollis*), etc.

The condition of an affection for persons of the same sex and for intercourse with the same is homosexuality in the strict sense and is called perfect sodomy. Although usually anal, the simulated intercourse may take place in any part or orifice of the body of the accomplice[33] and does not specifically distinguish the sin. Female

---

33. Oral insertion is called **irrumatio**, anal is **pedicatio**. **Uranistae**

sodomy or homosexuality is also termed lesbianism, sapphism, tribadism; it is accomplished by one party with an unusually large clitoris assuming the role of a man, or by the employment of an artificial penis (*phallus*), or in the common manner of mutual application of the labia genitalia (*fricatio*). Imperfect sodomy is carnal union between two persons of opposite sexes but unnaturally accomplished, i.e., anally. Coition between man and woman which is not anal is not presumed to be sodomy but rather fornication in intent or affection and pollution in effect or fact.

Sodomy, more grave because more unnatural than pollution, is reprobated by Scripture[34] and penalized by the Church.[35] In addition to the malice of pollution it adds the malice of affection for the same sex and/or for the *vas indebitum*, i.e., for a part of the body not destined or apt for copulation and generation.[36] Charity is violated because of cooperation in one another's sin, and other malices may be added inasmuch as there is involved the circumstance of marital bond, consanguinity, etc.

Since affection for the same sex is more repugnant to nature than for the *vas indebitum*, perfect sodomy is specifically distinct from and graver than imperfect sodomy. Also, consummated or completed and unconsummated or inchoate sodomy differ specifically.

Homosexuality (or uranism) in its various forms and degrees is widespread in modern cities; it is frequently found in military forces, prisons, ships, etc. Among a certain percentage of homosexuals (also called inverts, perverts, sexual deviates or gays) the vice is organized. The priest is called upon to deal with this type of sin in the confessional for the most part. Those who are inveterate homosexuals, even professionals, seldom contact the priest. However, even hardened cases can be helped and at least brought to a stage of cessation of overt acts and to the constant striving to maintain chastity, although a heterosexual condition or inclination may

> are adults involved with each other, **paederastae** are adults with youths, **gerontophilia** is toward old men.

34. Gen. 13:13; 18:20; 19:1-19; Lev. 18:22; 20:13; Deut. 29:23; Rom. 1:26-28.
35. Cf. cc. 2357-2359.
36. Cf. **Summa Theol.**, II-II, q. 154, aa. 11-12.

be impossible of realization in the particular individual. Some, particularly adolescents, engage in some homosexual activity, but it is transitory, i.e., a phase of weakness or immaturity which they can work out with help; they are not in the condition of a homosexual, i.e., they are not homosexual at heart. Others are in the condition of homosexuals but manage to maintain chastity and refrain from overt actions (or have overcome the vice). It is important for the priest to try to discover the actual situation of the sinner, as far as he discreetly can in this difficult and delicate matter, in order better to assist the sinner to regain grace and confidence. The same qualities of kindness, understanding, patience, and perseverance, as with the masturbators, is demanded of the priest with the care of homosexual sinners.

Here also the absence of moral responsibility or of serious subjective culpability must not be presumed. The deeper the habit is rooted in the individual the less the moral guilt may be in an individual action, as noted above in the case of masturbators. However, the removal of all responsibility would be the more advanced or extreme case. The homosexual is capable of controlling his sexual desires and impulses as also the heterosexual must. Although he may be responsible for the origin of his habit, if he has good will and effort he can set his will against the habit and with help under grace can improve and succeed. The sympathetic priest will treat this type of sinner in a manner similar to those with masturbatory or other sexual problems. The occasions of this sin must be vigorously avoided and care taken not to substitute other vices in its stead. He must be docile in rectifying an erroneous conscience.

C. *Bestiality*

Bestiality is copulation of a human being with an animal, regardless of its sex or of the manner by which it is accomplished. The touching of an animal, even with venereal satisfaction or pleasure, is not bestiality if there is no immoral affection for it.

This sin is condemned in Scripture[37] and penalized by the Church as with sodomy. It is the worst of the sins of unchastity in itself,

---

37. Lev. 20:15-16; Exod. 22:19.

since it is the extreme deviation from the natural order and most degrading of human dignity, not preserving even the human species. Completed and uncompleted sins differ specifically.

E. *Some sexual conditions and perversions*

Anaesthesia: an inability to arouse the sexual appetite by any means; more commonly found among women as frigidity.

Hypothesia: a languid and weak sexual appetite often found in women of devout purity and dedication to family life and sometimes in men of the sexually peripheric type who are content in their job and leading a good life.

Hyperaesthesia: a morbidly intense sexual excitability more acute in women in whom sex features strongly in their lives and which at times is connected with an abnormal inclination to venereal things or with sexual paresthesia; the insatiable carnal ardor in men is called *satyriasis,* the unbridled libido in women *nymphomania.*

Paradoxism or sexual paradox: the condition of abnormal sexual disturbances before the usual age of puberty or before the seventh or eighth year and in advanced senility, and often accompanied by self-abuse; a form of hyperaesthesia.

Religious paranoia: a manifestation of hyperaesthesia mostly found in women, especially the unmarried, who find libidinous satisfaction in a religious fanaticism directed toward confessors, images of saints, etc. Such hidden mixture of religiosity and sexuality offers great danger for confessor and priest who must always be on guard against such people, as they have not infrequently been the source of great grief and disasters. Morbid egoism, abnormal inconstancy, and mendacity, the signs and symbols of this abnormality, escape easy categorization, and, as is usually stated, in hysteria nothing is constant besides its inconstancy.

Paraesthesia: a condition existing when the sex life is not affected by venereal matters but by objects quite foreign to them. It takes many forms.

Symbolism: the use of the symbols of persons themselves in order to satisfy the sexual drive, e.g., underclothes, a shoe.

Fetichism: the excitement of sexual passion by things which in themselves have no relation to sex nor imagined in connection with any person, e.g., the imagination or sight or touch of a hand, hair, garment, shoe, etc., without any further desire. Sometimes this is connected with transvestism.

Exhibitionism: an impulse to show off the private parts to a member of the opposite sex, even with long delays suffered in order to seize the most rewarding occasion. It is more frequent with men.

Sadism: venereal pleasure which is aroused by real or imaginary actions on another that are actively and poignantly cruel and which inflict pain, e.g., striking, whipping, cutting, stabbing, strangling. It is found more in men and was named after the Marquis de Sade, an eighteenth century aristocrat, who described his own perversions.

Masochism: sexual pleasure derived from the real or imaginary suffering of pain, e.g., being struck, kicked, whipped, cut. It is less frequent in men than in women and is named after the novelist, L. von Sacher-Masoch, who described this perversion in several of his works.

Erotic mysticism: a union or mixture of typically sexual affections and actions with religious worship, such as occurred among ancient pagan religions and practices. True mystics, on the other hand (as well as Scripture itself), sometimes employ terms taken from sexual life to express desires and experiences which cannot be otherwise made intelligible regarding the heights of spiritual intimacy they enjoy in supernatural love.

Narcisism: delight in one's own body and an indifference to that of others; an autoeroticism or autism, even to the kissing of one's own image in a mirror. It is more frequent in women than in men.

Transformism: also called transvestism or the inclination to be transformed into the person of the opposite sex or the desire to be treated as one by accommodating or conditioning one's senses and actions to this tendency, e.g., wearing the clothes of the opposite sex, by promoting bodily changes such as the development of breasts in a man or by surgery.

Necrophilia: a rare and perverted affection for dead bodies. A similar perversion is *statuophilia* or a perverted affection for statues. This is probably pollution with the desire for the type of person whom the corpse represents or substitutes for.

Voyeurs have a tendency to peep at objects of sexual interest ("peeping Toms"); *renifleurs* and the *coprophilous* are attracted to excrement.

Pastoral concern:

The influence of sex upon the lives of individuals differs greatly (in addition to the difference of sexual tendency between man and woman), both by reason of temperament and environmental influences and by reason of deliberate attitude. Some people are very little aroused by spontaneous sexual tendencies or stimuli, others are so disturbed that sex seems to be the main focus of their life, while still others are positively and vividly disturbed by sexual drives and stimuli from time to time but not so as to absorb their whole attention. Similarly the deliberate attitude of some toward sex matters is libidinous or fully engaged, others are ascetic in outlook with their thoughts and affections above the considerations of sex, while still others seek sexual interests now and again but without being habitually or wholly absorbed.

The priest and confessor is bound to be most cautious in treating matters of sexual deviation. Mental diseases and pathological conditions can diminish and even destroy responsibility. Although the sinner may be at fault for the origin or acquisition of his vice, in long-term and advanced cases at least responsibility will be lessened in individual acts by reason of insufficient reflection or full and free consent. In some cases of hypersexuality the slight and trivial things which cause sexual excitement may be allowed inasmuch as these things of themselves have little or no influence on sexual concupiscence and there is no proximate danger of consent. Sexual sinners should be encouraged in their struggle and helped from falling into discouragement and depression; where they return to the same confessor they should be able to show evidences of their sincerity and purpose of amendment.

V. *Internal sins against chastity*

A. *Morose delectation*

Morose delectation is the deliberate complacency taken in an unchaste action as such thought of as present but without any purpose of carrying it into execution. It is not merely the fact that bad thoughts, obscene imaginations or representations of unchaste things, are in the mind, but rather the complacency or enjoyment of the will in them. Thus deliberate pleasure is called morose (from *mora*) even if protracted for only the briefest space of time.[38]

To think over or to analyze things which are unchaste (or merely the technique or skillful manner of accomplishment) on a merely theoretical level for the sake of knowledge, study, etc., is not sinful or only slightly sinful if there is not sufficient reason and this is done out of mere curiosity or levity. Care, however, must be taken in such matters since, given the concupiscence of fallen man, the jump is not too difficult between delight in a knowledge of such things and pleasure in the things themselves with attendant danger of carnal disturbance and consent.[39]

Morose delectation in venereal satisfaction itself with full advertence and consent is seriously sinful, being sinful affection. Often full deliberate action is not verified and at most the sin is one of negligence in not repressing such thoughts or images. In doubt of consent presumption of lack of consent or of full consent can be given to one who tries to combat such temptations and is displeased with any failure, whereas the opposite presumption is given to one who easily falls into or is given to libidinous things. To provoke such thoughts and images out of levity or curiosity or to entertain or retain them out of neglect or idleness is seriously or slightly sinful in the measure of the influence they have in exciting the passions and the proximity of danger of consent.

B. *Sinful desire*

Sinful desire is the deliberate act of the will to do something

---

38. Cf. **Summa Theol.**, I-II, q. 74, a. 6.
39. **Ibid.**, aa. 7-8.

unchaste, or complacency in an unchaste act unlawfully to be performed in the future. The desire is efficacious if there is a genuine intent to do it, inefficacious if the purpose is to do it except that the action is seen to be impeded and cannot be fulfilled or the intention depends upon a condition to be verified.

An absolute or efficacious desire is seriously sinful in the same species as the unchaste object desired, e.g., to commit adultery, even if it does not take place. An inefficacious desire that is hindered of fulfilment is similarly sinful, e.g., to fornicate with a particular woman desired by a man in prison for life; to be saddened over having missed a particular opportunity to commit an unchaste sin. A conditioned desire is not sinful if the condition removes the malice of unchastity from the object, e.g., to marry a certain person if she were not already married, but not if only part of the malice is removed, e.g., a desire to commit an unchaste sin if there were only no hell, to commit fornication if the person were not in religion.

Whereas morose delectation generally is not concerned with circumstances changing the nature of a sin, sinful desire can take this into consideration, e.g., to entertain unchaste desires toward a single or a married person. Confessors may judge it prudent not to question about the ultimate species especially where it would be fruitless for the particular penitents.

C. *Sinful joy*

Sinful joy is the pleasure taken in a previously committed sin of unchastity, a complacency in an unchaste act unlawfully performed in the past (but not in a past lawful act in marriage).

Sinful joy is of the same species and gravity as the past recalled sin, as a sort of deliberate continuation. The object and circumstances affecting the malice should be confessed, but often a sinner has abstracted from the circumstance and enjoyed recalling merely the act itself. A confessor may question a sinner confessing "bad thoughts" (by which term people generally mean all internal sins) to ascertain if the thought was of a past sin and also about the object, e.g., adultery, fornication, sodomy, or if it was not a past sin but morose delectation, whether any desire was also present.[40]

VI. *External uncompleted sins against chastity*

A. *Carnal disturbance*

Carnal disturbances or venereal motions of the sexual organs are those which are in some degree deliberately caused or approved for the venereal pleasure which they afford. Thus they differ from the carnal movements which arise from natural physical or mechanical causes without pleasure. Carnal disturbances which are directly willed or willed indirectly or in cause are judged by the principles already explained.

Resistance to involuntary sexual disturbance is of obligation insofar as there is danger of consent present, and a grave duty if the danger is proximate. Normally, slight and quickly passing carnal disturbances should not be bothered about lest the imagination be aroused or the association of ideas stimulated and the disturbance aggravated. Often an internal act of displeasure will suffice. In more vehement disturbance stronger positive or active resistance is necessary, although usually of an indirect type and especially if experience has shown that direct attack tends to aggravate the problem. When there is proportionate cause and no proximate danger of consent, in necessary or useful activities simple displeasure will suffice.

B. *Impure actions*

Impure or immodest actions are those which of their nature are apt to excite venereal pleasure, although not venereal in themselves. They are morally indifferent and become sinful through an intention to excite or because of their strong or slight influence in exciting venereal pleasure. In judging the lawfulness or the

---

40. Innocent XI (4 mart. 1679) condemned the proposition: "It is lawful for a son to rejoice over the patricide of his parent which he perpetrated when drunk, because of the immense wealth that resulted from it by inheritance." Denz.-Schön. 2115.

degree of sinfulness in concrete cases consideration must be given to the character and circumstance of the action, the temperament and condition of the agent, his previous experience, and the sufficiency of the reason for acting. Thus judgment will vary by reason of the action in question and the person affected. The parts of the body are divided in their influence upon sexual pleasure into non-stimulating or decent (*honestae*) parts which normally offer no danger of unchastity (face, hands, feet), lightly stimulating or less decent (*minus honestae*) which are commonly covered at least partially (breast, back, arms, legs), gravely stimulating or indecent (*turpes*) (sex organs and adjacent parts).

It is a serious sin to *touch* any part of one's own or another's body with an impure desire or intent; it is a slight sin to do so out of sensuality, unless done passingly. A proportionately reasonable cause of necessity or true usefulness permits the handling even of one's very stimulating parts, even if incidentally orgasm should take place, keeping the danger of consent remote, e.g., to bathe, relieve irritation, use medication. If done from a less adequate reason, from curiosity or levity and not prolonged, the sin is usually not more than slight.

Regardless of sex, it is seriously sinful to touch the indecent parts of others, even over the clothing, unless with sufficient reason, e.g., a physician; if done passingly or from levity or jest without evil intent, it is usually a slight sin. To touch the less decent parts of the same sex is usually a slight sin but serious regarding the opposite sex, unless done passingly from levity or jest without evil intent.

Decent *kissing and embracing* as accepted custom among honorable people as a sign of friendship, politeness, relationship, or noble love is lawful between persons even of opposite sexes, barring any evil intent or desire. Consent must be withheld from any incidental venereal satisfaction that might result. These actions which may occur in honest recreation or games are not necessarily to be judged serious. Ardent, prolonged, and repeated kissing and embracing is frequently a serious sin (excluding parents and children). In company-keeping with a view to marriage ordinary kissing and embracing within the bounds of moderation and motivated by a pure affection is permissible, even if some incidental sexual excitement should result which is resisted and not consented to. Even the slightest degree of venereal pleasure as such may not be intended or consented to.

Kisses and embraces which are not in themselves indecent but evidence a sensual or sexual motivation by the other party are to be resisted; they may be in some measure tolerated to avoid embarassment or defamation of either party, as long as they are disapproved and scandal is avoided. They must be avoided and actively resisted if they are indecent and also because of the duty to avoid scandal. Kissing with the tongues is usually seriously sinful as gravely stimulating and dangerous; kissing the genitals is absolutely forbidden.

For any reasonable cause it is lawful to *look* at one's own indecent parts. To do so out of curiosity or levity is usually not more than a slight sin. Unless done intentionally for some time or with evil intent, to glance at the indecent parts of another of the same sex out of curiosity or levity is usually not more than a slight sin. Unless for a reason of necessity or great usefulness, e.g., in the case of a physician, to gaze at the indecent parts (naked or thinly veiled) of the opposite sex is usually a serious sin, unless done unexpectedly by chance or hastily or at a distance or regarding little children (also prolonged gazes on female breasts or thighs are usually provocative to men). If there is no sexual affection, gazes upon the less decent parts of one's own body or of that of another of the same sex is usually no sin or at most a light sin. The same may be said regarding the opposite sex, although a more strict judgment regarding circumstances and intent must be made here. To observe animal mating out of curiosity or without reasonable cause is slightly sinful barring venereal intent or disturbance, but it is more serious to gaze at human coition except perhaps passingly and from a distance.

It is lawful to look upon nude or lightly covered statues or pictures which are artistic and not lascivious in intent or representation and which distract from the venereal, at least for the majority of viewers with prudence and right intention who are accustomed to view these representations. To view the truly lascivious or obscene representation is generally a serious sin, unless done passingly or without venereal desire or by those who from experience are not disturbed. Sensual curiosity in these matters would be a slight sin.

Unchaste *speech* and *songs* are gravely or slightly sinful in the degree of influence they exert in arousing carnal pleasure. This very often depends upon the people involved, e.g., among older people or adolescents, in mixed age or sex groups, and upon the intent and circumstances, e.g., evil intention, scandal, sinful joy, or levity. It is probable that the number of listeners need not be mentioned when confessing the sin of scandal, but it is at least recommended for the good of the penitent and the judgment of the confessor. It is not a sin to overhear obscenities when this is not voluntary or not a positive encouragement to the speaker or singer and no scandal is given. Voluntary listening is judged by the degree of influence in arousing sexual pleasure, or the curiosity or human respect involved. It is not necessary for one to change his occupation in the presence of the foul-mouthed but rather to do what is possible and prudent in order to discourage such language, etc. Merely vulgar talk concerning the needs of nature, etc., is not unchaste but rather uncharitable insofar as it wounds sensibilities. Certain words of endearment may be sinful among particular persons.

The *reading* of books which excite passion or sexual pleasure is sinful in the degree of influence of the book or passages in it. That which is slightly indecent and read from curiosity, etc., is at best slightly sinful, unless grave temptations are frequently aroused. Some excitable literature may be read for proportionate cause by those who must acquire necessary knowledge, such as physicians, censors, teachers, etc. The reason must be proportionate also to the danger of consent.

Company keeping with the intention of early marriage can be considered as a necessary occasion of sin, since in our society at least people do not marry strangers. However, those keeping company and especially the engaged are not allowed any sexual liberties, since these are forbidden to all outside the married state. They must use the ordinary supernatural and natural means whereby the proximate occasion of falling into sin (especially after unfortunate experience) is made remote, notably in regard to circumstances of being alone together. Juvenile steady dating or "going steady" should be discouraged, since it can be dangerous. There is no intention or possibility of early marriage. In the confessional or in counselling, the individuals and circumstances, their past experience, etc., must be considered proportionate to the dangers involved, as serious sin or proximate occasion is not necessarily verified for all cases.

THE CELEBRATION OF THE ANOINTING OF THE SICK

I. Role of the Sacrament of the Anointing of the Sick

The sufferings and infirmities of man, especially those which trouble his conscience, affect the Christian as well. But, Christ's disciple is aided and sustained by his faith in the measure that he penetrates the mystery of suffering and courageously bears his sufferings, for which reason also he is beloved of Christ. Sickness and infirmity, not unconnected with man's sinful condition and present despite his diligent care, fill up for the Christian what are lacking on our part of the sufferings of Christ for the salvation of the world. Moreover, the ill and the infirm by their witness are a reminder to others of what is essential and is above; they show that the mortal frailty of man is to be redeemed through the mystery of Christ's own death and resurrection.[1]

Thus, by the sacred anointing of the sick and the prayers of her priests the whole Church commends those who are ill to the suffering and glorified Lord, asking that he may lighten their suffering and save them. She exhorts them, moreover, to contribute to the welfare of the whole People of God by associating themselves freely with the passion and death of Christ.[2] In this sacred Unction, connected with the prayer of faith, there is expressed that faith which is to be aroused in him who administers and above all in him who receives this sacrament. The faith of the sick person and that of the Church will save him—a faith which is mindful of the death and resurrection of Christ whence all sacramental efficacy derives and which looks forward to the future kingdom pledged in the sacraments.[3]

1. **Ordo unctionis infirmorum eorumque pastoralis curae**, nn. 1-3, S.C.C.D., 7 dec. 1972.
2. Vat. II, Const. **Lumen Gentium**, 11. This sacrament has usually been called Extreme Unction, because it is normally the last of the holy oils to be administered in life (cf. Const. **Sacrosanctum Concilium**, 73). From its matter it is sometimes called "holy oil" or "prayer with oil," or "oil of the sick" or "sacrament of the dying" from its recipient.

The work of reconciliation with God and with his Church which has taken place in the sacrament of Penance is brought to fulfillment, therefore, in the sacrament of the Anointing of the Sick, which is celebrated in the circumstances of dangerous personal illness or old age. It has always been understood in the Church as the sacrament which completes not only Penance but also the whole Christian life, which ought to be a continual penance. Our benevolent Redeemer has always provided salutary remedies against the weapons of all man's enemies, especially in the sacraments whereby the Christian may during his lifetime keep himself free from spiritual harm. Notably in the circumstance of dangerous and debilitating illness the adversary of our soul strains more vehemently to bring us to utter spiritual ruin even by tempting us to lose faith in the divine mercy. In a period of such illness (or old age), when strength is weakened against the onslaughts of the devil, the inclinations and anxieties of wounded nature, and the impact of worldly factors, this sacrament, imparting its own special grace, is the strongest defence in the preservation of union with God in grace and charity.[4]

It is of faith that the sacrament of Unction of the Sick was instituted by Christ[5] for the remission of sins and the comforting of the sick.[6] It has three effects: the principal effect is to strengthen

3. **Ordo unctionis infirmorum eorumque pastoralis curae,** n. 7.
4. Cf. Trent, Denz.-Schön. 1694, 1696.
5. **Ibid.,** 1695; cf. 1716. Const. Apost. **Sacram unctionem infirmorum,** 30 nov. 1972: "The Catholic Church professes and teaches that the Sacred Anointing of the Sick is one of the seven Sacraments of the New Testament, that it was instituted by Christ, and that it was 'alluded to in Mark (6:13) and recommended and promulgated to the faithful by James the Apostle and brother of the Lord'."
6. Const. Apost. **Sacram unctionem infirmorum:** "This reality is in fact the grace of the Holy Spirit, whose anointing takes away sins, if any still remain to be taken away, and the remnants of sin; it also relieves and strengthens the soul of the sick person, arousing in him a great confidence in the divine mercy whereby, being thus sustained, he more easily bears the trials and labors of his sickness, more easily resists the temptations of the devil 'lying in wait' (Gen. 3:15), and sometimes regains bodily health, if this is expedient for the health of the soul."

the soul to overcome the remains of sin or the weakness in the soul, due to a proneness to evil and a languor in the pursuit of good, anxieties, fear, torpor, and all such debilities left behind in the soul from original sin and accentuated by personal sins, and to withstand the final assaults of the devil; secondary effects following upon the grace of strength are the remission of sins and, if expedient for spiritual welfare, bodily health.[7]

As a sacrament of the living the Anointing of the Sick presupposes divine friendship and grace in the soul,' but accidentally, if sins are present, they are remitted, with at least attrition on the part of the recipient, both as to guilt and punishment. This is most important in the case of the dying who are unconscious and unable to confess or receive Viaticum. When, in the disposition of divine providence, it is expedient for the welfare of the soul, sometimes bodily health is restored by aiding and sustaining the natural forces combatting the dangerous sickness.

Although it is not a necessary means of salvation, no one is allowed to neglect this sacrament.[8] It is commonly taught that there is of itself a light obligation to receive it, in the absence of a grave divine or ecclesiastical precept. However, failure to receive the sacrament due to contempt or serious negligence when it is most needed or with resultant scandal would be a serious sin.

II. Requisite Material

The material of the sacrament of the Anointing of the Sick is olive oil, or, if opportune, another vegetable oil, properly blessed for this purpose by a bishop or by a priest who has the faculty to do so from the law itself or by an indult of the Apostolic See.[9] Besides the bishop himself, the law also grants the faculty to bless

Cf. Denz.-Schön. 1696, 1717.

7. **Ordo unctionis infirmorum eorumque pastoralis curae**, n. 6.
8. c. 944.
9. **Ordo unctionis infirmorum eorumque pastoralis curae**, nn. 20-21.

oil to be used in this sacrament to one who in law is equivalent to the diocesan bishop, and, in case of real need, to any priest who may thus bless the oil in the actual ceremony of the anointing.[10]

An admixture of extraneous matter renders the oil invalid material, if it is no longer olive or vegetable oil.[11] Although it is not certain that the Oil of the Infirm alone renders the celebration of this sacrament valid, in practice and outside of necessity and in the absence of the proper oil, another sacred oil may be employed under a condition ("if this is valid material"), but the sacrament must be later repeated with the properly blessed oil.

The oil is customarily blessed on the Holy Thursday of the same year by the bishop, from whom it must be obtained even by exempt religious.[12] New oils should be obtained promptly by the pastor either personally or through another, even a trustworthy layman, if there is a good cause.[13] Old oil is burned in the sanctuary lamp; oil that is soaked in cotton is to be burned and the ashes placed in the sacrarium, e.g., in the case of a priest who blesses oil for the conferral of this sacrament in the case of true need.[14] The sacred oil should be kept in a decent and appropriate phial sufficiently filled with oil-soaked cotton. It should be kept, when not in use, in an honorable place. The supply of sacred oil should be renewed as often as necessary, if the supply obtained from the bishop of Holy Thursday becomes inadequate.[15]

Although the minimum of a drop of oil is valid material, the thumb of the minister should be dipped into the holy oil for each anointing in order better to secure a sufficient amount for each unction. It must be spread on the forehead and hands (usually in the form of a cross) or, because of the particular condition of the sick person, on another more suitable part of the body (not merely dropped or touched to the sense), the whole formula being

---

10. **Ibid.**, n. 21.
11. If the supply of blessed oil becomes too diminished, other olive oil may be added, even repeatedly, but in a lesser quantity. (c. 734, 2)
12. **Ordo unctionis infirmorum eorumque pastoralis curae,** n. 21.
13. Holy oils should not be sent through the mails or entrusted to an express company.
14. **Ordo unctionis infirmorum eorumque pastoralis curae,** n. 22.
15. **Ibid.**

pronounced. Both hands are anointed while the second part of the formula is being pronounced.[16] If a hand is mutilated or cut off, the anointing is made on the nearest portion.

Thus, in a case of necessity it is sufficient to make a single anointing on the forehead or, because of the particular condition of the sick person, on another more suitable part of the body, the whole formula being pronounced.[17]

III. Prescribed Words or Formula

The prescribed words or formula of the sacrament of the Anointing of the Sick are: Through this holy anointing may the Lord in his love and mercy help you with the grace of the Holy Spirit.
The sick person responds: *Amen.*
May the Lord who frees you from sin save you and raise you up.
The sick person responds: *Amen.*[18]

IV. Minister of the Celebration of the Unction of the Sick

The proper minister of the Unction of the Sick is only a priest and every priest, even those censured or degraded. The ordinary minister is the bishop, the pastor and his parochial cooperators, priests to whom is committed the care of homes for the sick and the elderly, and superiors of clerical religious communities.[19]

Other priests, with the assent of the ordinary minister, may

---

16. **Ibid.**, n. 23. Particular Rituals in the future may provide for additional unctions (ibid., n. 24).
17. **Ibid.**
18. Const. Apost. **Sacram unctionem infirmorum; Ordo unctionis infirmorum eorumque pastoralis curae.** n. 25. NCCB 4 ian. 1974
19. **Ordo unctionis infirmorum eorumque pastoralis curae.** n. 16. The clerical religious superior may anoint the ill novices and professed who are outside the religious house (PCI 16 iun. 1931). In a monastery of nuns the ordinary confessor or the one taking his place has the right and duty to anoint (c. 514, 2). In lay religious institutes it pertains to the local pastor or to

confer this sacrament. They may also anoint in a case of necessity and with presumed assent of the pastor or chaplain of the home, whom they later inform.[20] To act outside of necessity without at least presumed permission is seriously prohibited and of itself a serious violation of a pastoral right.[21] In prudent doubt of the presence of necessity or of required assent, the priest may always lawfully anoint.[22]

When two or more priests are attending a sick person, one may say the prayers and perform the anointing with its formula, while the others may perform the other parts of the rite. All priests may impose hands.[23]

The ordinary minister is seriously bound to celebrate the sacrament of Unction of the Sick personally or through another.[24] To delay the conferral with exposure of the ill person to dying without it would be a serious sin. However, the minister is not bound to confer the sacrament with special danger to his life, unless it is morally necessary for salvation or more certainly valid than Penance in the case, as in the situation of the unconscious who have not confessed for a long time. He is not so bound in the latter case if the disposition of the candidate (and thus the effect of the conferral) is not certain, or even if certain, a greater evil to the common good would result from the death of the priest (e.g., where there is a scarcity of priests, or in mission territories).

The ordinary minister is to prepare the faithful in general and families in particular in such a way that they are led to look

>the chaplain to whom the local Ordinary has granted this right (**ibid.**, 3; 464, 2). It is the right and duty of the rector in a seminary (c. 1368).

20. **Ordo unctionis infirmorum eorumque pastoralis curae,** n. 18. It belongs to the local Ordinary to regulate those celebrations where the sick from different parishes or homes for the sick are brought together to be anointed (**ibid.**, n. 17).
21. cc. 462, 3º; 451.
22. Cf. c. 939. No priest may anoint himself (S.C.P.F. 23 mart. 1844).
23. **Ordo unctionis infirmorum eorumque pastoralis curae,** n. 19.
24. Cf. c. 939; also Pius XII. Discourse "The Foundations and Norms of Christian Morality for the 'Exercise of the Mission of Health'," 12 nov. 1944.

forward to this sacred anointing and to receive it promptly and at the opportune time with great faith and devotion. Moreover, those who assist the sick should be taught the role of this sacrament.[25]

V. Candidates for the Sacrament of the Anointing of the Sick

As soon as anyone of the faithful begins to be in danger of death from sickness or old age, the appropriate time for him to receive this sacrament has certainly already arrived.[26] Thus this sacrament can be validly conferred only on a person who has been baptized by water, who has or at least has had the use of reason, and who is in danger of death from sickness or old age.

Being the completion and consummation of Penance, the Unction of the Sick acts to strengthen the soul against the remnants of sin and the assaults of the devil, all of which the infant (and the perpetually demented) is incapable, not having attained the use of reason. The sacrament therefore requires the existence at some time (although the person may be presently unconscious or demented) of *some use of reason* and thus of a capability of temptation and inducement to commit at least a slight sin; it strengthens against them. It is not required that sin has been actually committed but only that the person is capable of sinning. Thus the sacrament may be conferred immediately after the Baptism of a dying adult[27] in order to strengthen against temptation, such as the fear of death. It is conferred also on the sick who have lost their senses or use of reason but when in possession of their faculties had, as faithful, sought the Sacred Unction.[28]

Children in danger of death who have reached their first use of reason should be anointed, even before they have made their

25. **Ordo unctionis infirmorum eorumque pastoralis curae**, nn. 13, 17.
26. Vat. II, Const. **Sacrosanctum Concilium**, n. 73; **Ordo unctionis infirmorum eorumque pastoralis curae**, n. 8.
27. S. Off. 10 maii 1703; S.C.P.F. 26 sept. 1821; presupposing a sufficient intention of receiving this sacrament (S. Off. 10 apr. 1861).
28. **Ordo unctionis infirmorum eorumque pastoralis curae**, n. 14.

first Confession or Holy Communion, in order to be strengthened by this sacrament.[29] As a norm the use of reason is presumed at the age of seven; before that it must be shown to exist, and where it does, it is an abuse to refuse to confer the sacrament.[30] In doubt as to the attainment or the sufficient use of reason the sacrament may be given conditionally ("if you are capable").[31]

The candidate must be *in danger of death* from *sickness* or *old age*. The danger need not at all be imminent or mortal; a prudent or probable judgment as to its gravity suffices and will eliminate any anxiety on the part of the minister as to its presence. The latter may take into consideration the judgment of others, especially the physician.[32] The sacrament may be given as long as there is true illness which is presently and actually serious and dangerous, thus, for example, excluding the person simply insensible merely from inebriation. Thus a sick person may be anointed before undergoing a surgical operation, as long as a dangerous ailment is the reason for the surgery.[33] Elderly people whose strength becomes much weakened, even though no dangerous illness is observed, may be anointed.[34] Since the danger of death must arise from intrinsic causes, no other cause whatever justifies the conferral of this sacrament, e.g., shipwreck, sentence of death, impending air raid or battle, the mere accumulation of years; a pregnancy must present an extraordinary difficulty or danger.

Eastern Christians who are separated in good faith from the Catholic Church, if they ask of their own accord and have the right dispositions, may be granted the sacrament of Unction of the Sick not only in cases of necessity but also in special circumstances when it becomes materially or morally impossible over a long period of time for them to receive the sacraments in their own church, thus depriving them without legitimate reason of the

29. Ibid., n. 12; S.C.Sac. 10 aug. 1910.
30. S.C. Sac. 8 aug. 1910.
31. c. 941.
32. **Ordo unctionis infirmorum eorumque pastoralis curae**, n. 8; cf. Pius XI, Litt. Apost. **Explorata res**, 2 feb. 1923 (**AAS** 15 [1923], 103-107).
33. **Ordo unctionis infirmorum eorumque pastoralis curae**, n. 10.
34. Ibid., n. 11.

spiritual fruit of the sacraments. Catholics on their part may request the same sacrament from those non-Catholic ministers whose churches possess valid sacraments, as often as necessity or a genuine spiritual benefit recommends such a course of action, and when access to a Catholic priest is physically or morally impossible. The regulations of the local Ordinary are to be observed.[35]

Separated Christians (who are not of the Eastern Churches) who are not one in faith in the sacraments, and in the Anointing of the Sick in particular, are forbidden the ministration of this sacrament. However, this may be permitted in danger of death or in urgent need (during persecution, in prisons), if the separated brother has no access to a minister of his own communion and spontaneously seeks the sacrament from a Catholic priest—so long as he declares a faith in this sacrament in harmony with that of the Church and is rightly disposed. In other cases the judge of the urgent necessity must be the local Ordinary. A Catholic in similar circumstances may not request this sacrament except from a minister who has been validly ordained.[36]

As a sacrament of the living, the Unction of the Sick presupposes for its lawful and fruitful reception the state of grace. At the same time, the greater the reverence and devotion, the richer the spiritual fruits that accrue to the soul. If time and the condition of the ill person permits, the sacrament of Penance normally precedes and Viaticum follows the reception of this sacrament, in accordance with the rite of the conferral of the several sacraments.[37]

VI. Repeated and Conditional Celebrations

The sacrament of the Anointing of the Sick may be repeated or given again to a sick person who has already been anointed

35. Vat. II, Decree **Orientalium Ecclesiarum**, n. 27; Secr. ad unitatem Christianorum fovendam, **Directorium**, 14 maii 1967, nn. 42, 44.
36. **Directorium**, n. 55.
37. **Ordo unctionis infirmorum eorumque pastoralis curae**, nn. 30, 115.

but later suffers a relapse after a period of convalescence; it may likewise be repeated if, in the course of the same illness, his state becomes more critical.[38] In cases of doubt of the existence of the above circumstances, the minister of the sacrament must form a reasonably prudent judgment on whatever evidence he has, giving the sick person the benefit of the doubt, since the sacraments are for men.

The sacrament is to be conferred absolutely on the sick who while conscious requested it at least implicitly, or who very likely would have desired it even though afterwards they became unconscious or lost the use of reason.[39] Such a necessary and at least implicit habitual intention is considered to be present in the will to live and die a Catholic; it need not have been formulated in the present illness. It is presumed a Catholic would always request the sacrament if he could, unless there is sure basis for a contrary presumption in a particular case. Bad Catholics and those who have become unconscious in the very act of sinning (e.g., in a quarrel or a shooting) may be anointed conditionally ("if you are capable") on the basis of a habitual desire to die as a Catholic, unless they have positively manifested the contrary. Those who remain contumaciously impenitent in serious sin (e.g., an invalid marriage) and those who refuse the last sacraments before lapsing into unconsciousness should be denied the sacrament, since they have given no indication of a minimum intention. In any doubt of final impenitence or obstinacy the sacrament is conferred conditionally ("if you are capable").[40]

If a priest is called to a sick person who has already died, he should offer prayers to God that he might be absolved from his sins and admitted by the divine clemency into the heavenly kingdom. He is not to anoint him. If he doubts whether the person is truly dead, he may confer the sacrament conditionally ("if you are alive").[41] In cases of sudden death, life may linger for some time after the apparent death of the person. Thus conditional anoint-

38. **Ibid.,** 9.
39. c. 943.
40. c. 942.
41. **Ordo unctionis infirmorum eorumque pastoralis curae,** n. 35.

ing may be given up to one hour after apparent death, or even two or three hours if the person was in full vigor at the time of demise. Where a lingering illness has gradually consumed the person, it is considered that real death occurs shortly after all signs of life have ceased. Thus anointing may be given up to one half hour of apparent death. In all these cases it may be expedient to explain to the bystanders that the actual moment of death is uncertain and that the sacraments are for men.

VII. Visitation and Communion of the Sick

All the faithful should share in the solicitude and charity of Christ and his Church toward the sick and suffering by visiting them, comforting them, and offering brotherly help. In particular, pastors and those with the care of the sick should impart the teaching of the faith regarding the role of suffering in the mystery of salvation as it is joined to the sufferings of Christ and sanctified and strengthened through constant prayer. It is helpful to pray over them and also to recite with them and others who are present suitable prayers, together with Scripture readings and reflections. The sick should gradually be led to frequent reception of the sacraments of Penance and the Eucharist, and, when opportune, the Anointing of the Sick and Viaticum.[42]

Pastors of souls should be solicitous that the sick who are of adequate age, even though not seriously ill or in imminent danger of death, frequently, if not daily, and especially during Eastertide, receive the Eucharist, which can be administered at any time of the day under the usual safeguards and in accordance with the prescriptions regarding Communion outside of church and without a Mass. The sick who cannot receive the Eucharist under the form of bread may receive under the form of wine, as long as the proper care of the sacred species as prescribed is observed. Those who assist the sick may receive Holy Communion with them.[43]

42. **Ibid.**, nn. 32-37, 42-45.
43. **Ibid.**, nn. 46-48, 56, 62, 95. Communion under both species **may**

The liturgy provides a rite for the Communion of one sick person[44] and a shorter rite when many are to be communicated in different rooms.[45]

VIII. Rite of the Anointing of the Sick

The priest who is to anoint should try to become aware of the condition of the sick person, if possible from the latter or from the family, and to explain the significance of the sacrament. Sacramental confession, where necessary, should take place some time before the rite of anointing, or at least at the beginning. Otherwise the penitential act within the rite is performed.[46]

A sick person who is not confined to bed may receive the sacrament of Unction in the church or some other convenient place where there is an apt seating arrangement for him and where at least relatives and friends who will take part in the celebration can gather. In homes for the sick and rest homes, the priest will have to take into account the situation of the other residents.[47]

The ordinary rite of Anointing[48] is used in anointing several sick people using the plural form. However, both the ceremony of imposition of hands and the anointing with its formula are conferred on each one singly.[49]

When the condition of the sick person allows, especially if Communion is to be received, the sacrament of Anointing may be conferred during Mass in a church or, with the consent of the

> be given to the sick person who is being anointed and to those present only when the Eucharist either as Communion or as Viaticum is administered at a Mass celebrated in a church **or lawfully in a home of a sick person or in a rest home (Missale Romanum, Instr. Gen., n. 242; Ordo unctionis infirmorum eorumque pastoralis curae,** nn. 80, 82, 99).

44. Ibid., nn. 49-58.
45. Ibid., nn. 59-63.
46. Ibid., nn. 64-65; cf. also 40-41.
47. Ibid., n. 66.
48. Ibid., nn. 68-79.
49. Ibid., n. 67.

local Ordinary, in a suitable place in the sick person's home or a rest home. It is conferred after the Gospel and the homily and in accordance with the prescriptions for this ceremony. Communion may be received by the sick person and those present under both species.[50]

On the occasion of a large gathering of the faithful, when in the judgment of the Ordinary many sick persons may be anointed at the same time, the rite of celebration of anointing a large gathering of the faithful[51] may be used. This may occur during a large pilgrimage of a diocese, a city, parish, or pious association of the sick, or if suitable, in homes for the sick. An apt pastoral preparation and catechesis is to precede the ceremony, and usually the sacrament of Penance is made available. If several priests are present who are designated for the ceremony, each one imposes hands and anoints with the proper formula some of the sick. The ceremony of unction may take place within or outside of Mass.

IX. Viaticum

Communion received as Viaticum is considered a special sign of sharing in the mystery, celebrated in the sacrifice of the Mass, of the death of the Lord and his passage to the Father. It is the duty of pastors and those with the special care of the sick to provide them with the strengthening comfort of Holy Viaticum when they are in proximate danger of death, and especially when they are in full possession of their senses. This may, in accordance with the prescriptions of the rite, be administered within or outside of Mass. The Sacrament of Penance is usually to precede. The Eucharist may be received under the species of wine if it cannot be received under the species of bread. All who participate in the celebration of Mass may receive Communion under both species.[52]

The ordinary ministers of Viaticum are the pastor and his

50. **Ibid.,** nn. 80-82.
51. **Ibid.,** nn. 83-92.
52. **Ibid.,** nn. 26, 27, 93-114.

cooperators or curates, a priest with the care of the sick in rest homes, the superior of a clerical religious community and, in case of necessity, any priest with at least the presumed permission of the ordinary minister. In the absence of a priest Viaticum may be brought to the sick by a deacon or even by a lay person who has been duly deputed by the Bishop to distribute Communion. The deacon follows the rite of the Ritual, the others follow the usual rite for distributing Communion but pronouncing the formula of giving Viaticum.[53]

X. Continuous Rite of Sacramental Celebration in Danger of Death

The sacramental confession of the sick person in danger of death should be heard, if he is willing and able, before the celebration of Unction and Viaticum. If it is to be made within the celebration itself, it should be done at the beginning of the rite, before the unction. Otherwise, the penitential act is performed within the rite.[54] The confession or penitential act may be concluded with a plenary indulgence in the hour of death.[55]

It should be noted that, unless there is obvious serious sin, the sacrament of Unction may not be refused because the sick person has not gone or will not go to confession. Each case for the reception of this sacrament must be judged on its own merits and any danger of scandal avoided. The benign indulgence of the Church toward her children in face of the presence of danger of death should be kept in mind.

In urgent danger the sick person is given the opportunity, if possible, to confess his sins at least generally. Otherwise, he is quickly anointed with one unction and then Viaticum is given. At the approach of death, if the other sacraments cannot be given, Viaticum (which all the faithful are bound to receive in danger of death) is immediately given so that the dying person might be

53. Ibid., n. 29.
54. Ibid., n. 115.
55. Ibid., n. 122.

strengthened with the Body of Christ and fortified with the pledge of the resurrection as he leaves this life.[56]

The sacrament of Confirmation, when conferred on a sick person in danger of death, is usually given separately from the other sacraments. In the legitimate absence of the Bishop the law grants the faculty of confirming to pastors and parochial vicars and, in their absence, to their cooperators or curates; likewise, to those who have the charge of duly established special parishes, vicars econome or administrators, substitute and auxiliary vicars. In the absence of all of these, any priest free of censure or canonical penalty may confirm in these circumstances.[57]

Since in both sacraments, Confirmation in danger of death and the Anointing of the Sick, there is an anointing, they are not usually to be conferred in a continuous rite. If it is necessary, however, Confirmation is immediately conferred before the blessing of the Oil of the Sick, but the imposition of hands that pertains to the rite of Anointing is omitted.[58] The short rite, or in extreme necessity the simple formula with the anointing, may be used.[59]

The rite of commendation of the soul of the dying should be used in order to assist those who are about to leave this life.[60]

---

56. Ibid., nn. 30, 116.
57. Ibid., n. 31.
58. Ibid., n. 117.
59. Ibid., nn. 136-137.
60. Ibid., nn. 138-151.